The Shouting Signpainters

The Shouting Signpainters

A Literary and Political Account of Quebec Revolutionary Nationalism

by Malcolm Reid

(MR)
New York and London

Acknowledgments

Sections from *Les Insolences du frère Untel* reprinted by permission of Jean-Paul Desbiens and Les Editions de l'Homme, copyright © 1960 by Les Editions de l'Homme.

Extracts from *Journal d'un inquisiteur* by Gilles Leclerc reprinted by permission of the author and Editions de l'Aube, copyright © 1960 by Editions de l'Aube.

Extracts from *Le Cassé* by Jacques Renaud reprinted by permission of the author and éditions parti pris, copyright © 1964 by éditions parti pris. Extract from *Electrodes* reprinted by permission of the author and Les Editions Atys, copyright © 1960 by Les Editions Atys.

Extracts from *L'Afficheur hurle* and *L'Inavouable* by Paul Chamberland reprinted by permission of the author and éditions parti pris. *L'Afficheur hurle* copyright © 1964 by éditions parti pris, *L'Inavouable* copyright © 1968 by éditions parti pris.

Extracts from "Ex-Socialist" by Henry Moscovitch, from *Poésie/Poetry 64*, reprinted by permission of the author and Ryerson Press/Editions du Jour, copyright © 1964 by Ryerson Press/Editions du Jour.

Extracts from "La Semaine dernière pas loin de pont," "La Chair de poule," "Le Beau Pétard," and *Le Cabochon* by André Major reprinted by permission of the author and éditions parti pris, copyright © 1964 by éditions parti pris. Extracts from "En ton cri tous les cris," from *Le Pays*, reprinted by permission of the author and Librairie Déom, copyright © 1963 by Librairie Déom.

Extracts from the poetry of Gason Miron reprinted by permission of the author.

Extracts from *Journal d'un hobo* by Jean-Jules Richard reprinted by permission of the author and éditions parti pris, copyright © 1965 by éditions parti pris.

Extracts from *Zone, Florence,* and *Les Beaux Dimanches* by Marcel Dubé reprinted by permission of the author and Les Editions Leméac, copyright © 1969 by Les Editions Leméac. Extract from *Un simple soldat* reprinted by permission of Les Editions du Jour, copyright © 1967 by Les Editions du Jour.

Extracts from *Nègres blancs d'Amérique* by Pierre Vallières reprinted by permission of the author and éditions parti pris, copyright © 1968, 1969 by éditions parti pris.

Extract from *Les Cantouques* by Gérald Godin reprinted by permission of the author and éditions parti pris, copyright © 1966 by éditions parti pris.

Extracts from *Sonnets archaïques pour ceux qui verront l'indépendance* by Jean-Robert Rémillard reprinted by permission of éditions parti pris, copyright © 1965 by éditions parti pris.

Extracts from Raymond Lévesque, Gilles Vigneault, and Claude Dubois reprinted by permission of the authors.

Letter from Charles Gagnon to his father reprinted by permission of the author.

Extracts from articles that appeared in *parti pris* reprinted by permission of *parti pris*.

Copyright © 1972 by Malcolm Reid
All Rights Reserved
Library of Congress Catalog Card Number: 75-158922
First Printing
Manufactured in the United States of America

Contents

1. Watch out, tu vas vwere . . .   9
2. Flat broke   48
3. The alphabet of revolution   97
4. A man of letters   146
5. Wanting men to know what I have known . . .   182
6. The revolution not yet   254

The Shouting Signpainters

1
Watch out, tu vas vwere...

I go down from my room into the center of Montreal and turn east. It is 1966, the summer, although it could be a summer or two before or a summer or two later. Montreal is an island; in the middle is a hump of parkland, and it is at the foot of this hump that the city's two million people are clustered. The city I have explored is on the south side of the island, between the hump and the St. Lawrence. This is the downtown part of the city, and I am almost at its dead center. To the west is the part of town you would direct a tourist to: the shops are best, the buildings tallest, and the clerks speak English.

But I walk eastward, following the boulevards that thread the city east and west. I begin to look up the cross streets of east Montreal, narrow slits going north, I find it hard to guess how far. Each veers slightly and disappears well within the eye's range into a tangle of outdoor staircases and board fences, perhaps the odd tree.

I turn up one: it could be Beaudry, or Amherst; let's say the indicator reads "RUE DE LA VISITATION." Who or what has visited here of late? I walk past the church, tiny, trying to be gothic, at the south end of the street. A little further on I cross St. Catherine Street, a bright, brave business street in the west part of the city. Here it offers a record store dimly displaying an album jacket on which a young Frenchman in blue jeans swings aboard a boxcar in a scene meant to evoke the American West. He is a rock'n'roll singer; his pose is his reaching-out to the American origins of his genre. There are people who speak French in an American landscape, who want to hear rock'n'roll in French, but they are mostly here, in this Atlantic port; they rarely ride the rails west.

On the other corner, opposite the record store, a chips and hot dog restaurant with an arborite counter, no chairs, a man who shuffles his metal basket of potato slices and re-immerses it in grease. Not one of the proud pizzarias further west, where the cooks flip their dough for display and the windows are lit by neon and framed with vases of wriggly pasta staffs.

La Catherine is a plainer girl in the east than she is in the west, but the easterners have a compensation: her sister, Ontario Street, is a commercial main drag out here too, and just a few blocks up from St. Catherine you again traverse a line of snack bars, taverns, tobacco shops, where among the doctor-and-nurse novels you can sometimes pick up *Manon Lescaut* for a dime (*"Le chevalier s'avilira-t-il de plus en plus par amour? Texte intégral et complet."*). But then I know these streets a little—I know *Manon* occasionally turns up on Ontario Street, and I know what picturesque details to anticipate in the way of relief from the purgatory as I walk north. I've walked up Clark, my street, and I know to expect, on a wall a few blocks from my apartment, the graffito "A BAS LA CONSCRIPTION/VIVE HOUDE." Houde, an anti-conscriptionist machine mayor, is long dead, and I don't even know if the slogans are for real; this is a beatnik district. But somebody meant to say something out of the ordinary, and I know enough to watch the brick warehouse walls for it.

Here on Visitation Street there isn't any space on the dwelling walls for long slogans, the purgatory is unpicturesque, hardly relieved. Visitation, however, is famous. Just above Maisonneuve, just before Ontario, you used to come upon the gym of the Chevaliers de l'Indépendance. Did the knights sink low from love, or did they just go bankrupt? Their gym is closed and I always promised myself I'd come back when Reggie Chartrand—the organizer of the Chevaliers, their boxing teacher—was in to talk to him about how the neighbors liked him, how he had done recruiting the neighborhood kids. Now it is too late. But the building lightens Visitation Street for the walker, however it is seen by the residents; there are still some inscriptions in the storefront, Quebec flags, two fighters in combat, and:

FOR A FREE QUEBEC
LEARN SELF-DEFENSE
THE KNIGHTS OF INDEPENDENCE
MONDAY TO FRIDAY 8–10 P.M.

There is little else to relieve the grimness of Visitation—an Académie Garneau with a bit of Greek decoration on the façade. I've noticed, on my way down a parallel street (Visitation and its neighbors glide slowly up the Montreal hump as they go north), a small, inordinately fine sign indicating that a sculptor has his studio in one of the street's sheds; I've visited a ceramic workshop in a basement a bit further east, but Visitation has only "Brillo Signs—Truck Lettering."

At Maisonneuve, a third commercial cross street, I catch a glimpse, far to the west, of the ship's-prow-shaped Place des Arts, the new hall of high culture in Montreal. At the top of the street I will emerge onto the boulevard of dignified French-Canadian institutions, Sherbrooke East, in front of a fancy new teachers' college just old enough to have been the scene, in 1961, of an educational scandal in which old clashed with new, cleric with layman. And into Lafontaine Park.

But there you are out of purgatory. What is the life of Visitation before it leads to these open spaces?

How to evoke it? The one celebrated thing about east Montreal, the outdoor staircases, do not give the sharpest impression. An outdoor staircase is a buffer between you and the world, between you and the spy; you must climb to get into your dwelling, but he must climb to see you stretch out in front of your TV. No, the jolt comes from the downstairs flats, their stoops opening right from the sidewalk into the living room. It is summer, it is hot, people are sitting on those stoops—but they at least have chosen to display themselves. The sad ones are those who merely want a little air, but who by opening their windows put themselves unavoidably on display. Every burst of cowboy gunfire on the TV, every scrape of the feet, every clink of a beer bottle, is accessible to the passerby without even eavesdropping particularly hard. The floors, you can see from the outside, are linoleum, slick and dot-patterned, ragged at the entrance. There may be a bit of a rug. There is a couch; there is probably someone sitting on it in an undershirt.

The kids do not accept this circumscription, choose the slightly broader one of the street. They walk up and down the sidewalks, they run errands to the store on the corner of Ontario, they carry transistor radios, they shout from balconies to the ground, to the opposite balconies. Are the girls prettier or less pretty here than on the buses going up to the University of Montreal, where well-off French-Canadians send their daughters? It is hard to say, it is hard to establish what they call in the sociology classes at the university an *échantillon*. The boys here wear their hair slicked back, at the U of M it's tousled over the forehead; here they wear black leather windbreakers, there black leather sports jackets.

Visitation is what is called in conventional journalese a residential street, what we call in left journalese a working-class district. A place where people come home from work to talk, eat, make love, doze, wake. Where do they work? For later, this question, though there is on Visitation a factory, Jack Miller Inc., Mfr. of Ladies' & Children's Lingerie, a great brick block.

What do they say? Hard to bring it back, hard to keep it out of your ears. The remembrance of things past is hard enough when it is your own past, when it is your own street's folkways you wish to revive; it requires enough circumlocution and analogy even then. When it is someone else's? When you pass through, smile at a grammatical construction that doesn't correspond to the textbooks, repeat it to yourself and then lose it a minute later when your attention is taken by another.

A child will chase a ball into the street. Cars are going by. A parent's warning will follow him and his friends: *"Fais attention à twey là, vous aut' là!"*

Children will be knotted in one of the slots between stretches of lodgings where rotting planks lead into dark rear courtyards of mud surrounded by the twice-ugly reverse sides of these ugly buildings. Greeting each other: *"Shu fais là?"* Arguing their way out of a fight: *"Kessay j'ai fait? Dis-le en premier."* Fighting over a spitting contest: *"C'est pu pareil!"* Or flirting: *"Shsrai ta femme, eh? Ou ta fiancée, ou bahn kekshose."*

From an upstairs window, a teenager to a friend in the street: *"Hey, ti-Guy, veux-tu aller m'acheter deux hot-dog?"*

Or here are some I took down in a tavern on Panet Street, a few blocks over from Visitation. The Taverne Panet, with yellowing Canadian Pacific Railway prints of the Rockies on the walls, a beaker of pickled eggs on the bar, little round tables, concrete floor:

"*Disons que l'game est dans un mois d'ici.*"
"*Pi mon chum a bu deux, trois coups de vin. Là est heureux. Lui a payé.*"
"*Watch out, tu vas vwere!*"
"*C'est ça ké pas bon.*"
"*Sah même marque, tsi?*" (In a conversation about trademarks on some product or other.)
"*C'est pour ça que j't'd'mandais talurr.*"
"*Font pas l'dyawb, eux.*"
"*Mwey itou j'ai rentré.*"

The first example means: *Watch yourself, you there.* In conventional French it would be *Fais attention à toi, vous autres là.* The pronunciation *twey* for what is pronounced in conventional French as *twa* is standard in proletarian French in Quebec, so standard that French-Canadian writers have established a standard spelling for it, one which doesn't seem to me quite to render it: *toé.* What other deviations from the norm in this sentence? *Vous aut(res)*, perhaps, *you others, you all,* a favorite but not exclusively Canadian expression in French; and the traditional French-Canadian abuse of *là, there,* tacked on everywhere in a spoken sentence where a bridge seems needed. But these characteristics, not out-and-out faults, simply give a folksy, rustic air to the speech which uses them. The same might be said of *twey,* which I have been told was, along with *mwey* for *moi,* the standard pronunciation up to the highest levels of society in the France of Louis XIV (*l'Etat c'est mwey*).

Shu fais là? is *Qu'est-ce que tu fais là?* (*Hey, whatcha doing?*). In other words, the whole opening expression has been merged into *shu,* as *qu'est-ce que c'est* (*kess kuh say*) in the following sentence has become *kessay,* and the *que* which would conventionally go after it has been dropped to swing directly into *j'ai fait. En premier* is, again, a rustic-sounding way of saying what conventional French would render by *d'abord,* and may spring from English's use of the ordinal number *first* for *right off, immediately, first of all.* (The whole example means *Wuddid I do? Tell me that first.*) In *C'est pu pareil* (*But that's not the same thing any more*) the negative has been trimmed from *n'est plus* to simply *plus,* and even this has lost its *l* sound, to become *pu* (the *s* is silent even in the standard version). This, incidentally, seems to give almost the same word as the Italian for more, *più*. Ellipse, slurring, rustic pronunciation: the same traits turn up in the girl's refusal to cuddle up until she's "Your wife, or your fiancée, or anyway something like that." *Je serai* has become scarcely more than a single syllable in *shsrai;* what I have written as *bahn* is put on paper by French writers as *ben*. It is pronounced exactly as the French for bath, *bain* (ending in the French nasal), and should correctly be *bien* (*bee-ehn*). *Kekshose* is *quelque chose*.

For the full development of that hint of English influence we come to the boy's request to his friend to buy him a couple of hot dogs. The sentence is completely correct French, with the piquancy of the ultra-Québécois diminutive *ti-* (*petit*) plus the one syllable abbreviation for the name. But the hot dog appears to French-Canadians as a manifestation of the English-speaking structures around them, and they have simply integrated the expression. And wisely: the expression can be translated—*chien chaud*—but barbarously.

Why, though, assimilate *game,* as the tavern customer did in his proposition (*Let's say the game is a month from now*), when every French-speaking person knows *partie?* The French in France felt their own anglicizing influence in sport—they say *match*.

Pi is *puis,* "*then* my pal drank two wines," simplified of one of its sounds much as was *plus*. *Chum* is one of those English words French-Canadians use though English-Canadians have discarded it. *Là est heureux* means *then he was happy;* the *il* is dropped, the ever serviceable *là* has been stretched to suggest *then* in time rather than *there* in space. *Lui* (*him, himself*) paid the bill, rather than *il* (*he*)—a slight ungrammaticality for emphasis which could perhaps have been heard in France too.

But *watch out?* This is out-and-out anglicization, although not the most barbarous integration of the verb *watch* into French-Canadian French. The folklorist Jacques Labrecque, who specializes in the quaint and rural, sings that in one of his old Quebec songs: "When we're married, your old lady won't always be around *pour nous watcher*." Here we are into creole: the root word is English, the ending French—and the creolization, as I said, is not even very recent. *Vwere* for *voir* (in *you'll see*) is a lengthening of vowel sounds long characteristic of Canadian French. I have heard it alleged, but never established, that this stems from the English environment; it seems to me as likely that it is just a course taken by the French language in America that diverges from what is heard in France without moving toward any extra-French model.

C'est ça qui n'est pas bon (*that's the bad part*) has been shortened in two steps: *qui n'est* becomes *qui est,* dropping the first word of the two-word negative, and then the two remaining words collide into *ké.*

Similar slurring in *sah* (*c'est la*) and *tsi* (*tu sais,* which with repeated quick pronunciation slides very close to the English *see*)—*it's the same brand, y'know?*

Talurr is (*tou*)*t à l'heure: That's what I was asking you for a few minutes ago.* And on the structure of this sentence lies an elusive but unmistakable English stamp: *demander* is good French for *ask, pour* is indeed *for,* but *demander pour* is not *ask for.* This is a straight copy of English forms in which only the individual words are French. The idea would have to be expressed in a completely different way in conventional French: *C'est ça que je t'ai demandé* . . .

Pas le diable is a fine old French-Canadian expression. *They don't do a devil of a lot; they aren't worth a damn, they aren't.* And it is often slurred as indicated.

Finally, *Me, too, I went in.* And in spite of appearances, *itou* for *too* is not an anglicism, but one of those survivals from medieval French which the Québécois keep alive while Frenchmen have gone over entirely to *aussi* (which, of course, is used in Quebec *aussi*). *J'ai rentré* is a simple grammatical error; the auxiliary should be *être: je suis rentré.*

Thus: slurring, shortcuts, bad grammar. So far, things that all languages do (I think of the French actress Danielle Darrieux, singing, in the film of Zola's *Nana,* "*Il faut que ça saute*" contracted into *Fau'k'ça saute*—nothing particularly Canadian or recent there), things all schoolteachers worry about and try to stamp out. That they survive most persistently among the poor, these lapses, is no peculiarity of Canadian French either.

But what if they are coupled with other veerings from the norm which are invariably in the direction of a foreign language? In Quebec the poor are here, on Visitation Street; the English words and forms that enter their language are no graceful cultural borrowings, but the imprints of an English-language-using industrial system, owned partly by English-speaking Canadian entrepreneurs to the west, partly by United States holders and managed by English-Canadians. What if the teacher finds he himself is enmeshed in language-deforming surroundings he cannot uproot; if the privileged French-speaker finds his speech subject to strains that do not weigh on the impoverished English-speaker? If, even after conscientiously weeding all the grosser anglicisms from his vocabulary, he utters, unaware of any incorrectness, sentences like: *"J'ai réalisé que c'est devenu crucial de supporter la lutte contre le joual."*

Cheval is French for something you rarely see in Montreal, a horse. *Joual* is a slurring of *cheval* you rarely hear in Montreal or elsewhere, but the schoolteachers and other worriers in Quebec have taken it up as the epitome of the phenomenon. How did this rural reference come to epitomize what is happening to the French language on Visitation Street, to cover both the slurring and the even more bothersome anglicization? Many English-Canadians, even without knowing French, are aware of the story; its outlines have often been sketched in polite journalistic terms as an act of bicultural decency to a French Canada that seemed obsessed with it.

The obsession dates back to 1960. During that year I was working for the Canadian Pacific Railway, one of the big transport systems that have their headquarters in Montreal. It is a good example of the English-speaking control of the industrial order in Quebec. Promoted by Scotch bankers and rammed across the country by a Wisconsin engineer, it belongs to the nineteenth-century capitalism that called forth the Dominion of Canada. My contact with French Canada at that time was the group of French-Canadians in the cubicle next to ours in the public relations department who rendered our press releases into French for the French papers. My contact with intellectual life was the book department of Eaton's, a department store between my office and McGill, the English university I'd flunked out of the year before. It was at McGill that I had begun to think a lot about Quebec, its politics, the fact that it was a place of English owners and French workers.

In Eaton's one day, looking over the new French things, I spotted a paperback with a khaki jacket picturing a cartoon priest, starched collar flapping, beret on head, flesh colored blue, glint in eye and snicker on mouth, kicking a tin can with the clodhoppers which stuck out from under his cassock. The title was *Les Insolences du frère*

Untel. The publisher was Les Editions de l'Homme, the outfit that put out all the topical best-sellers of those days. They had done a biography of Maurice Duplessis, the boss of Quebec provincial politics for twenty or thirty years, that had helped defeat the old man's party after his death in 1959. They had done a book by two university priests against ballot-box stuffing under Duplessis's regime that had played a similar role. And the publisher, Jacques Hébert, had written denunciations of a doubtful murder conviction in the Gaspé peninsula and of the long detention of a sane teenaged boy in the insalubrious section of a Montreal jail reserved for the mentally ill.

And now *Les Insolences*, with preface by André Laurendeau, an editor whose essays in *Le Devoir* I admired. (*Le Devoir* was the Montreal daily which represented about the same viewpoint as Hébert's publishing house.) Even without looking inside I got the idea: tart-tongued young priest criticizes our social mores; from a nice left-wing position within the church, he knocks down the fuddy-duddies. I had already been introduced to Laurendeau's idea of the Negro king, the native despot who delivers his people into the factories of the occupier, his campaigns financed by the factory owners, while his people imagine him to be defending them against these foreigners. This idea seemed to suggest that my homebred socialism and French-Canadian nationalism were beginning to coincide. And so when I came upon *Les Insolences*, I told myself that Quebec was further ahead than that; that it could do better than a nonconformist curé. I let the book go.

The controversialists of French Canada did not. Frère Untel kept his anonymity for a while; then it became known that he was Jean-Paul Desbiens, a teacher at a school in the Saguenay country north of Quebec City, and that he had paid for his insolence by an imposed period of study in Switzerland. Meanwhile his book ran through edition after edition into the hundreds of thousands of $1.00 copies, the all-time Quebec best-seller. The papers were awash with debate over his criticisms of the province's clerical school system (Desbiens returned to grace a couple of years later as an officer in the Liberals' education department, helping them modernize), and with the new name for the language spoken by his pupils: "joual."

Frère Untel had begun his book:

On October 21, 1959, André Laurendeau published an editorial note in *Le Devoir* in which he called the speech of French-Canadian schoolchildren "joual" speech. It was he, therefore, and not I, who invented this name. It is a well-chosen one. There is an evenness of proportion between the thing and the name that designates it. The word is odious and the thing is odious. The word joual is a one-word description of what it is to speak joual: to speak joual is to say *"joual"* instead of *"cheval."* And it is to speak as horses might speak if they hadn't chosen silence and a Fernandel grin.

Our pupils speak joual, write joual, and do not wish to speak or write anything else. Joual is their language. Things have deteriorated to the point where they do not recognize an error that is pointed out to them by the teacher. *L'homme que je parle: the man I'm talking* for *the man I'm talking about—nous allons se déshabiller: we're going to get undress—*these examples don't faze them. They even strike them as elegant. Spelling errors are not quite the same; if they are circled by the teacher they know how to correct a disagreement of endings or a dropped *s*. So the vice is deep—it is at the level of syntax. It is also at the level of pronunciation: of twenty pupils whose names you ask at the beginning of the year, only two or three will you catch the first time. The others you will have to ask to repeat. They utter their names as one confesses an impurity. . . .

This lack of language that is joual is an example of our great French-Canadian nonexistence. You can never study language too closely. Language is the arena of all meanings. Our inability to assert ourselves, our rejection of the future, our obsession with the past, all this is reflected in joual, which is really and truly our language. I note in passing the abundance of negatives in our speech: instead of calling a woman beautiful, we say she's not ugly, instead of saying a pupil is intelligent, we say he's not so dumb, instead of saying we are well, we say things aren't getting any worse, and so on . . .

I read my class Laurendeau's editorial when it appeared. The pupils recognized that they spoke joual. One, almost proudly, went so far as to announce: "We've founded a new language!" They saw no need to change. "Everybody talks like that," they said, or: "People laugh at you if you talk another way from other people." Or this diabolical objection: "Why bother speaking any other way; we understand each other." It is not as easy as you might think for a teacher to improvise an answer to that last remark, which was in fact made to me that afternoon.

Yes, horse-whinniers can understand each other. The question is whether one can live one's life among horse-whinniers. As long as it is simply a question of chit-chat about the weather or sports, as long as you only want to talk about sex, joual is amply adequate. For exchanges between primitives, a primitive language serves; animals get by on a few growls. But if you aspire to human dialogue, joual is no longer good enough. To paint a barn, you may find a stick of wood dipped in whitewash will do; to paint the Mona Lisa you need finer tools.

This brings us to the heart of the problem, which is a problem of civilization. Our schoolchildren speak joual because they think joual, and they think joual because they live joual, like everybody in this fair land. The joual life is rock'n'roll and hot dogs, partying and bombing around, etc. It is our whole civilization that is *joual*. Nothing can be corrected at the level of language itself (competitions, campaigns for Good French, conferences . . .). It is at the level of the civilization that we must work. Easily said, but reflection on the question leads to a desperate wondering: what is to be done? What can a teacher, tucked away in the back of his school, do to halt the catastrophe? All his efforts are ridiculous. All he wins is as quickly lost. From four in the afternoon on, reality contradicts him. The whole civilization negates him, negates what he defends, derides what he urges. I am not an old man, and not all that crotchety a one; I like teaching—and yet, I find it demoralizing to teach French.

Take the elements to which I had been exposed and put them together. Laurendeau, a liberal, not a revolutionary, editor, had spoken of French Canada as an African colony: puppet ruler, foreign sponsor, native clientele. Frère Untel, a still-frocked cleric, had written from the backwoods after a change of rulers, a change from reactionaries to modernists but no basic change in the system, and described the condition of the native population. Its poverty comes out of its mouth every time it speaks. And then I could look around me. Montreal bunches its French poor into grim eastern streets—some of them actually named for the English conquerers (Wolfe, Amherst), others flattering the religious culture of their inhabitants (Visitation, Ste-Dorothée)—and into another grim area to the southwest. In these two areas are the big plants—General Electric, Dominion Textile; American, Anglo-Canadian—where the residents of the French quarters work if they don't work in the center of town in industries like the railway I wrote publicity for, English-owned again, whose shareholders, executives, managers lived north and west, up or over the mountain from the proletarian French. Modify this with some mixed areas, where there are English speakers among the working class, or French speakers moving up into the middle levels, and a central district inhabited by recently arrived European poor of neither French nor English culture who are still learning English. The pattern is colonial.

Colonial by what conquest? There is one more element, one which Laurendeau and Desbiens took for granted, for it is taught to every French-Canadian child. It is that the society in question was militarily defeated in 1759, when Wolfe took Quebec from the French Empire. But no part of America was sovereign at that time, and neither Laurendeau nor Desbiens evoked a clear link between the conquest and the present state of things. Constitutionally Quebec—like, say, Pennsylvania—had since emerged from colony, not to nation, but to a subdivision of a nation which in its totality was sovereign. References to African kings and French-Canadian nonexistence were only figures of speech: Laurendeau had said that English-speaking capitalists in Quebec behaved *as if* they were in an African colony, Desbiens that his pupils spoke *like* primitives. We aren't *really* a colony, they seemed to be saying, but we've got problems. Such metaphors help us face them.

This was roughly my own view through the early 1960's. Men like Laurendeau and Desbiens were looking approvingly at what the Liberals were doing: nationalizing electricity, reforming education. These, they felt, were attacks on the ills they had diagnosed. At the same time a separatist movement had come into existence and was challenging Liberalism with the idea that what Quebec needed was *real* sovereignty. I moved back to my home town of Ottawa for a time, and even in this outside-of-Quebec federal capital I found a pattern much like the Montreal one: French manual workers in the east end, English suburbs to the west, some French moving up in a federal civil service which, because of the French-Canadian vote, was more open to them than the private economy. Even when I finally read *Frère Untel*, I still saw only the modernist denouncing obscurantism, missing the reference to French-Canadian nonexistence. In 1962 I moved to Sherbrooke, a small industrial city in the south of Quebec, to work on the English newspaper. I found French slums and English elegance all the more juxtaposed there.

I continued to argue that the English-speaking capitalist domination of Quebec in the 1960's did not follow from the English conquest of Quebec in 1759, that Quebec, like the rest of America, had since inched forward from colonial status. The Québécois had been colonized anew in recent times, yes, but it was in a businesslike Yankee way, without the Union Jack presiding. The remedy was socialism, an end to all capitalism in English Canada. The demand for political independence was a diversion of energies: I didn't buy the half-measures of Laurendeau, Desbiens, Lévesque (who was now a minister in the Liberal government), but I agreed with them on that. (A drama student I was interviewing in Sherbrooke was full of admiration for Marcel Chaput, then the main separatist leader—his fundraising fasts, his patriotic ideals. Couldn't I see that the Québécois had to fight for independence before anything else? No, I said. Why, he asked. "Because there are more important things to do," I answered.)

And when the bombs of the Front de Libération Québécois echoed down to Sherbrooke from Montreal, I, like everyone else, insisted on hearing a different explosion than the one the FLQ had set off. A Belgian named Schoeters, settled in Catholic Quebec, was involved, so the whole thing was probably right wing, probably modelled on the Flemish autonomy movement or the Organisation de l'Armée Secrète. And violence wasn't among the great popular impulses of this province that had resisted Ottawa-imposed conscription in the two big wars, was it?

But the Front de Libération Québécois took its name from the Arab rebels of Algeria, the Front de Libération Nationale of Ferhat Abbas and Ben Bella, not from the French diehard reaction to it, or from anything else white, Christian, or European. My jolt at André Laurendeau's exposition of the idea of the Negro king should have taught me better what sort of revolt to expect to spring from Quebec society. And the truth about the politics of the FLQ eventually penetrated my and the respectable press's wrongheadedness. The captured terrorists, word went around, swore by a book called *Les Damnés de la terre*. This manifesto of the wretched of the earth had been published two years before, in 1961, by the anti-colonial Paris publisher François Maspero. Reading it would have given any doubter an idea of the lines along which the terrorists' minds were working. Its author, Frantz Fanon, had said he was trying to help the underdeveloped world start history over again, make a history in which it would play an active, aggressive part, rather than merely submit to the will of Europe. Similarly, for the FLQ, the recital of history on which I was basing my belief that Quebec was, well, not exactly a colony—was mystification. Quebec had been conquered in the past, and its state at the present moment was that of a bowed people; any intervening account which said that this nation had been freed, rendered sovereign or at any rate a participant in a sovereign partnership with others, that it had gone through a peaceful revolution from colony to self-government, was mystification.

The FLQ manifesto was published in the papers; it spoke of an armed alliance of Quebec peasants and workers and it made clear that the metaphors of Desbiens, Laurendeau, and Lévesque were being taken literally. A society which had been conquered, bypassed by the creative movement of modern history, one which served only as a labor force for productive structures set up by others, which showed the marks, in impoverished bodies and impoverished spirits, of this exclusion, was a colony. The worthy response of the member of such a society who had awakened to his situation was anti-colonial revolution.

There was something else which should have warned me that this kind of revolt was to be anticipated. My reading in this period included *Cité libre*, a monthly magazine bound in cardboard, with few illustrations and no ads, to which I, like everybody else, had become accustomed to looking for a dependable progressivism. To *Cité libre*, to *Le Devoir*, and to Jacques Hébert's publishing house, now called Editions du Jour; Hébert's name appeared on the masthead of *Cité libre*, Frère Untel said he never missed an issue ("What reading habits you have, brother!" he parodied the reactionary clergy in advance), and the preface to *Les Insolences* was by André Laurendeau of *Le Devoir*. The members of the group in a sense acknowledged themselves as a single tendency. And in the early 1960's it was no longer as forlorn a tendency as it had once been. The biggest Montreal daily, *La Presse*, had been drawn into it; a newly founded paper, *Le Nouveau Journal*, was clearly part of it; *Le Magazine Maclean*, the French-language subsidiary opened up around this time by a fairly bland Toronto slick magazine, felt obliged to get with it; some of the traditionally dull native Quebec attempts at periodical journalism had jazzed up a bit. Indeed, you could speak, as *Liberté*, a literary magazine which challenged *Cité libre* a little in youth and audacity, did, of "the forty-year-olds in power," for if old, clerical Quebec was not dead, progressives had seized many organs of power at its intellectual center and the Liberal regime was carrying out largely their program.

The biggest gun *Cité libre* had ever fired at Duplessism triumphant was published in the mid-fifties, when alone with the unions, *Le Devoir*, and people like Lévesque at Radio-Canada they formed a very forlorn left indeed. It was aimed at the greatest scandal of the whole long reign of that unsubtle king of the Blacks. It was called *La Grève de l'amiante* and was a series of essays by men of that left on the insurrectionary strike in Quebec's asbestos-mining Eastern Townships in 1949. That strike hammered into existence a small social conscience within the French-Canadian Roman Catholic church, and most of the essays in *Cité libre*'s book were signed by believers. Eyewitnesses like Gérard Pelletier, who had covered the strike for *Le Devoir*, recounted the events, stressing the martyrdom of the strikers—who laid down their sticks of wood when the army of cops sent by Duplessis arrived with guns and clubs—rather than on the dynamite that did, mysteriously, go off. Analysts like Pierre-Elliott Trudeau, who had started *Cité libre* the year after the strike, sketched in the social history that had led to Asbestos (the name of one of the towns as well as of its product).

It was to Trudeau's thoughts on French-Canadian ideological history that I should have paid closer attention. Never, he said, had democracy been born among the French in Canada. This seems to me to be true. They were governed within constitutional forms, they had parliamentary politics and habeas corpus law courts and freedom-of-the-press, but none of it had they won by their own efforts, it had all been slapped on by the British Empire and the majority-English Dominion of Canada. When Duplessis went too far and legislated himself the right to padlock buildings where he judged Communism to be afoot, it was the majority-English Supreme Court in Ottawa that called him to order. The French didn't mind, their judges on the court were in the habit of being the right-wing dissenters on such issues. Provincial autonomy, you know. Their priests had always deplored capitalism, preached a return to the soil. The French-Canadians had been feudal peasants at the moment the British took over, had gone on being farmers for a long time after, and then had entered the newborn industrial order as workers for the English and Americans; never had there surged from their midst a capitalist class which might have pushed for bourgeois liberties among them. Catholic unions were set up solely to fight secular ones (at Asbestos they rebelled). And so, when the crisis of 1929 and the thirties came the doctor-lawyer-notary notables, the only bourgeoisie ever to come into existence in French Canada, were more intrigued by Mussolini's, Franco's, or Salazar's remedies than by Franklin D. Roosevelt's—not to speak of the Communism which enlisted many of the Jews freshly arrived in central Montreal from Europe.

If French-Canadians had never awakened to their own liberty, if they lived uneasily in a democratic-way-of-life thrust upon them by their economic masters, surely this awakening must eventually come, and in a form firmly outside the embrace of English approval. "When the colonizer speaks of Western values," Fanon could have told me—but I didn't know him then—"the *colonisé* fingers his machete."

Trudeau didn't agree. When the Liberals came to power he was more skeptical than most members of the *Cité libre* school: the adherence of René Lévesque did not convince him the Liberals had changed from machine to reform movement. The magazine was still moving around the theme of the fragility of English democracy in French Quebec, but Trudeau's hope nevertheless lay in French-Canadianized fundamental-freedoms and social-progress; in French-Canadians, so to speak, one day applying themselves to being apprentice Anglo-Saxons.

And then, at the beginning of the 1960's, just as the Duplessis machine died, the separatist movement came into existence. It had three tendencies: the Alliance Laurentienne on the right, the Rassemblement pour l'Indépendance Nationale in the center, and the Action Socialiste pour l'Indépendance du Québec on the left, with some future FLQ people and Marxists around the center and left tendencies. *Cité libre* would not have it that separatism was in any way a progressive movement. It was the new treason of the clerks, they said in a famous 1962 issue on separatism, it was the return of the elite's mussolinian dream. The real issues were above ethnic divisions. They were The Bomb, U.S. investment, automation. When the FLQ came in 1963, *Cité libre* saw only madness.

Whom had the madness afflicted? Who was taking the colonial metaphors literally, trying to bring the people-with-no-tradition-of-democracy into history, putting the finger on the Algero-Cuban machete? Well, there were the score who were captured as the FLQ. But the terrorists were not the only young people who were beginning to apply anti-colonial thought to the Quebec situation. Since the separatist movement began a milieu had been developing in Montreal in which this thought was discussed. Pierre Bourgault, a feature writer for *La Presse* who was active in (and later chief of) the Rassemblement pour l'Indépendance Nationale, made a famous speech in which he confessed that many of the terrorists had been in the RIN and had come to consider its demonstrations ineffective. In the RIN and out (other terrorists had been in pan-Canadian left organizations: the Communist Party, English-dominated even in Quebec; the New Party clubs meant to lead to a big, new labor party; the one left-separatist group, the Action Socialiste), those who had planted the bombs and been captured had friends, comrades, fellow anti-colonialists, and the arrests did not halt the development of the larger group. This larger milieu produced the separatist left of the rest of the 1960's: not only later groups of terrorists—for a time using the name Armée de Libération du Québec, mostly readopting the name FLQ—but also the multiplicity of above-ground left separatists. A nation called Quebec was emerging from the snack bars of the east end of Montreal where it had been trapped under the name French Canada. It was painting slogans on the walls, bombing federal buildings and monuments, flowing into the streets chanting *"Le Québec aux Québécois."* What would be the nature of this repossession? "Our great French-Canadian nonexistence," said Desbiens, the teaching brother from the Saguenay, but that did not mean he would agree to an Algero-Cuban kind of coming-into-existence. "We must recommence the history of man," said Fanon, the black psychiatrist become Arab revolutionary, but those who proposed a new history for Quebec were often singularly poor in socioeconomic thought. (This was the case of Marcel Chaput, a scientist in the federal military research organization, living across the Quebec border from Ottawa in the proletarian city of Hull.)

A friend who was in on the discussions among the emerging anti-colonial young after the capture of the FLQ in the spring of 1963 put it to me this way: "I can't remember the order of things exactly, but there was a period when everything clicked into place. We had read the *Communist Manifesto* and it had its point but it didn't seem to apply to us, here and now. We'd listened to Marcel Chaput, and again, he didn't seem to tell the whole story. Then the FLQ, Fanon, discussing all these at about the same time, and a synthesis took place. It was possible to be socialist and independentist without feeling torn in two. The two overlapped, merged. I recall sitting at a meeting where the title *Les Damnés de la terre*, the name Fanon, were tossed into the conversation. I had not heard of them, though already I was frequenting that group, leaning in that direction, trying to put together that synthesis. I soon got hold of the book, of course, and it did its work, it played its part."

The public expression of this new grouping, the separatist left, appeared in October 1963 as a magazine called *parti pris*. The usual use of this expression in French is derogatory: *"T'es plein de parti pris!"* an exasperated mother will say to her child—*you're so pigheaded, your mind is always made up ahead of time. Parti pris* is the prejudice every partisan starts his partisan remarks by vowing he has set aside. But writers have occasionally taken pride in proclaiming their *parti pris*, as did Sartre (whose preface to *Les Damnés de la terre* was not the least of Fanon's recommendations to young French-Canadian intellectuals) in his 1947 questioning *What Is Literature?* "Some may say we are petty bourgeois hesitating between the ruling class and the workers. False. *Notre parti est pris.*" This cocky pride in one's basic prejudgments was clearly the mood of the editors of *parti pris*.

My own first memory of *parti pris* is of spotting its announcement in *Le Devoir* while I was in Sherbrooke. I remember thinking: "Not another frank, outspoken liberal sheet." The advance description, while probably simply an attempt at exposing what the publishers had in mind, discouraged me: *parti pris* would be "separatist, socialist, and secularist." But so many left intellectuals were separatist, so many open minds were "socialist," meaning vaguely sympathetic to popular wishes and willing to talk about Marx and planning. And wasn't everybody in Quebec now for separation of church and state? —from Cardinal Léger on down, passing importantly by *Cité libre*?

The magazine became real suddenly. I was in the Parti Socialiste du Québec, which shortly before had declared its independence from the pan-Canadian labor party I spoke of, the New Party, now founded and named the New Democratic Party. I was in Montreal for a weekend, attending a PSQ meeting in an English Catholic high school in eastern Montreal. Pierre Maheu, smiling, peddled me a copy at the door and I leafed through it as the meeting proceeded. Everything about it was small, square, and chunky. Its name, one word tucked above the other to make a block of type, was in lowercase letters over a black dividing rule; white above the rule, red below. On the red, the table of contents: "OUR PERSPECTIVE . . . from revolt to revolution—pierre maheu; from duplessism to the FLQ—jean-marc piotte; toward a total revolution—yvon dionne /POEMS: andré brochu, paul chamberland, andré major . . ." Price: 50 cents. A price only asked at that time for little magazines, not for popular ones. Highflown, I decided as I leafed, but not the just-another-liberal-rag I'd feared. When it tackled religion it was from the point of view of atheism: not from agnosticism or from a dismay at the abuses of the clergy, but from the idea that religion was, yes, the opium of the people. This was new. The socialism was Marxist; the separatism struck the tone of the FLQ's manifesto; and it was anti-colonialist. *And somehow it was all one thing; not three.*

(The introductory editorial: "We fight for the political independence of Quebec because it is an indispensible condition of our liberation; we believe that political independence would be a fraud if Quebec did not at the same time acquire its economic independence; and we believe that the control of the economy, the means of production, cannot be authentic unless it is in the hands of all Québécois, in the service of a total transformation of our economic system." Piotte: "No need to insist that independence gained by the clerics would not liberate us. Our economy would still be run by foreign capitalists. Our policies would be independent only in law, on paper: the decisions of our representatives would be dictated by foreign finance. Also, capital would go on exploiting workers, as at present and as in other countries. But the recent formation of the PSQ, the chance that it may become independentist, gives hope that political independence can be the start of liberation for the workers." Dionne: "So let it be stressed that 'socialism, people's democracy, and independence' are three terms of a single reality . . ." Or Denys Arcand in his entertainment column: "No longer does it matter if this or that play is universal, written in good French, stands a chance of success in Tokyo, Paris, or Tobruk. No, now the essential thing to pin down is the place of that play in the revolution." Or Camille Limoges on education: "This democratization of the schools corresponds to the politicalization of the masses; we need them both at once . . .")

Yes, this was philosophical stuff, but not the Voltairian commonsense of the Trudeau school: *Cité libre* was even the main target of lampoon. I savored the longest piece, by Maheu, a complex description of the mental effects of the Quebec situation, a psychoanalysis of the colonized Québécois. This was truer if less smooth than the old *Cité libre* logic, I thought, and the language was beautifully turned here too. Listen:

> The first Thursday of the month, a while back, my mother used to make me recite—aloud—my recent sins, in preparation for the ritual of the following day. According to their gravity, she would cry a greater or lesser quantity of tears over my evil nature, something which didn't prevent her from using my confessions to keep a sharper eye on me the next month.
>
> Last summer, the arrested members of the FLQ, twenty years old, delivered up their confessions to brave policemen while our charitable souls—cabinet ministers or editorial writers—throbbed over the youth gone astray whom they called to "dialogue."
>
> Decidedly, *nothing ever changes in the land of Quebec.* The similarity is no coincidence. It is the real structure of a society, expressed at once in individual life and in politics. The members of the FLQ are the first to live at a political level what we have all experienced at school and in our families. The judiciary, the "toughened" police, solitary confinement and the psychiatric ward, have replaced the principal's strap or the papa's; the humanistic jeremiads of André Laurendeau have replaced the tears of the *maman;* but it is the same structure which reveals itself, the same mush, the same gush that englobes us, and which camouflages the same violence that has been done to us since our childhood.
>
> Our childhood: there indeed is where it all begins; so much so that to speak of it properly one would have to speak of everything at once, for childhood was our first contact with the alienation that an alienated society imposed on us. The family incarnated the society for us; the

family, that all-important institution, foundation-stone of our society, primary cell of the Church—primary place of the fucking-up of things, for our parents and hence for us. The French-Canadian people, dispossessed of their chief political institutions, had undertaken a kind of cultural retreat into a family become the main social institution; this retreat had taken place under the aegis of the curés, who also profited from the political void and replaced all social ethic with a morality of fear. And they had taken over the family, served it up with a sweet sauce of religiosity. In the convents young girls were prepared for their "maternal role" and these were the privileged; the majority one didn't bother giving an education, unnecessary in any case for the mothers they were to become: the "Children of Mary" prepared them adequately, "Ladies of St. Anne" that they were to be. The boys, they were taught to see in the girls eventual occasions for sin among whom, miraculously, would appear "the future mothers of your children." Marriage took them out of their "boyhood," which was ceremonially and bawdily buried, and into the world of the Mother, of "responsibilities," of submission to morality. True, true, the man kept the authority of daily family life; but precisely, daily life was denied in favor of an order of eternal values incarnated by the Mother. The wife, confined to her kitchen in the life of reality, took refuge in Moral Values, while the husband, submissive to that authority with its stamp of approval from heaven, was robbed of the real sense of his daily struggles. The one and the other, short of total degradation, ended up contenting themselves with that gray life wherein "the greatest satisfaction," they said (and it was our parents themselves speaking), "is duty accomplished."

Our parents were of the generation that emigrated from the country to the city; parish structures here dissolved in pluralism, economic necessities rebelled against big families: the old family order was obsolete. Tradition had left the father the out-of-the-house world, work; but here work had become an enslavement and our fathers were left with a long dissatisfaction, the anticipation of vacations. As for our mothers, they felt their authority slowly lose all meaning, slip away from reality; reality was the kitchen, the baby's cry, a strange mixture of exasperation and resignation. They had been promised they would be "queens of the household"; cheated, they became the martyrs. Recriminating ("what did I do that God should . . ." and "now don't go and make your mother cry"), they possessed us by weepiness, enclosure under the sign of misfortune, an order which was the only one within which they conceived life possible. Thus the most unworldly elements of the system were the most important: we learned to say "Jesus" before we learned to ask for what we wanted. And, the system becoming less and less real, more and more a summons to duty, we very soon were told that the Jesus in question would cry if we were bad: this is how our sniffling God was born from our frustrated mothers. But childish spontaneity and the city prevented us from conforming entirely; we soon learned that we were different, and this was one reason for the many tears around us; we awoke to sociability marked with guilt. Soon the bogeyman moved in front of the weeping Jesus; we discovered the violence, the threats, that the sobs had hidden.

I pass quickly over this, because for one thing it really calls for much longer study, and for another each family's life, despite constants, has its variations.

But the major lines of what I have tried to evoke came out even more clearly at school. The *sisters* and *brothers* who replaced our parents dwelled even farther from the real. Morality dictated: boys and girls apart. A segregation reflecting the closed world of the adults who taught us. It was all very complicated, huge, frightening: behind the school there awaited the Church, behind the teaching brother the parish priest, behind the alphabet the fires of hell and the insignia of first communion; the system, omnipresent, swallowed us up. Not content to drum into us prayers and catechism, it invaded arithmetic, history. This system still exists, recent books have described it.

What strikes me most are the techniques used to make us adhere. First, persuasion, sweetness, paste: stars and cherubim in pink decorated the workbooks of the good pupils; on the board were the number of masses one had attended "for the missions" and the number of little Chinese whose salvation one had purchased at twenty-five cents apiece; in order the better to fly to the throne of the Holy Virgin, a small airplane represented each pupil. And of course the children with the richest parents could buy the most Chinese, and what with the secondary importance of actual school marks, the best pupils always turned out to be the mightiest sinophiles! This made us understand, as we discovered the existence of Others, that they were Evil: outside the system, nothing but pagans who abandoned their little Chinese, miscreants who tortured missionaries. We had the choice of being little angels, or else burning out the eyes of missionaries, martyrs still more pitiable than our mothers. The principal's strap helped us make our choice. Once a month, in the school I attended, the teacher pointed out to the principal, on his visit to the class to read out the marks, three or four bad pupils to be made an example of; all of us trembled, all knew themselves guilty of some vague sin. This was the reverse side of the system, the fear which filled out our education. Elsewhere the good sisters required a punished pupil to say "Thank you, sister"; the punishment had to be accepted, the self recognized as punishment-worthy, the guilt internalized. This was the height of the rape of the conscience, for the *thank you sister* could not be in good faith. Little Jesus still wept, but now he was backed by God-who-sees-all-and-judges-us: I know more than one who, at the moment of a confession, literally pissed in his pants. Our being was stolen from us, the system, via our teachers, decided what we were. But we well knew we did not coincide with this image of what we should be presented to us by our teachers and society. The system demanded an absolute adhesion that was ontologically impossible; and even our particularity (the simple fact of being unlike others) we accepted in bad conscience, as *he-who-is-other-than-the-others;* we purged ourselves of our vestiges of personal life, our *mauvaises pensées.* Stripped of our very selves, we were nevertheless haunted by the need for that condemned identity; we lived it as a secret chink, a hidden weakness that ruined in advance all effort to render ourselves acceptable: even those who succeeded knew in their shameful hearts that they passed under false pretenses.

THE BIRTH OF REVOLT

The school changed its name, became the college; the system refined itself and persisted. It was traditional, for instance, for the disciplinarian who had just administered a student his first whacks to send him to the "spiritual director" on duty. This latter specialist in sweet-talk was moved, understood, spoke of sex, did his best to provoke the salutary softening. "The great family of our college" they used to say and indeed, the priests, whom we called fathers and who wore skirts, incarnated the profound ambiguity of parental authority; they used all methods, from corporal punishment to the gooiest "comprehension." For there were penalties for not turning in one's "director's notes" regularly. Inversely, some students were surprised to learn that the authorities knew about things they had mentioned only to their "director." At college, as elsewhere, concern for the salvation of our souls excused many a small complicity. . . .

The oldest among us, people of the generation of *Liberté,* for example, had to wait a long time for this awakening. In their rebellion they still felt isolated, which explains a certain temptation to aestheticism, an escape like any other. The youngest, contrarily, arrive at the ripe moment; they know that history is *ours* to shape. Their revolt immediately becomes action, and to affirm *our* existence they take on frontally, violently, the structures which still interfere with our solidarity. Thus the members of the FLQ, seeking to proceed, bet on the solidarity that youth would feel toward their violence. Those who profit from our alienation, the elites in power, well understood the explosive force of their action; the members of the FLQ were "dangerous": this they were clearly made to see. The public in the courtroom during the coroner's inquest manifested its sympathy for the detainees: the public was excluded. The accused were made to feel isolated: it took several days before they could see their lawyers. They formed a group: they were separated into different cells, a means was even found for preventing them from meeting in the courthouse, they were forced to testify against each other; the unity of the group had to be broken. Those who yielded, recognized themselves as bad boys, juvenile delinquents, were accorded the "protection of the court" and freedom on bail; the mucky-understanding method, this, the "spiritual fathers" and the pasted angels of our childhood. For those who refused to incriminate the other members of the group, who affirmed their political convictions, it was the "comfort" of solitary and the psychiatric wing; here we had the strap, the violence that completed the pattern. And so it is that these young people incarnate our dilemma; like them, though less tragically, we must all choose between pride, anger, and revolution on the one hand, and doubt, shame, and submission on the other; the FLQ prisoners, mistreated and humiliated, have won their bet; they are our mirror and we cannot fail to recognize ourselves in them.

And as for the *parti pris* group, it would not displease me to say it seeks to be an Intellectual Quebec Liberation Front. And since the Quebec revolution is now in its awakening phase, our first task will be one of demystification; our critique will do violence to established myths, we shall attempt to destroy, by discovering their contradictions, the morality and the legality of the system, and open the way to authentic relationships between men.

It will be said, it has already been said, that we are going through the "adolescence of the mind," revolt, negativism. But we know that there are moments when the most urgent tasks are tasks of negation. Or they will apply the "brilliant new literary generation" label to us, they are already applying it to some of us: it's the flattering-comprehension trick and we know all about it. Above all they'll call us isolated intellectuals, representing a tiny minority of youth. They will try to put us in solitary, like the others. Those in power are so lacking in imagination that we can predict their responses to us. It's easy, because to deactivate the explosion this time they will use the same old tactics we have been defending ourselves against since childhood. Not twice in the same trap. And defending ourselves is all the easier because of one new fact, for which they're unprepared: we now form a group whose interest lies in solidarity.

Everything, now, centers around this new fact. We constitute ourselves in subject-group, our adversaries become our object-group. Henceforward it is we who are the essential; we do not write for "dialogue," for comparison of our ideas and, more and more objectively each day, our enemies'; but to build with those who become each day more objectively our brothers a thought which will serve us as a weapon. For revolutionary thought is no prefabricated theory: it is the group in fusion which, discovering itself, surpasses its alienations and defines its hopes, invents its future as it sheds its past. *Parti pris,* well, it will be an instrument at the service of this group's self-definition. And we shall try to behave in such a way that this group extends itself gradually until it embraces everyone: for that is what the revolution is.

There was a difference between this and almost any previous writing about the subject, the details of the conservative Catholicism of French Canada. It would not be approved by the English-Canadians; it would not be anthologized in English Canada as the bright new sound from Quebec. Even the English-Canadian left would have its reservations. (It was old left, it was Thomist, it was totalitarian, the new left would say; and the old left would say it was classical college, it was Thomist, it wasn't working class enough.) No, there was something new here.

There had been previous treatments of conservative Catholicism. If a history of French-Canadian literature were composed by an adherent of the colonial interpretation of Quebec, it would decipher the repressed personality, the muffled shouts of liberation, back through all that has been written in French in America. (*Parti pris* itself has partly undertaken this task, a worthy one.) The American critic Edmund Wilson has done something of the sort for Anne Hébert, a poet of the preceding generation, and other French-Canadian writers of his selection, in *O Canada.* And in general rebellious books like the *Insolences du frère Untel* have been well received in the English-speaking world, which sees French Canada as backward even by bourgeois standards, needing to be brought up to date—that is, up to the level of consciousness of the English-speaking world itself.

But this is precisely the point: Anne Hébert's cries of liberation are muffled, surrounded by fantasy, scarcely recognizable (take her poetic novel *Les Chambres de bois*) as having anything to do with day-to-day French-Canadian reality. The clashes she draws can be regarded as being entirely within the French-Canadian soul, nay the human soul, not out in the world of power relationships between this or that group and its neighbors. Indeed, is her work not written-in-good-French? Has it not been published-in-Paris? And who knows, hailed-in-Tobruk? Is it not, in a word, as much a proof of resilient French-Canadian health as a diagnosis of French-Canadian ills? Anne Hébert has lived many of her adult years in France, far from that day-to-day reality, and has never (that I know) felt the need to take a political position that would express her revolt against the oppressive forces she only hints at. (Some other writers, whose works have undoubtedly been light in the Quebec darkness, have specifically repudiated the new Quebec left. This is the case of Jean-Charles Harvey, whose libertarian writings between the wars Edmund Wilson particularly valued as blows to obscurantism, but who turned to the right in his old age; and of Roger Lemelin, whose *Plouffe Family* television scripts, produced in both English and French for several years by the Canadian state networks, are one of the few authentic inside views of French-Canadian working-class life large numbers of English-Canadians have ever shared, but who, too, frequents the right in politics.)

As for the liberating cries of Frère Untel, they are clear enough and clearly enough public political stands that go beyond the individual soul; but they liberate only to the level of, say, Protestantism, asking for tolerance, openness of spirit, but not revolution, overthrow of the economic order on which the not-Good French he regrets rests. ("Michel calls himself a Communist; this is because he is ignorant of Christianity," Desbiens wrote in the dedication of the *Insolences* to a Ukrainian friend. His own reaction to the youthful left that has brought forward extreme solutions to the malaise he diagnosed was oddly noncommital: Quebec, I read of his saying in a speech he made after he entered the education department, is going through a great philosophical resurgence, "*parti pris* for the youngsters, and a few of our best editorial-page writers for the graybeards." Later his reaction turned hostile.)

What was it about *parti pris* that disqualified it from the English approval that fell upon the Hébert fantasts and the Frère Untel reformers? Even Maheu's stripping-down of colonialism in the classroom could, after all, elicit an Anglo-Canadian endorsement: "Just as I said; their own schools mess them up for any kind of modern life." The difference was that Maheu and his comrades went beyond the classroom out into the factory, analyzed beyond the colonized psyche into the colonized economy, condemned the material context for the cultural shrivelling. The schools taught submission because the children would have to submit when they became adults; the children would have to submit because their ancestors had come late to the capitalist table—*but the circle could be smashed, the latecomers to capitalism could come early to the evenly divided table of socialism.* No longer the dreams of slipping out from under the oppression through Good French, acceptance in Paris, English liberal-mindedness: the *partipristes* would found their own publishing house, in Montreal, to publish books that might be in bad French if that was the kind of French that existed in Montreal, but that would consciously take their place in the revolution, that would take on the whole descriptive and transforming task of nailing down the old order and clearly stating the new. No longer the aestheticist's limiting of oneself to words on paper, to oblique hints of revolt against oppression. If heavier weapons were needed to accomplish the revolution, the *partipristes* would try to forge them: they would found a political movement, with office, mimeograph, paintbrushes, dues to pay bail if need be; they would take their message to trade unionists and street gangs, they would take their verses into the streets, paint them on walls, shout them to crowds, melt them down in the furnace of action until they were arms for the oppressed in their war with the oppressors. Writers had not been heard announcing such a program of intent in Quebec before. For the reader who seeks more than hints, the history of revolutionary literature in Quebec begins in October 1963, with the first issue of *parti pris.*

For the French-Canadian reader, I judged from my reading of French-Canadian political literature during the preceding few years, the newness could be measured in the new vocabulary. The adversary was summoned not only to answer to new charges but to learn a new language. There was, of course, the usual language of political and racial debate, including Marxist terms not favored by the *cité-libristes* but not unfamiliar either—exploitation, imperialism, means of production, solidarity. But I am speaking more of words which emerged from the conjuncture of Marxism, psychiatry, the French existentialists of the left, above all Sartre, from Fanonist anti-colonialism which had already put those first three European ideas to anti-European uses. A glossary might have run:

aliénation (aliéner, aliénant): A term from Marxism—capitalism *alienates* the worker from his product, his labor is *alienated* labor—which is strengthened in French by the fact that *aliéné* is the standard French term for a mentally ill person; he is alienated from himself, he is *out of his mind*, one puts him in an *asile d'aliénés*, an asylum for the alienated. This was an answer to the compassion of the French-Canadian establishment psychiatrist who, after the FLQ, had come to the troubled notables' aid with an explanation that made the young terrorists neither bad nor good: they were illuminated souls, mental cases. This madness of the oppressed was often evoked with another word—*aberration*—and opposed to the notions of *coincider, nous rendre à nous-mêmes,* coinciding with, being returned to, oneself.

ambiguïté: This lurked everywhere in the forests of alienation unveiled by the *partipristes*. It was in Maheu's introductory description of how the self-accusation of the French-Canadian schoolchild turns into the self-assertion of the Québécois intellectual; more recently he has spoken, in reference to the popular and semi-fascist *créditiste* movement in Quebec, of *l'ambiguïté du peuple*.

assumer: Not the English "assume," and a bit more than the usual French use (to assume a post, a job, a title, a responsibility). From existentialism, this, and meaning to look squarely at one's life, surroundings, strengths, and sufferings, and to accept the battles they thrust upon one; being, using another Sartrean word

authentique: Unauthentic, for example, is the French-Canadian who becomes fluent in English, joins a Rotary Club, makes a bundle in business: he has solved his problem, but by being less himself, by sliding away from a fight, by leaving his compatriots behind in the collective deadend.

canadian: Spelt that way, in English, but with the small *c* that is customary for adjectives in French, this was an assumed anglicism which meant: there is no such thing as *canadien,* Canada is a thing not adaptable to French needs, within which no authentic French life can be lived, the only way to retain our Frenchness is to cast Canadianness to the English, *les canadians.* The irony here is that for a long time French-Canadian nationalism expressed itself in an attempt, still heard in the mouths of old French-Canadians, to reserve Canadianness solely to the French—they were *les canadiens,* the others were *les anglais.*

clérico-bourgeois: A portmanteau adjective which was yet another *parti pris* attempt to stress that for it the Church's domination of the French-Canadian spirit and capital's domination of French-Canadian labor were not two problems to be dealt with in the analytic liberal manner, but two sides of one synthetic reality. The regime which ruled French-Canadian life was not the clergy plus the petty bourgeoisie; it was *clérico-bourgeois*—the Church using the notables, the notables using the Church, both being used by English-speaking capital.

colonisé (colonisateur): Not only was Quebec a colony, the brand was on the forehead of every individual Québécois; each was a *colonisé,* a colonized person. And every English-speaking occupier, whether a big or little fish in the domination, was a *colonisateur,* a colonizer. The terms were Fanon's, Albert Memmi's (whose *Portrait du colonisé* was another basic text for the new Quebec anti-colonials), Jacques Berque's (whose *Dépossession du monde,* published in 1964, would actually list Quebec among the colonized nations, one of the first recognitions from France).

déshumanisation: The *partipristes* shared this term for what the regime does to its victims with young English-speaking revolutionaries in North America. Another was *dépossession*—*Dépossession du monde*— and another, a good one this, *décolonisation.*

démesure: The heedlessness that *parti pris* at first found almost a virtue in the FLQ terrorists; their pain at the oppression around them was measurable in the immoderation of their acts. The outrage was unbearable; the action must be *inconditionnée, irrémédiable.*

démystifier (démystification, démystificatrice): Formerly this would have been the reader of a murder mystery, the man at a loss before a point of etiquette. Here, though, the mystification was the fake justification, the false feelings and fraudulent defenses the regime threw up around it, drilled into its victims: "democracy," "biculturalism," "violence." To demystify was to tear down the defenses, to uproot the feelings in the victim, to understand. To *dévoiler,* to bare to the oppressed man's eyes the real ways out.

dépasser (dépassement): Ordinarily, simply to overtake, go past, leave behind, as in a race or with an outdated clothing style. Here, however, something more like *to surpass oneself,* to comprehend one's oppression and to strive to burst out of it. *"Dépassement vers le monde,"* said Paul Chamberland in the second *parti pris.*

essentiel: The regime had always said that something else outside the Québécois was this: heaven, said the Church; the country, said the *canadians.* Now the time had come to turn this around, to make oneself the essential, the rest the can-be-changed. But it is better still—and here, of course, we are at the heart of this entire outlook —to toss out the whole search for essentials and to live *exist*entially; with oneself still the starting-point, but making even of that self something changeable, still-to-be-created.

historisant: History become a verb: *historisant* is the act that is history-making, the man who does something rather than having something done to him, having history made on his back. Fanon again.

humanisme: A joke. So often pressed into service by the mystifiers that the *partipristes* could no longer use the word in any sense but Fanon's: "This Europe which never stops talking about Man and shoots him down on every streetcorner where it meets him."

inventer: Not the steam engine or the cotton gin, but one's life, one's future.

moment: A step in the revolution, a stage in the invention of oneself.

praxis: The fitting together of those moments: first understanding, then acting, and knowing just when and how to do each. To be wished for devoutly.

prise de conscience: Before one can take sides, before one's *parti* can be *pris,* one must *take up consciousness* of one's situation; the beginning of everything, thus, this moment of the *colonisé*'s awakening.

And finally, most Sartrean of all,

situation: Unsituated, freedom doesn't know what to do; no will to freedom and the situation overwhelms: it is the freedom in situation which can do something.

But this was the view from French Canada. For myself, an English-speaking watcher, the newness of *parti pris* was still most plain in the surprising effect of its responses to the old English-Canadian taunts at French Canada. These taunts seemed to hurt *Cité libre*'s feelings. A *citélibriste* like Gérard Pelletier, a Catholic for all his fights with the reactionary clergy, could not abide English talk of the "priest-ridden province"; he would sermonize these bigots for their outdated picture of Quebec. But *parti pris* admitted the stereotypes were fundamentally true; preparing to go beyond them, it could bear cruel pictures of the present. Thus:

First of all, to the bigoted schoolteacher in one of the two evocations of French-Canadian life in English that have moved me, Robert Fontaine's *The Happy Time* (the other is Jack Kerouac's *Visions of Gérard*): "This is an English nation."

"Yes," reply the *partipristes*, "and that is why we no longer want to live in it."

"You lack business sense, you are poets, or simply strong-backed simpletons," says the Anglo-Montrealer.

"Indeed," respond the *partipristes*, "history so far has given power, cash, stocks, bonds to you, words to us. Our muscles have become profits in your factories, and now we want the factories to produce for us, for all, and we shall use our words to plan how to take them from you."

"Priest-ridden," they said of Quebec, its own fault, not ours.

"True," say the *partipristes*, "our priests have helped you shear your wealth from our backs, and when we correct that we shall not be Protestant individualists like you, but materialist sharers like those other Latin Catholics, the Cubans."

And finally the Anglo-Saxon scoffed at the penniless poet's very words: "As for your distinctive language, it's not even French, it's a mongrel, and what it's becoming—need we say it?—is English."

"Right again," *parti pris* replies, "our language is yielding to yours, is inferior to yours, as are our teeth, our skin, our educational level, our per-capita income, our very vision of life. And all these inferiorities must be overthrown. Prepare yourselves."

During that 1963 Parti Socialiste meeting at which I leafed through the first number of *parti pris,* I had, before voicing an opinion, named myself as "Malcolm Reid, Sherbrooke." Maheu, speaking just after me, parodied my parliamentary pretentiousness: "Pierre Maheu, Outremont"—Outremont, over there on the north slope of the mountain, being the wealthiest Montreal district in which French-speakers predominate (and one which, interestingly, has almost no Anglo-Saxons; the English-speakers of Outremont are the upper-middle strata of that other underdog group, the Jews), he had also parodied his own petty-bourgeois roots. And those of *parti pris?* Certainly the enemies of the magazine did not lose time in saying so. By what right did this publication, whose very masthead gave an apartment address on Champagneur Avenue in Outremont, speak for Visitation's slums? What relationship existed between the stony misery of the slum-caged Quebec proletarian and the refusal of this misery by the less-hard-pressed, culturally armed Quebec intellectual?

Not all the *parti pris* group were Outremontagnard classical college products like Maheu. Some (Jean-Marc Piotte) had escaped from the east end and remembered it. Some (Paul Chamberland) were from neither extreme. There were about ten on the masthead of the magazine, perhaps twenty altogether in the group at the start. They partly sprang from, partly formed, a much larger milieu which I first brushed up against when I was simply reading the magazine, and got to know better after 1965 when I began to seek them out to write about them.

The newly literate youths from the slums and the *révoltés* from Outremont, plus, for example, village intellectuals come to Montreal in flight from the isolation which escaped, perhaps, the slum, but did not escape the parish, each approaching from his own direction, found their way to a strip of Sherbrooke Street West. A strip in the area between the Sherbrooke Street of respectable old French-Catholic institutions in the east and the chic Sherbrooke Street of art galleries and dress shops further west. On one side of Sherbrooke in this area is a restaurant, officially called the Swiss Hut; in fact a tavern which admits women. Its walls are varnished boards, its tables are masonite in log booths, but it is not sprightly, it is dingy, like a tavern, and it sells almost nothing but beer, like a tavern. Its clientele is not all bohemian; oddly, the lonely middle-aged drinkers who, I suppose, always went there, who would be likely to go for the music in the Country Palace next door, have stayed. But now half the place was taken over by youths living downtown, growing beards and wearing rough clothes, seeking comradeship in their rejection of bourgeois life.

Upstairs on the other side of Sherbrooke Street is the Asociación Española, a club which began as a gathering place for the considerable number of Iberic immigrants in Montreal. The Spaniards still come, there are flamenco performances on weekends, there are red-and-white tablecloths, but at the Asociación, too, more beer has come to be sold than any other drink. And more French to be spoken (as well as English, since the English-speaking bohemia of Montreal, once separate in its diversions, now joins the French here; it is near McGill University).

The Hut and the Asociación are symbolic, of course. It is not any one café that is revolution's cradle; indeed, the specific acts of the FLQ can be traced to conventional, plush-seated booth restaurants a bit further east—the trek out of the slums was less advanced, as was revolutionary thought at that moment—on St. Denis Street, for example. And the terrorists were many of them below drinking age and below a bohemian level of self-consciousness.

There are other downtown meeting centers besides the cafés which brought young rebels together: the Jacques Cartier Normal School, a Catholic teacher-training institution which I have already situated in Lafontaine Park just above the most intense slums, is one. At least three on the masthead of the first *parti pris* had been students there. But the process was that: the converging, both intellectually and geographically, in mid-Montreal of young French-Canadians who felt obscurely that to fulfill themselves they must demolish the hold of the Dominion of Canada, the capitalist economy, and the Roman Catholic Church on their personalities and their society. And even if they happened to come from a well-off Montreal district or a mill town in the Ottawa Valley, their gesture was a symbolic burst westward. From the old unquestioning French-Canadian universe to the new uncertainties. From a thoughtless conviction of one's Frenchness in the midst of its erosion, to a terrible defensiveness of it in a situation where one had a surer conscious mastery of one's culture, relaxed contacts with non-French life, but a comprehension of the slow death of French, the long entrapment that is French life.

Walk *west* across Montreal and you can imagine the process. From the dark neighborhoods of the east to the lit-up restaurants on still-French, slightly old-fashioned St. Denis, then to the cosmopolitanism—and the skid-row social disintegration—of St. Lawrence. Here on the official mid-band of the city life is materially worse than further east. The rock-bottom-priced cafeterias and hot-dog stands will be where he eats now, the traveller out of east end alienation, living in physical misery for the sake of his new glimmer of self-understanding. For the horizon of history that was invisible in the sad uniformity of Panet Street surges up on St. Lawrence: bums, whores, abjection, vs. driving music, driving people, skyscrapers coming into view. From there to the bohemian center-west, where the French take on the English at their own brainy games. Then to the sharp new apartments still further west where the people *Maclean's* and *Holiday* talk about live. Now the majority of your neighbors will be English; you know that the majority of your old neighbors couldn't have made it this far, would be seared, lost dumbfounded in this sleek foreign world.

"Most of us from the working-class districts couldn't move back there." It is a twenty-year-old socialist-separatist militant, not particularly literary or arty, who is telling me about the feeling. "When we were kids we spoke no English, we never saw further east than Bleury, never saw the stores on St. Catherine West. To live here is to have escaped. But we all know that things are still at zero-level back in the workers' districts; as far as political awareness goes, the work is still to be done, and it will have to be done there." He was talking about the same colonial division of Montreal I saw on my walks through the city. An accounting course had taken him out of the French slums, *parti pris* had taken him out of the slums' resignation. He lived with friends in a comfortable west Montreal apartment, but he knew the west hadn't embraced him for all that: the masters of the economy had built their Montreal still further west.

He and his friends were typical of the young men of working-class origin *parti pris* had brought to political consciousness. The scene that comes to me when I think about this process involves one of the friends he lived with. Highly strung, muscular, very crisp and grammatical in his speech, this young man is a self-educated intellectual from Valleyfield, a textile town near Montreal. He worked in the book business at the time, by day surrounded by theory, but attending all the demonstrations, those nights of practice.

This particular night, though, we were in a booth at the Hut. The table was crowded, prickly with beer bottles; with us is the secretary of the Mouvement de Libération Populaire (the group *parti pris* formed to bridge the gap between theory and practice), a girl who will later go through the courts over one of the revivals of the FLQ, and Gaston Miron—Miron, poet and precursor of *parti pris,* the kind of intellectual who seems to know everything. He was discoursing on the incorrigible bourgeoisness of the theater: "A bourgeois form, always has been, always will be; it was invented for the bourgeois when they came into existence and it is they who have kept it alive. Bertolt Brecht tried to make it serve the workers, wrote plays explaining surplus value, everything you want; the workers couldn't have cared less." The young man from Valleyfield intervened to ask who Bertolt Brecht was. Gaston said quietly that he was the greatest dramatist of the Communist world, that he had organized the Berliner Ensemble, that he wrote, as he'd said, didactic Marxist plays. The young man was ignorant but interested; the older one was interested in informing him, going on with his point, hearing the reaction to it. It was one scene in the meeting of popular anger and literature in colonized Montreal in the 1960's.

Literature had wanted to become action, to act upon the colonized city it sprang from. In 1964, *parti pris* had assigned itself the above-ground work of awakening the colonized man in the slum, of engaging the intellectual in bohemia (colonized too, even if partly free of the slum culture). An important part of the action of the Mouvement de Libération Populaire would be helping to rally demonstrations. The Canadian federal holidays were occasions. Especially the "24th of May"—Victoria Day—which derives from Queen Victoria's birthday and by convention marks that of the current British monarch; it accordingly enrages the separatists. In 1965 the Montreal police department was jolted by disturbances on this holiday in Lafontaine Park, that big open area on the northern rim of the slums. *Parti pris* revolutionaries were involved. Jean-Marc Piotte, thin, bespectacled, thin blond hair and moustache, author of "From Duplessism to the FLQ" in the first *parti pris,* spoke to the crowd through a bullhorn, trying to bring out both the national and class character of the protest. Rounded up with other agitators by the police early in the evening, he promised in court some weeks later to keep the peace for a year from that date. Jean Racine, also thin, but bushily black-haired, communicated with other demonstration leaders with a walkie-talkie which resembled a transistor radio, and avoided arrest to the end.

Parti pris regarded Victoria Day 1965 as a date in the revolution in Quebec. More so, perhaps, than even the FLQ arrests in 1963, or Nightstick Saturday in 1964 (when demonstrators went to the downriver capital of Quebec City to greet Queen Elizabeth), for in neither of these cases had there been so clear an appeal to the *colonisé*-in-the-street. On Victoria Day 1965, a number of policemen had been injured in late-night brawls with leaderless demonstrators from the slums. It was new to the police, this action in the slum streets, and frightening.

A month after that Victoria Day swarming-into-the-streets the same separatist and socialist swarm, now largely stripped of leaders, felt the police's reaction to the wounds they had been dealt in May. It was July 1, the ninety-eighth anniversary of Canadian confederation. The demonstration had been announced by word and handbill at the festivities on the French-Canadian holiday that comes *between* the two Canadian ones, the feast of John the Baptist on June 24. The police formed themselves into walls around each of the two parks in which, one after another, the youths tried to group for a charge, and dealt them clubbings each time they made contact with a wall.

It seemed suddenly to be a tradition, however, the federal holiday demonstration in Montreal. A year later neither Piotte nor Racine was on hand, the one bound over until several days later, both now involved in a search for other ways to awaken the colonized worker, among trade unionists in the cooler-tempered Parti Socialiste du Québec. But something calling itself in a leaflet the Mouvement 23 Mai was going to demonstrate, leaders or no. The east was going to have its night of breaking-out. "The 23rd of May Movement seems to be rather young," one English-speaking friend said as I made my way across Lafontaine Park. "Three thousand Rolling Stones," said another. And in fact it was teenagers, even the ones in the lower half of their teens, long hair and tight pants, joual-speaking French-Canadian youths from the eastern part of the city's heart, Visitation

Street and the blocks and blocks of slums around it. Such youths gather in Lafontaine Park every holiday. They come to listen to rock'n'roll on transistor radios, to eat hot dogs from the municipal snack bar. The grass is soothing and the canoes glide nicely on the artificial lake. When there is a demonstration, they join it. I listened for the slogans they were chanting, and though it was often a straight separatist Quebec-to-the-Québécois, sometimes the demand was made in the name of the workers: *"Le! Qué! bec! aux! ouv! ri! ers!"*

The adolescent mass swung around the lake, to a corner of the park where there is a monument to Dollard des Ormeaux, a French-Canadian clerical hero massacred by the heathen Iroquois in New France's fur wars. (He's no Québécois hero.) A guy in a scarlet synthetic-fabric polo shirt was on somebody's shoulders shouting, unaided this time by microphone or bullhorn. It was the young man from the Hut who'd wanted to know about Brecht: "We have assurances from our lawyer that anyone arrested will be defended. We came to demonstrate and we shall demonstrate!" As he slid to the ground the crowd filtered through the trees to the street, and he grabbed me by my sweater front and told me: "I'm proud, man, I'm proud." He had written a Marxist paper against that anarchism which counted on the angers of the proletariat, especially the lumpen. Now, his red shirt standing out, he was leading a streetful of teenagers westward from the park in the proletarian-to-lumpen east. The sun was just descending, the slogans cut through the dusk, and the motorcycles of the police zoomed alongside the flood they could not halt.

The flood flowed into Sherbrooke Street East, a major thoroughfare, and occupied it. But this the police could not tolerate and a roadblock of paddywagons diverted the tide north a little, into back streets. After regrouping it dribbled back down to Sherbrooke again. Its new occupation of a main street had audacious moments: the moment when a youngster shinnied the post supporting a balcony on this very respectable and very French eastern avenue and tore away the canvas of a banner proclaiming a traditional party ward-boss's candidacy in the provincial election then underway. Cheers. (Later, a tossed stone knocked over a placard in a window for the nonsocialist and election-participating Rassemblement pour l'Indépendance

Nationale, and this pleased the *parti pris* militants.) At another moment the bulk of the demonstrators sat down on the pavement. But they were too anxious for action to carry through on this tactic. Again the youngsters were pushed into side streets, again they worked their way west in splintered rivulets. The direction still was clearly west, and the red-shirted militant later told anyone who would listen: "My objective was McGill." The gray-stoned campus on Sherbrooke Street West was a nice representative institution of the money-making, decision-making, English west of the city.

The crowd was onto St. Lawrence Boulevard—the Main, watershed of east and west, a main drag of restaurants, warehouses, billiard halls, flophouses. Jewish traditionally, but more and more the Greek alphabet replaces the Hebrew on storefront signs. For a moment, here on the Main, I wondered if we were beyond the anti-Jewish vandalism of earlier, prewar days of French-Canadian popular agitation. A few rocks are tossed, but the word was, "Don't touch," and the demonstrators moved their open palms toward an automobile which threaded through their forward movement, as if to rock it, but did not. Past the Carpenters' Hall, past the Elysée art cinema. Once again onto Sherbrooke. They swing west again, now over the line, now into the west half of town, now within sight of the skyscrapers and gray stone, but here the most determined police roadblock awaits them and they filter down into side streets south of Sherbrooke, toward St. Catherine, as close as they will get to the heart of town. Past a Greek Orthodox church, past the once-beatnik cafés near the state art school, into the rubble-covered rear yard of the freshly constructed Place des Arts. Here nightsticks reach them, and paddywagons and windowless black police buses swallow them up, or they head back eastward.

The return east is not organized, it is done in small chanting bands, and there is talk of regrouping in Lafontaine Park. Once in the park the returning pockets mill around, but no strong leadership shows itself and the police are now confident. Slowly, nightsticks in hand, they herd the small groups diagonally back across the park, through the trees, over the paths, and out the southeastern corner, where the park adjoins the slum streets. Boys in jeans put their arms over the shoulders of girls in jeans; quarrels break out between the herded: "Hey, lay off, I'm a separatist, too," says an English-accented voice in reply to a joual taunt. The thrust into the west is over, the retreat to the east complete.

The intellectuals who led it are talking it over at the Hut. And a month later, on Canada's ninety-ninth birthday, the cops are so thick around the edges of Lafontaine Park that you can't even wander in from the sidewalk after a certain hour before the announced demonstration time. Only the French-Canadian picnickers from the east end streets who have been there all afternoon are allowed to munch on. They do so as if under glass, shielded from the Québécois anger that might come at them out of their own eastern streets.

2
Flat broke

When a writer has been born in a country far enough away from the one where his language came into being to have developed a distinguishable speech, but is not confident enough to write its own grammar and hurl it at the motherland, he does not know how to write about his country. He will probably want to put the kind of speech he hears every day into the mouths of his characters. Why should his faraway reader, once told of the locale of the story, not be willing to make the effort to catch on to this regional divergence of the tongue, as Faulkner, Joyce, or any Latin American novelist ask their readers to? But what about the rest of the text, the narration? What if his writing is not of a kind that makes this distinction, if the whole text is the author speaking, as with a poet? Who sets the standard there? To write in the manner of the native land of the language, he will have to speak in a foreign accent, to assume a foreign elegance, perhaps cut himself off from his countrymen as readers. And if the hope of catching the attention of the motherland is in any case faint?

On the other hand, the hope is always there. And the other choice, renouncing the international standard and international hopes for faithfulness to the spoken language one is surrounded with, means one has to force oneself to believe in the completeness and serviceability of one's local speech, to capture it, to delineate it, to consider it not a dialect but a language. And this implies further political responsibility: to consider the people that speak it a nation, able to legislate its language as well as its civil code. Thus Noah Webster fought the British in the militias of the American Revolution: the one era saw the United States declare their independence and the American language its. And it was the long years of American political, economic, and linguistic self-assertion that dealt with the problem and put it out of the way for the great American writers. With an Irishman like Joyce there was a nuance: the national self-assertion of the country was part of the climate he came from, but there was a contrary process in the language itself: the acceptance of the dominant country as arbiter in matters of language, the abandonment of the local tongue to concentrate on surpassing the colonizer in the superimposed one, prepared the way for international recognition of the Irish masters. The two possibilities find expression in a single sentence in Albert Memmi's *Portrait du colonisé*: "Colonial literature in European languages seems doomed to die young." This theorist of anti-colonial revolt, writing from Arabic-speaking Tunisia, affirms the local tongue as the only authentic idiom for a literature of the colonized, but does so (like Fanon, like Aimé Césaire) in French.

In Quebec, the largest community of French-speaking people outside France, the problem exists for writers in this general sense and in a brutal special one too: almost all of the deviation of Quebec French from French French can obviously or possibly be attributed to the nearness of English.

The problem is as old as the carving-out of the French and English empires in North America, but it is not quite that simple. It cannot really be said to have been confronted in its full grittiness before the 1960's, when attempts were being made to cut through all the other problems of French Canada. Past campaigns for pure French —or, the opposite, in defense of the perhaps impure Canadian habit against some fancier, more pretentious European norm—were always based on undisputed assumptions. There was the assumption that correct French did exist; that its repository was France; that purity could be checked against French grammars, dictionaries, speech patterns. There was the assumption that this was indeed the more serviceable tongue; that to come down for Canadianism was to accept (perhaps, mind you, with aggressive pride) a backwoods status; that only people who were trying to *be better than they were* would strive for another kind of French than that which sprang to the lips. There was, in other words, French, and Canadian French; you took your choice and you acted accordingly.

In September 1963, with the founding of the magazine *parti pris*, the whole question of what Quebec had to learn from the rest of the world, what it owed to the rest of the world, and what the rest of the world owed it, was up for re-asking. Where previous movements for French-Canadian advancement had appealed to rights established in pacts between French-Canadians and those with whom they had had to deal historically, *parti pris* said that the pacts had never been more than disguises for plunder. Quebec was a colony. Where previous movements called for new pacts, *parti pris* called for revolution. Its program for the refrenchification of Quebec meant taking what the province lacked from those who held it. To separatism, not a new program for the province, it added socialism of a generally Marxist kind.

Parti pris said it was fighting for a Quebec "free, secular, and socialist"; its masthead carried the phrase *"revue politique et culturelle,"* but everyone knew this description was false—it was simply the lack of a single word for its position that prevented the magazine from saying it all at once. For it was all one thing, this enchainment of Quebec, it was the same complex knot of effacements described by the anthropologists of colonialism on the three poor continents. And the breaking of the chains would be one thing too, the freeing of poetry as well as labor, as indivisible as the bread-land-and-peace, or the *liberté-fraternité-égalité,* of great past upheavals. For the French language was one of those things the colonialists—juridically the English-speaking Canadians, part of mainstream American culture, holding authority in an economy in which French speakers were the work force; ultimately United States capital itself, the big presence in Quebec industry—were in the process of robbing from the French-Canadians. To restore the language, one had to restore the nation. Perhaps, in fact, the language was not a distortion, a mistake, a drifting from some French truth about Quebec, a mark of neglect or laziness on the part of the speakers, reparable by admonition, but rather a perfect gauge of where French-Canadians stood. Perhaps he who espoused Quebec nationalism had also to espouse Quebec speech.

The exploration of these themes was done in *parti pris* largely by classically educated youths who were at least within reach of standard French. Their education had been in the *collèges classiques* run by the Roman Catholic clerical orders for those French-Canadian petty bourgeois who could afford to pay the clergy's tuition fees. These advanced secondary schools or junior colleges granted the *baccalauréat*, the preliminary to the specialized faculties of the French-Canadian university, and were until 1967 the Quebec notable class's means of reproducing itself. In 1967 they began to be absorbed into a state system. They had for centuries enabled lawyers' sons to become lawyers, doctors' sons doctors, and, more recently, schoolteachers' sons sociologists. They were also the entry into the notable elite for a few workers' sons, according to the tradition whereby a working-class family would sacrifice so that *one* of its sons, the intellectual among a dozen, could *faire son cours classique*. But their main function was restrictive: as private institutions selling learning at private-enterprise rates, they assured that learning be the possession of one class, and since the universities (also clerical if less private) were geared to them, they long impeded the development of a public secondary-school sector of any intellectual solidity. Their own intellectualism was, of course, severely circumscribed by clerical control, but the youths they taught to read the classics in annotated editions usually found their way to the modern, and to the *maudîts*, masters in paperback. The lettered *partipristes* came from this milieu; they read the rebel French writers, took in French recordings and films, could think of visiting France some day. The line they took, however, was bound to reach some French-Canadians on the border between their privileged awareness and the unconsciousness that is the lot of the average speaker of Canadianized French, unaware which parts of his speech meet international norms and which derive from English-American influence, and unable to do much about it in any case.

It was two youths from this in-between category whose work formed the beginnings of *parti pris* as a school of imaginative literature, a publisher of novels that told the story of Quebec's colonization in concrete images from the life of the *colonisés*. And which did so in the language of the *colonisés* themselves, not in the French that was offered to the classical-college student as an ideal. This *défense et illustration de la langue jouale,* this refusal of the spring of universality proposed by the classicist, this coming down firmly for the local tongue, its expansion, literarization, legitimization, as the authentic way out of the rupture with the motherland, was adopted hesitatingly by Laurent Girouard, and wholeheartedly by Jacques Renaud.

It was, after all, natural that a magazine which saw language as a mirror of economics would contain poems as well as polemics, would have novelists as well as political analysts on its staff. And, considering both life and art as fields for forcible overthrow, it would want to extend its thrusts at the social order by founding a political party, its hackings at the literary order by founding a publishing house. *Parti pris* became a publishing house within the first year of its existence, in February 1964, by issuing a novel which announced itself as a failure, the proof of the impossibility of first-rate writing coming from within a community of second-class Canadians. To the extent that the writer had quit that second-class Canadianness for a still-to-be-founded *québécicité*, he might be free of this failure, but who could claim to have done anything but begin to quit the old, to find the new?

The novel was Girouard's *La Ville inhumaine—The Inhuman City—* and in the third issue of *parti pris* its author had already stated, in capital letters, the impossibility of art coming from the enslaved: "THERE IS NOT AND NEVER HAS BEEN ANY SUCH THING AS FRENCH-CANADIAN LITERATURE," meaning that writing that tried to meet the requirements of both ends of the hyphen tore itself in two: the only successes of the past had been reachings for that *québécicité*. This was December 1963 and there had been as yet no detailed treatment of the difference between French-Canadian speech and French, between *joual* and *cheval*. (Nor was there to be any between the beginning of the magazine and the beginning of the éditions, except for Girouard's note that French-Canadian newspaper critics like Gilles Marcotte of the mass-circulation *La Presse* could be counted on to check—and reject—all Montreal-published novels against the French grammarian Grevisse, and to publish their own novelistic efforts in France. Marcotte, nevertheless, found "presages" in *La Ville inhumaine* when he reviewed it.)

And *La Ville* itself did not clearly challenge the grammarians, clearly adopt an anti-French, undividedly Québécois voice. The saddest thing about it was that the author's statement, rashly used in the publicity for the novel by Girouard himself in his capacity as manager of les éditions parti pris, was fairly just: *La Ville inhumaine* read less like a novel than like the notes for one, the diary of a man who always meant to distill his baffled adolescence into a work of art but who remained baffled at the time of distilling. It switched back and forth between styles, clear and jumbled, literary and popular. At its least "French," its most *joualisé*, the book hit something like the tavern speech of French Canada, and the mood, the womanless, refugee mood, of French-Canadian tavern customers. (Réginald Boisvert, a writer of the just-older-than-*parti-pris* generation, nicely explained that mood in his "Importance and Meaning of the Tavern in the Cultural Context of French Canada," in *Ecrits de la Taverne Royal*, a mock-literary paperback collection of essays that appeared on the stands about 1960: "Our rural population migrates massively to the cities. The father's role changes radically. No more is he the boss of an enterprise; rather the bringer-home of the pay envelope. . . . He can, of course, hide behind his paper, absorb himself in the TV. But how to escape that feeling of uselessness, that malaise once the bacon has been brought home? And that inferiority before woman, whose prime hours of useful activity these are? He is out of place. He leaves the house. . . .") Laurent Girouard evoked it this way:

> The last buses leave. The cleanup man is waiting for me to lift my feet. I've been here all night just . . .
> "Move, Christ!"

The presentation publisher Girouard gave author Girouard was also an expression of uncertainty. Visually, the book had only one mark of the *parti pris* style, the lack of capitals on the jacket: *"la ville inhumaine/*laurent girouard/*parti pris."* But this was under a miniature abstract oil, reproduced on fine paper, in normal rectangular book shape—everything evoking high-class French publishing, right down to the uncut pages inside. The novel was described in a publicity release in the magazine as "a failure which attempts to assume itself, and to go beyond itself"; it was meant to have the ugliness of the colonized Quebec existence, yet it was dressed in the complacent clothing of a *belle lettre* ready for a "reading public."

Late in 1966 I sat down in the Royal Tavern to talk about these things with Girouard. The Royal was a gathering place of the just-before-*parti-pris* bohemians, a room papered with eagles and stars, far from the slums of the east in the downtown part of Montreal near the Radio-Canada studios. Girouard put his briefcase on the bench beside him and looked firmly at me from behind spectacles, neatly trimmed beard, and equally neat tie. He was twenty-seven, married, father of a child, commitments he had taken on early, before the socialist-independentist commitment was clear. He spoke of a background that set him apart even from some of his *parti pris* comrades:

"My father was a metalworker in St. Hyacinthe, and I remember things from home that are only words to some of the others—strikes, no work for months, nothing to eat in the house, that sort of thing. My problem I share with a whole new group here in Quebec, teachers and government employees as much as artists. We are proletarians who have become intellectuals and who must, somehow, try not to lose our balance."

He talked about *La Ville inhumaine*:

"My book was detestable, yes, but it was fitting for it to be so, it could not be otherwise, it sprang from a detestable situation. And our literature will be excessively detestable in this way as long as that situation persists. For we are faced with this dead end, that if literature is *literary,* if it idealizes, renders marvelous, it is nonsense, it does not represent us. I could strive to be a fine writer, a master craftsman, but having attained that I would have attained nothing, because the social and political alienation in which language is encrusted would still be there, my writing would be a beautiful machine going around and around within itself. I would have to publish in France, and there I would be some sort of sub-sub-Robbe-Grillet (just as, if I took the other way out and Americanized myself completely, I would be at best a sub-sub-Faulkner or Dos Passos). So what is left to us writers? We can play the clown, the bohemian scribbler, like Jasmin, or the maker-of-fine-phrases like Godbout—I know they hate each other's guts, consider themselves at the antipodes the one of the other, but . . . Or we can fight the alienation, write works that really do reflect us, even if they are for the moment doomed, and while awaiting the coming into being of possibilities for the work that will not be doomed, try to extract from writing its value as work, as a spark that may indicate future surpassing of the failed effort."

At this time, writing had become difficult even apart from the colonial curse, simply because of family and work. But the work was not without satisfactions:

"I teach in the South Shore school system just off Montreal Island —I've even been acting principal at my school for quite long periods over recent years—and my work there makes me the opposite of discouraged. There I work with youths, working-class kids still unformed, open to an explanation of their lives and problems. Even the authorities know it: I'm engaged in political indoctrination in my classes. How? You can go about it from almost any starting point. As a subject for an essay you assign Vietnam: you discuss the causes, the forces involved, the future. The kids start thinking about it, taking positions. Already students from my classes are participating in political movements, in the trade unions, in the student unions at higher levels of school. Youth are catching on: it's a matter of time before this shows, before these youngsters emerge and cough up all the ideas they've been accumulating. And as long as you are holding their attention, are getting the knowledge into their heads—and can answer the questions of the trustees—there is nothing the authorities can do.

"Another main interest of mine, you know, is archaeology. I spend my summers at a site on Lake St. Louis, near Melocheville, where some friends and I realized a few years ago that Indian encampments must have left their traces. We started as pure amateurs, now we have a University of Montreal grant and a staff. The precise shape of the past life we will be able to uncover is not yet clear, but already we have been able to modify some of the conventional classifications of Indian civilizations upheld by the northern United States archaeological establishment. I'm working on a paper now for one of their journals, telling of combinations we have found of elements of Indian culture they have always believed belonged to disconnected periods. I am studying nights at the university, yes, but the Melocheville digging is not for that; it is for something else, to satisfy a need I have to recapture the past, or part of it, of this colony that is my homeland. Lessons to be learned from the previous occupants, their fate before the French colonizers? That would be putting it too strongly: there is never an easy moral in a piece of pottery or an arrowhead. Simply a better understanding of what it is to be a man."

And yes, there is another novel. It's been off and on, this novel, and though Girouard associates the offs and ons with the repressiveness of the colonial atmosphere he has felt around him, some of what he says must sound sadly familiar to any writer: "It'll be a brick, three-four hundred pages. And of course I'll try it at *parti pris* first, but I don't know if they'll want it. *Qu'est-ce que tu veux,* it's another novel for intellectuals . . ."

For Girouard, founder of les éditions parti pris, is no longer their director. Work and family have forced him to give up even writing for the magazine. I could not help feeling there was a certain bitterness in Laurent Girouard at the relative unsuccess of his own novel amid the rather astounding successes of other writers he had tracked down and published—their successes, partly his handiwork but less his glory. And as for the landscape of failure in which the unsuccessful novel was the true one, it was odd to hear it so much insisted on by the greatest *reader* among the *partipristes.*

It was Girouard, for example, who had directed me to Albert Laberge. This man, who died an aged sportswriter in 1960, had left behind, though hardly anyone had noticed, a chilly, cynical, published-by-the-author novel written before World War I and called *La Scouine.* It was a series of sketches of turn-of-the-century rural life in which the meanness of the French-Canadian peasants is scarcely excused by the condition of their lives: *la Scouine,* the old maid title character (so called from schooldays by classmates who smelled the urine of her inevitable bed wettings, and finally from a shower of piss from the boys in the class, paying her back for a treachery—though Laberge also and contradictorily remarks that *Scouine* has no meaning and "takes us back to the very origins of language"), is mean-spirited even as a babe, and can only become exaggeratedly so as spinsterish mannerisms set in. Her equally spinsterish brother is more pathetic than mean: he falls from a ladder while topping-off a brick house his family has built in the hopes that he will install a bride in it and take over the homestead; crippled by the fall, he never marries, and his one roll in the hay is with a middle-aged female field hand his father hires one harvest season. He, too, acquires a nickname—it jolted me when I first read it—*le Cassé*, the broken one. But exactly what has broken Laberge's peasants is never defined: the clergy are there, arrogant and clownish, the English are there, but aside from the fact that they are to a man on the Conservative side when election time comes, they are placed in no particular power relation to the French-Canadians. The mutual hatred of the two groups is described with the same cold mockery as everything else.

There is a fraudulent merchant and a complacent judge, and the toil in the fields is itself murderous, but in the end the author (who notes in a dedication that his brother still tilled the soil of the Ottawa valley at the time of publication, and who at death preferred cremation to being buried there because of the acerbity of his judgments of his neighbors) seems to see the life of his people as summed up in his recurring image from the Charbonneaus' daily supper: a loaf of bread both sour and bitter, marked in the crust with a cross.

The whole is peppered with dialogue in a joual wilder, it seemed to me (though that was probably because of its archaism), than any of the *partipristes*':

>—*Mon vieux, j'cré ben que j'vas être malade.*
>—*A soir?*
>—*J'cré qu'oui.*
>—*Ça serait teut ben mieux d'aller cri le docteur.*
>—*J'cré qu'oui.*
>—*J'irai aprè manger.*

The exchange still largely rings true. Many working-class Québécois still say *j'cré* for *je crois*, *j'vas* for *je vais*. Québécois of all classes can be heard saying *ben* for *bien*. And the dropped-article contractions *à soir* and *après manger* could not be more Québécois.

Girouard's favorites are culled from more recent undergrounds, too, and include Gérard Bessette, a loner in French-Canadian writing, working out in Loyalist Ontario at a literature-teaching job at Queen's University in Kingston, producing characters of magnificent isolation, like the surly book clerk of his *Le Libraire*, guzzling himself drunk each night to shut out the poverty of spirit of the town where he works and to shuck off the burdens of one who would bring light. But Bessette is known. His closeness to English-Canadian academe even makes him one of the most promptly translated of the French-Canadian writers. Girouard's taste runs most of all to the obscure and the ignored—as a teacher obliged to teach the "Canadian classics" he detests, he perhaps makes a virtue of exclusion from this consecration.

And so he called my attention to the curious Mr. Gilles Leclerc—a "thinker" more than a philosopher, specifies Jacques Renaud, who also swears by him—and his curious *Journal d'un inquisiteur*. This densely written 313-page meditation appeared in 1960 just before the Quebec elections which brought the Liberals to power and made Quiet Revolutionary liberalism the philosophy of the regime. It is a long cry against Duplessism—never so named, though, and perhaps it would be more accurate to say against obscurantism, against clericalism, which were the climate of the Duplessis period just ending. Leclerc is a Christian believer and his pain at the abuses and worldliness of the Church is that of one who would like to see faith flower in liberty. For liberty is the great cause of this inquisitor, and one thinks of Pierre Maheu's remark as a *parti pris* representative at a conference on secularism, that a true act of faith, like true atheism, is impossible before the secularization of Quebec is accomplished. Leclerc's faith, in both liberty and God, is sterling, but there is, in his long, slow, and mightily abstract commentary, one great absentee: economics, the material context around Quebec spirituality, the presence of an English-speaking investing and managing class on the top level of Quebec society, hovering over the whole French-Canadian struggle for self-discovery. In a word, colonialism. Over and over again, Leclerc rails against theocracy and its

> total accord between Church and State. Both manipulate handily the club, or, euphemistically and according to fashion, the argument of authority, obedience, and the established order. Three magic notions that have as close relations the Purity of the Race, the Heroism of Ancestors, the Divine Mission in America. Unfortunately, the catastrophic people that we are can draw from these heavenly words only earthly nourishment. I say catastrophic because an accident of chronology and geography whereby the French language and the Catholic faith coincided has been shaped by the hierarchs into a new metaphysical necessity, thus managing to sully both language and faith and the pride that goes with them.

But never does he wonder what, beyond stupidity, arrogance, and ill-will, plus that coincidence of history, could have made French Canada's institutional elites what they are; nor does he look to popular revolt for a redressing of things in a more humane and libertarian direction. The people are sympathized with as "defenseless and voiceless" one second, and dismissed as "gelatine beneath the boot that stamps them" the next. Victims, yes, but then, Leclerc moans in a sort of one-sentence prologue that comes before his official, three-page prologue, "the majority will always find authority normal; a handful will judge it grotesque . . . and they alone will explore the paths of freedom." No new social structure can help, hope seems nowhere but in wiping-away the gelatinous stuff of men's physical life to make way for sheer spirit, nowhere but in the apocalypse announced in the title of a book of verse which I have never seen, but which Leclerc lists among his other works on the jacket: *La Chair abolie—The Abolished Flesh.* For him, and here no doubt he leaves his separatist admirers behind, "No more are we conquered, nor conquerers either! French-Canadians have their backyard now; they can do what they want in it."

For me, and I had to fight myself to admit this, the whole ground had been covered by Pierre-Elliott Trudeau and the liberals, so contemptible to *parti pris,* around *Cité libre.* There too the pious dictatorship which had so long commanded French-Canadian life had been taken apart, and four years earlier, in the book *La Grève de l'amiante.* It was written by a group of *Cité libre* contributors and edited by Trudeau, who did a long introductory essay on the priestly ideology of French Canada during the years that led up to the 1949 Asbestos strike. And no matter how pallid his solutions, Trudeau never had any illusion that the root of the problem was anywhere but in the hard-cash world which escaped the French speakers' grasp.

But perhaps Girouard's preference for the Leclerc version was more a matter of tone than of content. What *partipristes* could not forgive Trudeau, what seemed to them false and treacherous in his demolition of theocracy, was his cool, assured tone. How could he live in the smothering of liberty and not cry, not scream, not scribble on walls, not take to drink or dynamite? Such calm could come only from a basic coziness with the very English money which paid for this reign of darkness, an Anglo-Saxon confidence that all would be straightened out when the French-Canadians learned engineering, business administration, and behaviorist labor relations. And indeed, the man's eventual departure for Ottawa confirmed the impression that, for him, the light in Quebec theocracy was to come from the colonial capital.

"That's why I've always considered Leclerc, despite everything, despite the *Journal*'s vile style, despite it all, essential," Girouard was telling me as we sat in the Royal Tavern. Girouard was still dealing with detestability. He had announced in a *parti pris* special issue on writing that the birth of the socialist-independentist movement had freed him from his gloom enough to get him back to his typewriter, back in there trying to add to the "valid writing that has nevertheless come out of Quebec." Now there was hope of a day when the search would not have the cards utterly stacked against it. His work at *parti pris* had perhaps opened the way beyond detestability.

"To me," he said, looking back to his time as publisher, "book publishing is political agitation. The book should try to shake people, tell what the regime hides. But alas, books just don't get to the people who need shaking, the workers, the exploited. I consider *Le Cassé* an event in Quebec history—not just a literary event, but a social one. I'm proud of having put it into circulation. And it was a success, 6,000 sales.

"We know who bought it: it was classical college students, university students—young people, largely, and some who were not regular novel buyers. That's a breakthrough. But it's little enough with an attractive format, a good price, distribution on newsstands and all the advantages the book had. I consider *Journal d'un hobo* just as big an event in Quebec literature; it moved more slowly, but we had to bring it out. Those are the two big ones for me. Our output has had mixed reasons behind it. Jasmin's play I didn't really think was a natural for us, a must—I saw its value but at the time we were just groping in the publishing business, just seeing if we could get a book through the press and into the bookstores. My book and Jasmin's play were printed without a pre-defined idea of what a *parti pris* book should look like. Jasmin's name and the fact that the play had been done on TV did help. Then we tried the taxi book, and that was the biggest disappointment of all; it had a proletarian author, a topical, down-to-earth subject, a colorful, newsstand-style presentation, but still there was no breakthrough to a mass audience. Jacques Hébert was able to get that breakthrough with a thinner, more anecdotal book about the Montreal taxi driver's problems, but he could do it because of his huge established list of successes—they finance big printings of new titles. *Parti pris* really started with *Le Cassé:* we set our style—I'd asked a professional designer to do me a distinctive jacket layout—and we knew what kind of commercial distribution we could handle. The main lines of the program still apply, though Godin no longer tries to get out of the bookstore onto the newsstands."

Godin is Gérald Godin, who took over when Girouard quit as director of les éditions parti pris. *Journal d'un hobo,* by Jean-Jules Richard, was the last book Girouard published, late in 1965. The three other books he spoke of—Claude Jasmin's play *Blues pour un homme averti,* Germain Archambault's *Le Taxi: métier de crève-faim,* and Jacques Renaud's *Le Cassé*—followed quickly after *La Ville inhumaine. Ville, Blues,* and *Taxi* were the preparation for *parti pris*'s publishing; *Le Cassé* was its launching.

The second book published by les éditions parti pris resembled the first in its respectability. This time it was an established author, Claude Jasmin—the man Girouard had dismissed as taking the "clown" escape from the tensions of writing in Quebec—who had come to the new publisher. Jasmin, whose photograph, with fringe beard, was then appearing over his art column in *La Presse,* wrote scripts for the state television network—including this one, *Blues pour un homme averti,* blues for a grown-up, for a smart cookie. He was a bit older than the *partipristes,* had published other books with the apolitical publishers of Quebec, and had been reprinted in France. He worked, in this play, in a dreamy, symbolic style, presenting a man who seeks the origin of his miserable life in his fatherless childhood. Like much Quebec psychological fiction, the play was introverted to the point of omitting such elementary information about the concrete life of the characters as last names, occupations, precise places of residence, and moments in time. And like most previous French-Canadian literary dialogue, it was written in what the author appeared to consider simple, realistic, but universal French. French that could have been spoken by working-class French-Canadians, but that would also be understood by Frenchmen. A still from the Radio-Canada production decorated the jacket, but again it was a bookstore-intended binding, not a drugstore one. The establishment, through its TV network, could well claim to have gotten this "portrait of a colonized Québécois" to more ordinary Québécois than *parti pris*'s printed version would.

Next came *Le Taxi: métier de crève-faim—Taxi: A Sucker's Trade*—nonliterary writing in keeping with Girouard's strictures, but this time nonfiction as well, clearly announcing its agitational intent, printed on newsprint, bound in bright red, sold on newsstands. It was a formula which had been developed by Jacques Hébert, a Montreal publisher in his forties who had in the last years of the Duplessis regime made books almost a mass medium in Quebec by publishing topical nonfiction, modernist attacks on all that was medieval in Quebec—Church-controlled schools, payoff-controlled politics, uncontrolled birth—in pictorial jackets, selling for a dollar on newsstands. Hébert's politics were those of *Cité libre,* the magazine of Quebec liberalism, and *parti pris* considered him an adversary; in publishing *Taxi* it was offering a socialist polemic to compete with his center-left ones. Girouard wrote the foreword to *Taxi:* taxi-driver-author Germain Archambault's call for legislative reforms to enable the cabbie to keep from starvation was too timid; only a general revolution could provide a full life for the class he belonged to. And, added Robert Maheu, brother of Pierre and also a *parti pris* contributor, plugging the book in the magazine, proletarian openness to this view was indicated by Archambault—an old Marxist among taxi drivers—and his driver-collaborators bringing their manuscript to *parti pris.*

And then, in November 1964, the real life of les éditions parti pris began. The event was the publication of Renaud's *Le Cassé.* "PAROLES," the name of the series, was the biggest word on the cover: the book was a word, a voice, a shout—and there would be others.

Jacques Renaud—the first Quebec writer consciously to put on the sackcloth of joual—was also the one who had most recently learned to speak standard French. His father had worked most of his life in an overcoat factory as a collar-folder. Renaud did not go to classical college, but to a state-financed high school in the decent and dreary working-class section in northeast Montreal called Rosemount. At this school there was a mathematics teacher named Arthur Major, who, though living and teaching in these working-class surroundings, was sending *his* son to the Collège des Etudistes on Rosemount Boulevard. The two boys, Jacques Renaud and André Major, met after each had left school behind and begun the self-education which a third writer in their group, Paul Chamberland, says must be undertaken by all Québécois, whether schooled in elite institutions or in proletarian, who wish to free themselves of joual and the *joualisé* vision of life.

"But even before that, even at home, I used to write," Renaud told me in the fall of 1965. (We met and talked infrequently from then until the spring of 1968.) "Stories, yarns. My father and mother read them; they found them okay, and didn't mind the idea of their son writing."

At nineteen, Renaud worked as a clerk in the semi-intellectual surroundings of the municipal film library, but at the lowbrow salary of $35 a week. A friend of his worked at the same building, the St. Sulpice reference library on St. Denis Street, in the east but downtown. Jacques remembers the self-educative process:

"We had nothing; our only entertainments were walking and talking. We began to play a game: each thing we saw, we sought the right word, the precise term to describe it. From a speck of dirt to a church steeple. We walked and walked, all the downtown streets of the city, and I was realizing that writing, getting it down, is not an easy thing."

He remembers, too, the crossing of a threshhold:

"I had written in a story, *'Elle s'en fout.'* Then it struck me that no one says that; they say, *'Elle s'en sacre.'* The more I thought about it, the more I knew that the first sentence was unreal, taken from a book I'd read, not from the language I'd learned from people. I crossed it out and wrote it the second way."

The change from an expression about as conventional and old-fashioned as "She couldn't care less" to something about as violent as "She didn't give a damn" was not so terribly daring. Other writers had put stronger oaths than that in their characters' mouths. And it may not have been the birth of a literature—Renaud refuses to give himself so grand a role. This change, though, led to things happening in the literature of Quebec that had never happened before. By the middle of 1964, Renaud was writing in a manner which assumed not only the curses, but the sentence structure, the vocabulary, even an English spelling of the anglicisms of the people of his childhood and his more recent bohemian poverty. And by then the *parti pris* writers were known as such. In their magazine they had claimed the misery of the Quebec slums as their misery. They had claimed as their anger the anger of the young terrorists who a few months earlier, in the spring of 1963, under the name Front de Libération Québécois, had attacked hated federal buildings, mailboxes, and monuments with homemade bombs. They were looking for a kind of literature appropriate to this commitment.

The literary search was shown in the first issue of *parti pris* in the fall of 1963. Paul Chamberland called his four pages *"Poèmes de l'ante-révolution"* and dedicated them to Gaston Miron with a quotation from the older poet's erotico-political pronouncement, *Recours didactique:* "I hear within our great unconsciousness the splashings of our angers rising." The anger had emerged from the dead-end streets where Miron, in the 1950's, discerned it, out of the great unconsciousness and the prison-brain whose confines Miron had railed against, and was onto paper.

Later, in 1964, Chamberland returned still more intensely to the theme in a chant of revolution written for the publishing house *parti pris* had founded, and gave his new book the title *L'Afficheur hurle.* Literally, "The poster-hanger screams," but Chamberland explained what kind of poster-hanger:

"I thought of myself as one of those guys who write political slogans on walls," he told me. "A signpainter, a shouting signpainter." Slogan-painting preceded bombs as a way for separatist youths to leap into provocative action in the sixties; indeed, the bombers always signed their work with a dribbly "FLQ" on a nearby wall. (The most famous graffito was, of course, the one Charles de Gaulle was to fasten onto in 1967 to pique the Anglo-Saxons: *Québec libre.*)

All the *partipristes* were Shouting Signpainters, but Renaud is probably the only one who ever actually wrote on walls:

"I was in what was called the Réseau de Résistance—the predecessor to the FLQ. We wanted to hit the population with some sort of shock but had not yet envisaged violence. So we painted on the walls. You can still see some of our *Québec libres* here and there, signed 'R.R.' That was us."

This political apprenticeship was simultaneous with the literary searching Renaud had described, and companions for the two overlapped. Major, who prefaced *Le Cassé* ("I give you Jacques Renaud, a *cassé*. . . . If you're one too, flat broke in every sense, not a cent in your pocket and not a Truth to bash over people's heads, that's the way it is with you, you'll be solaced for a moment in reading this, for Renaud has undertaken to avenge at once himself and you."), hung around the middle-aged Raoul Roy's socialist-separatist magazine and discussion group. Major published articles in the first *parti pris*, did the jacket notes for Girouard as well as that preface for *Le Cassé*, and followed up Renaud's book with two volumes of his own in joual—not as thoroughgoing as Renaud's—for les éditions parti pris. In pre-*parti pris* days Renaud had seen Major regularly and lodged in a rented room next door to another friend whose searchings were less literary, more political: they led not to polishing-off a protest novel, but to the Front de Libération Québécois. Renaud described it this way:

"One of us was always in the other's room in those days, talking, talking, going around and around the ideas that were working in us. And the discussions went on right into the FLQ period: I remember a conversation at a moment when—let's put it this way, I didn't yet know he was tossing bombs—in which we started all over again from scratch, put our entire political position in doubt and tried to see things afresh. We weren't complacent.

"There are some things that are pretty solidly established with us now—and this had a lot to do with the FLQ—established in a way that English-speaking friends like yourself, who have perhaps studied the problem, who have sought to understand, who have even approved the separatist solution, probably find hard to grasp. A mental *click* has taken place in us that has not, I think, taken place in you. There is no going back.

"This is true about independence. Among younger guys we're in touch with, writers who'll be coming along soon, following us, it isn't even a matter for discussion any more: it's assumed. It's true also of the dismissal—by those of us who are in solidarity with the FLQ—of pacifist objections made by some observers in the English-Canadian left. Their testimony against the system is expressed in demonstrations against nuclear warheads, against the war in Vietnam. They are at pains to be fair-to-both-sides. But I'm not that way; I'm not against-the-war-in-Vietnam; I'm against the Americans there. I don't want the Vietcong to be fair, to negotiate, to find the middle way, the peaceful way, I want them to wipe out the Americans, to the last one who's there. Quite simply to reduce them to nothing.

"And so, yes, there was a certain consciousness of the political extension of the linguistic scandal we were bringing out in our writing. You don't write to prove something, it wasn't like that. But it's true that if the *cassé* is short of words, he is also short of everything else, of physical comforts, of psychological ones. He has a limited vocabulary and a limited emotional gamut, a limited ability to define his own feelings, a whole limited life. I still know what it was like to speak joual, to feel trapped within it and within the slums. But what are you going to do, I've attained Culture since then."

I could hear the capital "C" as Renaud said this last sentence, and there was also a little smile of mockery. It was as if he were saying: I know this vaunted culture is shit, doesn't really make me any better than my old schoolmates; but damn it, it's just enough to make me privileged, cut off, condemned to sympathize paternalistically with those who are still in it up to their necks.

"Major says that the new turns Quebec literature has been taking —*parti pris,* joual, the rest—are attributable to the phenomenon I've just been speaking of: guys like us, from working-class families, remembering the joual scene but also having made it, as formerly only the classically schooled part of the population made it, into the world of culture, articulation, literacy, putting on record how one feels. I think that's pretty much true."

As for Girouard and the other Shouting Signpainters, for Renaud the politico-literary commitment was accompanied by a family one. But not a success. Renaud set up housekeeping with a woman named Diane, fathered a son, Tristan, whose photo he would show you in proud-papa style. He was still committed to paying Tristan's upkeep when I met him, though he had split with Diane. His attitudes toward women have never really recovered from this misadventure. Handsome, almost the romantic picture of the poet—curly red hair, pale skin, boyish features, snub nose—a success with the girls, he is torn between a constantly resurgent misogyny and an image of himself as understanding of feminine sensibility, able to sense women's needs and cater to them, able to write fiction from their viewpoint, to imagine the stream-of-consciousness within a female head.

At the moment *Le Cassé* was accepted by *parti pris* (unlike Major and Girouard, he had published nothing in the magazine but the fiction that later went into his book), Jacques Renaud's routine personal life was in fairly total disrepair, everything concentrated on the completion of the manuscript:

"I was at it more or less uninterrupted three days and three nights. And my intake of food was down to something like an egg for a whole day. *Cassé*, that I was. The publication of the book was important not in the sense that it was a financial windfall—I've not yet gotten my royalties, the movement is too broke itself—but in the sense that it opened up other possibilities: I got my reporting job on *Métro-Express* on my reputation as author of that novel. That got me out of the hole. And at the publication party I was, let's say, thin."

Things had pulled together all at once for this ex-*cassé:* "First wife, first child, and first novel, all before the age of twenty-three," griped a twenty-two-year-old friend.

The publication party took place in November 1964. By January 1965, the book had been reprinted once; it was reprinted again in 1967. The first printing carried an apparently self-written biographical note: "Born Nov. 10, 1943. Fought stupidity, his own and others. Appropriately paid for his efforts. Became mistrustful. Kept his intransigence, lost face on occasion. Determined to survive. Too well loved not to know how to hate. At work on a novel. Piling up his manuscripts." The second printing carried press quotes which give an idea how Renaud's intransigence, multiplied by *parti pris*'s, was received by the French-Canadian literary pontificate: Jean Ethier-Blais of *Le Devoir* for the liberal elite, and Brother Clément Lockwell for the clergy, found it powerful but not really literature, while François Hertel, an old Voltarian exiled in Paris, provided one of those bourgeois damnings *parti pris* loves to wear as medals. "This work," said he, "is in my opinion a foul act against the French language. Unreadable in France, Belgium, and the entire French ethnicity, it forces to the limits of delirium and ridicule the need to soil everything at hand, even one's native tongue."

There was a slight change in the cover design from the first to the second printing, but with this fourth book les éditions parti pris had found its style. Like the magazine, the books were square, or almost so, rather than the traditional rectangle, but a bit smaller than the magazine, almost small enough to fit in the palm, so that *parti pris* books formed their own eye-catching corner in a newsstand display of paperbacks and newspapers. Some later, thicker volumes were almost cubes. And, during this first period, badly bound. Held together only with glue, they had the sad tendency to fall apart with even the gentlest leafing once the binding had dried out. But that was part of what enabled them to bear the newsstand price of a dollar.

At the top of the jacket, the word *paroles,* in capitals on the first edition, brought down to lower case in the second, but still the largest word on the jacket. At the bottom, *parti pris,* in a miniature reproduction of the one-word-piled-atop-the-other style that was the magazine's logotype. In between, also entirely lower-case and sanserif, "jacques renaud/*le cassé*." The word *cassé* is the past participle of the verb to break, hence an English-inspired joualism for broke, penniless. But since, unlike the English *broke,* it is not an incorrect form assigned a special meaning, it has all the other meanings of the verb, too: broken, smashed, dispirited, crippled, destroyed. Even fractured, as in fractured French. Renaud was going to give us a man who was all those.

As for the overall title *paroles,* advertisements in preceding issues of *parti pris* had announced it as one of three series to be instituted by the publishing house: *paroles* would be literary, *aspects* would be informational—the sort of thing that had already been done with *Le Taxi* (though the jacket of that book spoke of the series *"documents"*)—and *raisons* would be philosophical, essays in separatist-socialist theory. This program for the compleat revolutionary publisher, however, was bound to be followed according to the real loves of the revolutionaries in question, and it was *paroles* that was the vital collection in the early days (*aspects* has since appeared; others have remained mainly good intentions).

The reader who opened *Le Cassé* found himself, though, with a document as well as a novel. André Major wrote a preface which spoke of the book's backdrop, a "banal portrait of east Montreal." Then came Renaud's own *"manière d'introduction,"* in which he yields to self-pity, asking that his body be burned if he dies, that his ashes be given to Diane and Tristan, and by them to the City of Montreal for sprinkling on sidewalk ice. There is a suicidal streak in Renaud's writing. In one of the five brief stories added at the end of *Le Cassé*, he says: "Jacques Cartier Bridge? Too tired. This is the fall, it's cold. And I don't feel like walking all the way over there. Anyway, I can swim. Y'never know, I could be drowning nicely and then it'd hit me how I wanted to come up." But he modifies this with: "Always putting on this here big act, eh?"

The novel itself opens on a note of affirmation, life keeping just ahead of squalor: "This room cost him five bucks." That was cheap for a week's room rent in Montreal in 1964, cheaper than I was ever able to find in searchings from 1960 on. Renaud tells in an article on his work which appeared in *parti pris* just after the joual writers broke upon the bookstores that it was something else in the opening sentence which, at the book-releasing cocktail party, gave him trouble with the literary judges: "Mr. Renaud, why do you spell the word *piastre* (buck) as follows: *p, i, a, s, s, e.?*" Renaud's only comment was that there were some sharp chicks at that bash and he wasn't too rational. (The reason he spelled it that way was simply that that's the way the Québécois who uses the word invariably pronounces it; if you are concerned about being correct, you say *"dollar."* It is in fact a word that is never correctly pronounced, and Renaud didn't even invent the joual spelling.)

Detail by detail, Renaud sketches in the world he is evoking. The room is more like a cupboard, the door is *"un pan de plywood"* which doesn't fill the doorframe, no heat, a mattress like a corpse, out of whose punctures a cockroach appears. What concierge would bust his ass fixing up a five-buck room? *"Ti-Jean comprend."*

Through the window, Ti-Jean locates himself—Jacques Renaud locates him—on the Island of Montreal, in the Province of Quebec (not in the Gaspé, though, where the girls have the softest skin in North America . . .), and in time: eleven o'clock, and Philomène is due. Philomène? No Gaspesian beauty but not bad; a brunette, unemployed, living off Ti-Jean, she is at that moment paying a cashier in a downtown restaurant, and, buttoning her trenchcoat (*"boutonne son trenche"*), she begins walking north to the address.

Begins hitchhiking (*"du pouce"*—some thumb—not the European *"auto-stop"*), is picked up by a young woman who renders her mute by speaking correctly ("Philomène is afraid of speaking badly") and puzzles her with homosexual advances. The woman is a student at the University of Montreal and speaks of poets (*"Bauglaire, d'autres"*). Philomène yields to the girl's gentleness, assurance, respectability. It is a further complication to her already conflicted sex life, and she cannot help thinking back to the night Ti-Jean took possession of her—when he chased a rival from her bed, declaring Philomène, at the top of his lungs, *"ma plote pour tout l'temps astheure!"*

This noun was explained by a writer friend who took Renaud in hand the evening of a small rampage of his own and apologized for him to others in the group. "Jacques is a writer who uses language as it is spoken by us in Quebec. He will use the word *plote,* which we apply to the vagina of a woman. I do not use the word when I write, nor have writers in Quebec done so up until now: but all the while it has been in absolutely universal spoken use, and Jacques decided he must use it." *Plote*'s secondary and usual meaning is, by extension, woman, broad, girlfriend, mistress. Perhaps "piece" would capture it in colloquial English. (It's original meaning is *ball,* the ball into which string or wood is wound.)

The modifier that Ti-Jean ends his sentence with, *astheure,* is a more characteristic Renaud revelation. *A cette heure* is a conventional, at least in Quebec, French expression for *now.* In joual, *cette* is minimized and becomes merely a linking sound between *à* and *heure:* the running together of *t* and *h* is no problem, since *th* is pronounced *t* in French; our aspirate does not exist. Renaud has brought off something that I cannot see being done merely at the urging of Major, who claims to be Renaud's spelling-corrector—Jacques being inclined not to bother seeking the most appropriate spelling for joualisms.

It is this quality of putting onto paper what everybody always knew, what was always staring us in the face but which always escaped our definition, that gives such enormous persuasiveness to the politics of *parti pris*'s literature. The cat is out of the bag, the slogan is on the wall, the tavern door is open. Writers before Renaud had attempted to suggest a popular French-Canadian way of saying things by adaptations of the "correct" spellings—*à c't'heure,* etc.—but the criterion was always unphonetic standard French. Jacques Renaud was the first to recognize that *astheure* was a single thought, a single sound, *a single word*. Like, let us say, the English word *astir*, from which it was scarcely distinguishable. The French themselves adapt their spellings when a dialect is to be suggested: *"P't'et' ben qu'oui, p't'et' ben qu'non,"* they write when evoking the Norman peasant's uncommunicativeness (the expression is in common use among the descendants of Norman peasants who live in Quebec). But always the criterion is conventional French; only Renaud looks the language in the eye, takes down what is actually said. And when, in another story at the back of *Le Cassé*, we discover a bum asking for ten cents—*"yenk ça"*—we have to furrow our brows and pronounce this un-French formation aloud before, of course, of course, we've heard it a thousand times—*rien que ça, only that*, written by a phonetic system which would make *p't'et' ben qu'* into *tet bank*.

All the way through *Le Cassé* Renaud looks things in the eye. This makes for a sexy book—a journalist confrère of mine recommended it to me as the frankest stuff that had ever been put into print in Quebec: "He describes guys standing on streetcorners putting their hands up women's dresses, *mon vieux*." Curiously, the one thing that is the obligatory subject of frank description in every sexy novel, lovemaking between man and woman, is absent from Renaud's. He finds it too noble, too triumphant for his attention; his business is the cold regard on the unbearable, the unutterable, the inglorious. So much is wrong, so unrepresentative is the exceptional success of a heterosexual love, that it would be dishonest to dwell on it. And so, when he brings Ti-Jean and Philomène's roommate together, we have this:

> Ti-Jean often arrives after Philomène has left. He corners Louise. Louise doesn't resist. The reader expects, no doubt, a nice juicy description. He may refer to his personal experiences. Not good enough? Then he can go to hell.

It is a world of faithlessness and mistrust, bargaining for concessions and fraud in the bargaining, this universe *cassé*, sexually broken, and emotionally, and socially, and in every other way. When we do get the sexual description we expect, it is only to demonstrate the poverty of the participants' hearts, the renunciation of the search for anything fine in the partner or even the rival.

Ti-Jean, toward the end of the book, is in a tavern, talking to another man about his sex life (a classic Québécois nonsituation), about an early experience in which *he* was the rival, feeling up another fellow's steady girl in the guy's absence, committing, at the girl's insistence, the *cochonnerie* of cunnilingus. The tone of the whole thing is sad: no coinciding of the yearnings of man and woman, only blackmail on both sides to extract what pleasure can be gotten in spite of the malaise, and, finally, the girl's boyfriend, while reclaiming his woman, being forced to be "dirty" too.

> He had to if he wanted to hang onto his chick. He was handsomer than me, and he still got *cochon* . . .

And a final miserable twist in this remembered scene that drifts through Ti-Jean's mind at the end of the story: he loses his audience for this recitation of what a passing acquaintance once bitterly called, before Renaud and me in a bar, with no greater provocation than the presence of the author of *Le Cassé*, "*la sexualité ratée du Québec*":

> The guy had gotten up and Ti-Jean had gone on talking all by himself just like he was walking by himself now, all alone in the middle of Lafontaine Park . . .

The plot of *Le Cassé* turns around a rumor that Ti-Jean's girl is also sleeping with a goofball pusher named Bouboule. As the rumor works on Ti-Jean we watch him, learn about his life, his spurts of anger at the unemployment insurance office (*"J'veux plusse que ça, c'est toute"*), his stretches of lethargy in his room reading detective papers ("some clean, some dirty"). Renaud gets in snapshots of the colonized environment, and they are always right. Ti-Jean listens to the radio: "*CJMS Montréal, le poste des Canadiens-français, vous écoutez le hit-perède américain avec* . . ." Bouboule drinks beer in a downtown tavern beneath Monsieur Cinquante, the immense cardboard trademark of an English-Canadian brewery, an unblushing use of the comic-strip French-Canadian Johnny Malotte in lumber boots, grinning from behind his thin moustache and tossing off a "by gar" or a "*sacre bleu*" as the real French-Canadians below swear away with their chalices and ciboriums.

Philomène is no longer with Ti-Jean; now he visits her for weekly or twice-weekly lovemaking at her friend Louise's place, and it appears—this is the closest we get to real eroticism—that their relationship is good, that they both enjoy themselves, that the only strain is that he wants to get away quickly afterward and she wants him to stay and listen to records, and used to, though she doesn't any more, want to go for walks with him. (The novel takes place in summer; many references to heat, sunshine, even the pleasure of sweating, come in.) But there is that rumor, and the nightmare of Philomène raped and his tearing her to pieces that it gives Ti-Jean. There is the awakening to the square of blue night offered by his window, and his thoughts, jealous thoughts. And the thoughts ring as true as the words to anyone who has lived in Quebec. Here is the colonized Québécois's self-accusation about sex, that saintly ideal which, when it proves unattainable, is not contested but is avoided by a piece of shamefaced colonized-Quebec cynicism. Translated:

> Bouboule, the rat, the way I figure, Yves is right about him, he's going to bed with Phillie. And she lets him, the bitch! Bouboule is nothing but a bum, he's that guy who sells dope. He makes me sick. Phillie's a good lay, and filthy, too. I bet Bouboule likes that. A lecher. I'm a lecher too, I guess. But it's him or it's me, damn it, that's the way life is. Phillie, I'm gonna bust you in ten pieces—ten, Christ! I'm gonna kill 'em both!

And he does kill Bouboule, tracking him to "that bearded hangout" where Bouboule pushes his drugs and where Ti-Jean feels scorned by the young bohemians; following him into Clark Street, to a dark place; stabbing with "a mounting, pleasure-giving motion of in-and-out." After an attempt to find Philomène, he simply wanders, a sort of purging wandering-till-dawn through his streets and through his life, turning much around that conversation in the tavern about the sexual struggle. That conversation had begun when

> this guy comes up to me and starts talking about politics, how I should get in and be militant.
> Militant, I've heard that word, I told him. A long time ago. A word I liked, too, when the teacher at school said we had to be militant. His was in the Church Militant. That was us, he said, men living their lives, women too, everybody together. But nobody seemed to be militant that I saw around. But I imagined everybody being like that, mili-

tant. It was beautiful. We went around showing people we had the right idea, giving an example, like. We believed in the Gospel, we didn't tell lies, we did like Jesus said you should, no jerking yourself off, no screwing women before marriage, you couldn't make fun of others, get what I mean?

Me, I said okay, I'm willing to try . . .

But Ti-Jean tells the man the story of his taking a girl away from his friend Robert by being more inventive sexually—dirtier—than Robert, and makes it clear he sees the world as a place where militancy gets you nowhere; only the dirt you do your fellow offers any hope of at least keeping you from falling behind in the general debacle. Ti-Jean feels the same and yet is amazed that the people he passes see nothing new in him now that he is a killer. He has broken the rules but has not broken with the belief that militancy gets you nowhere. He reaches into his pockets and finds that he is flat broke.

That's all. No police chase, no gunfight, no showdown. Why bother? Win or lose, killer-with-impunity or gallows-fodder, Ti-Jean has already lost by being born into the French slums of the east of Montreal. He has had his revenge, he has struck down a visible victim. "Little Johnny" has, not really matched his strength in any David-and-Goliath way, but at least had the better of big Bouboule.

His victim is not his oppressor, nor even a representative figure for his oppressor; he is a French-Canadian slum product like himself. And even dead he is a slum product who cuts a better figure than Ti-Jean: as a hoodlum of sorts, selling goofballs to the wealthy likes of Berthe, throwing around the money this provides, he will be thought by the police to have been wiped out by the underworld, not by the nobody who is Ti-Jean.

Are murder and pill-pushing, crime sudden and violent and crime long and crafty, the only revenges on the slums? Is there no key out of the prison? Major suggests a couple of keys, or a couple of other revenges, in his preface to *Le Cassé*—"the war cry . . . the bomb"— and another in an autobiographical bit that ran in *parti pris*'s issue on Montreal, *"la ville des autres"*: "I'll probably always have in me a bit of the punk from Ontario Street, that street that today spits rioters up toward Lafontaine Park, with the fleur-de-lys flag at their head." Nor is Renaud, finally, saying there is no way out, for his book itself is one.

Flat Broke 75

There is one hint in the plot of the kind of escape the book represents. It is in Bouboule's very different strivings to escape from *his* poverty. The restaurant where he pushes, from which he is emerging when Ti-Jean attacks him, is identified as being on Clark Street, just west of Montreal's rowdy center strip of St. Lawrence Boulevard, and it is recognizable as either one of two art students' coffeehouses, La Paloma or the next-door and extinct El Cortijo, both centers of French-speaking beatnik life in Montreal a few years ago. "The jukebox pisses Aznavour, vomits the Beatles, shakes Vigneault by the locks at the back of his neck to make him cough up his last great gobs of open air, the last pine trees in his head, his last scraps of himself," says Renaud, and though his tone is a bit sarcastic and the role of the café in the novel is incidental, we can guess that it would not have figured in the plot if it had not figured in Renaud's own flight from the life of the slums. Many who gathered at La Paloma in the early sixties were not in flight from poverty, and many, whether from rich parts of town or poor, never brought their revolt into very clear focus. But out of such places of intellectualization of discontent came some youths—it is said La Paloma attracted some of the future FLQ, and at El Cortijo they would have met Montreal Spaniards with memories of the Civil War—who were driven beyond intellectualism. And at least one—Renaud—who wrote.

(I went back to La Paloma one night with Renaud. We did a west-to-east march along St. Catherine, *la Catherine* of *Le Cassé*, in the mood of the only bit from his one previous book, a volume of verse called *Electrodes* that dated from about the time he was frequenting La Paloma, which he still likes:

> moonbeam and eyecatch
> hornhonk love
> under the weary smiles of snackbars
> laughing screams of the billboards
> coca cola and silk stocking
> optic nerve
> hurting throb of electricized stares
> drumbeat of i-love-yous in tin
> and the whole being swelled with wanting
> craving for something human
> in the dollared noise of the clubs

At Clark, in front of the windows full of stew at the Eldorado, the cafeteria of those poor-but-unbowed days, we turned to mount the street almost to Sherbrooke, and entered La Paloma. Renaud enjoyed himself, talking to me and the others in the group about getting drunk at the launching of a book by André Laurendeau, a long-time nationalist who was then proposing a patching-up of French-English relations within Canada, offhandedly telling us Laurendeau was a *fédéraste*, as if this *parti pris* pun on *fédéraliste* and *pédéraste* were standard usage. But his tweed suit no longer faded in among the jeans-wearers, even though the gang that still hangs out in La Paloma seemed to remember, or at least know, him: "Hey, how goes the novelist?" shouted a poet.)

Le Cassé, then, is a story of a savage, wordless man walking around Montreal as one would walk around a prison cell, but it is at the same time an escape key, a hacksaw for another imprisoned savage. Renaud was never the *cassé* he describes because he always had the words that Ti-Jean lacks, and because he learned to write them down. Ti-Jean could only strike out with a screwdriver, and only at a rival. The very fact that he's mistaken about Bouboule and Philomène says it: he's got *the wrong man*. Renaud, as slogan-painter and as Shouting Signpainter, had taken up the arms of revolution where Ti-Jean took up only the weapon of revenge. His words, on walls or on paper, were aimed at oppressors, not fellow victims. He says in his introduction that he does not believe in *"mots clés,"* a cliché for key words, illuminating pronouncements, but the identification of the book as an act of self-liberation is clear enough in his comments on it in a *parti pris* issue on the beginnings of a decolonized literature in Quebec: "This I can say, that if I hadn't written, I'd have killed the real Bouboule."

And if Renaud has struck a false note in exposing his *cassé* for a moment to the influences that helped liberate him, of placing him in a context of intellectualism just before he opts for violence, and thus making him for an instant more Renaud than Ti-Jean, more the author than the observed character, he has built up a steady melody of true notes throughout the book. Every page has one.

When Bouboule approaches Philomène, she puts him off with this argument: *"Philomène lui a dit à Bouboule que Ti-Jean je l'aime."* Literally: Philomène told him, told Bouboule, that Ti-Jean, I love him. It can be said directly: *Philomène a dit à Bouboule qu'elle amait Ti-Jean*—Philomène told Bouboule she loved Ti-Jean. In writing it almost always is, but in Quebec you will hear it the way Renaud put it down.

A few lines later Bouboule has this thought for exclusive men with their women: *"Gagne de caves."* Literally this has no other meaning than "win of basements," but here it is the English "gang (feminine, interestingly, though the French, who have also absorbed the word in the narrower sense of criminal mob, make it masculine—"We feminize everything," says a Québécois friend) of fools"—*caves*, hollow, empty-headed ones. Once again the resonance is authentic Montreal.

Meanwhile Berthe is pleased with her conquest of Philomène—"These working girls are so stupid"—and enjoying a life which Renaud summarizes as *"Littérature, auto, gouffebâles et papa."* Gouffebâles are goofballs, barbiturates which predated marijuana as a mild kick among Montreal youth, and were not restricted to, or even most characteristic of, the university student class. They were mostly ordinary prescription tranquilizer or appetite-killing pills which, swallowed with any fizzy drink, hard or soft, gave sensations that some sub-proletarians testified set them up for thefts or vandalism. In a moralizing 1962 paperback report on this "epidemic" in the Montreal slums, Marie-José Beaudoin presented this series of answers from three goofball users to the question "What would you do if someone gave you a lot of money?"

>   HÉLÈNE: I don't know.
>   YOLANDE: I'd travel.
>   GUY: Haven't got the slightest idea! Anyway, it's not something that could happen to me.

Which makes it clear not all goofball users were of the papa-pays-the-bills milieu. Berthe, in *Le Cassé*, is coarsened as a character by Renaud's evident hatred for her, but there is no doubt she is drawn from life, from a more and more existent Quebec middle-class youth, with, as an American friend sympathetic to Quebec but disillusioned with nonsocialist separatism put it to me, "their suede coats, their small cars, and their French cigarettes." And perhaps, though this would take more proof than one lesbian character in a novel, with a greater-than-average tendency to sexual experimentation.

Later in the book, Renaud offers a splendid parody of French-Canadian scandal journalism, which, same old Catholico-colonized story, is strong on gore and weak on sex: "What Ti-Jean likes is the beheadings. You don't see them too often anymore." But "Huguette will soon be found bathing-in-a-pool-of-blood. That's how all sex perverts end up, say *Detectives*, 15 cents." And similar quick parodies of colonized advertising and colonized radio. In all this, Renaud is very much in the *parti pris* vein of outdoing the depreciators of French-Canadian culture in the brutality of his account. "You say we're Americanized?" Renaud seems to say to the English-Canadian scoffer; "It's *worse* than you think." But he has not ingratiated himself with the English establishment for all that. No Toronto publisher has offered to bring out a translation of *Le Cassé*, though Renaud says an acquaintance of his, an anglicized French-Canadian living in Paris, has taken a crack at producing one in something like an English equivalent of its language. Preferred are novelists who lend a certain elegance to French-Canadianness, who take, when evoking the crudities of Quebec life, the same tone of detachment and irony the English-speaker himself would take. Or an even harsher one, based on horror that the pure flow of universal Frenchness should be so polluted. Renaud's offense is never to permit himself this detachment or this twitching of the nostrils; he is inside the problem, inside the skin of the reader of *Allô-Police*, the listener to CJMS, the drinker of the ale recommended by Monsieur Cinquante. "It's not beautiful, okay," he says with Ti-Jean, "but that doesn't mean it's not my life."

It's his life and it's his language, and he *knows* it as no Quebec writer has ever known it. Two last examples, two of Ti-Jean's thoughts during his all-night ramble through the streets. *"La ville, c'est pas disable, la nuit. C'est pas du monde,"* he marvels, and means: "The city, at night, it just isn't sayable. It isn't of the world." Poetry? Yes, but a poetry that is in the mouth of every ordinary Québécois, and that Renaud has taken down from a thousand hearings. Things that aren't doable, sayable, marryable, anythingable, come up over and over again in Quebec French. *The world*, in Quebec or any other French, means *people, the population of the world*. But the Québécois push this quirk further than anybody else. Hence the title of a later *parti pris* publication, a book of short stories by the Quebec songwriter and comedienne Clémence Desrochers, *Le Monde sont drôles*—The

World Are Funny. And hence the stock mother's reproach to a mumbling child: *"Parle comme du monde,"* "Talk like people!" Being like the world is to be as people are accustomed to your being. Not being that is to be strange, eerie, not of people, not of the world. Like east Montreal in the silence of three A.M.

The same sort of thought in *"C'est-tu drôle!"* "Isn't that funny," it means, but what it says is, "Isn't you funny?" This substitution of *you* (in the singular, *thou*) for *it* is universal in Quebec—"That machine, do you work?"—and I don't know whether it's just a twisting of the sound of *il* preceded by the *-t-* that is inserted when it follows a vowel—*fonctionne-t-il*—or whether there is actually in the speaker's head the notion of addressing the thing as a person.

Jacques Renaud's attitude in conversation about these and other things is never more than semi-serious. Grave utterances coexist with word-plays and superficialities, and even the grave remark can be gravely inhuman.

Thus: "But how are you going to bring about a revolution? A chief, a leader who can summon obedience, is the only way I see, because, after all, people are really so many ants in an anthill; they don't know what they want."

Or, in a less fascist vein, he can nevertheless hand down stunningly arrogant judgments: "France is a washed-up country, finished. Completely egotistical, sure it has nothing to learn from anyone and incapable of teaching us anything." (Which didn't rule France out of his travel plans.)

"The university? A sterile milieu, a place of the death of thought and creation." (Which didn't kill his interest in maybe taking up studies that would put him there, sometime when he had accumulated the money.)

Or stunningly mushy: "René Lévesque? I see him as a worker. By that I mean a builder, a man who laid the foundations for the national future in Quebec." (The word *ouvrier* is one with a strongly left resonance in French, but no such resonance was intended in Renaud's childlike image for the welfare statist who was then in the Liberal government.)

On another occasion he told me and a French-from-France acquaintance, a joke intended to needle me, but which again caught him miles from the *parti pris* outlook which I had presumed to be his constant: "Why is it best to place your garbage cans on the other side of the street? Don't know? So the English won't always be coming into your yard." But the racist joke, to bite, must be based on the social inferiority of the ridiculed group; a Polack telling an Anglo-Saxon story—unless it needled the snobbery, finickiness, etc., of the blueblood—would be pathetic rather than arrogant. That mystified *colonisés* in Quebec do on occasion tell jokes that assume a social superiority to their oppressors I have no doubt, but more characteristic are ones which have the English eternally drinking tea and exchanging how-do-you-dos—and I found it hard to grasp how an anti-colonialist perception of French-English relations could fail to reveal to any *partipriste* that the greater authenticity was in this strain of humor, that to be authentic the humor of the oppressed had to contest their oppression: only the oppressor could be an authentic racist.

The place of politics in Renaud's life is subliminal. The climate brought about by the socialist-separatist movement has touched him, shaped him, but the ordering of his political ideas is not a prime concern. At the convention of the Parti Socialiste du Québec some time later, when the *parti pris* group entered its ranks, I was surprised to hear the name "Jacques Renaud" among the paid-up members. When I asked him about it, he smiled and said, "Maheu insisted." Pierre Maheu, an editor of *parti pris,* worked in the same office as Renaud at the time.

Renaud is best talking about his writing:

"Look, here's my problem," he will say, seizing a pencil and pad. "I have a character. He is in his room, at grips with something that's bothering him. He walks around. He can go out, but immediately he comes into relation with other forces, this character, B, and this one, C." He is into a long, unclear description of the mechanics of his next plot, with a molecular diagram of it sketched onto the paper. He listens respectfully as I say that what I liked about his novel was that it wasn't like that, it wasn't just a character *aux prises* with his soul and his fellows, but the whole socioeconomic context came into it; that the great weakness of Quebec fiction that tries to copy twentieth-century European introspection is that it doesn't have behind it the factual backgrounding of nineteenth-century European realism; that even Proust, with all his wanderings in the hallways of subjectivity, doesn't omit to specify the stocks and bonds that keep Swann's revenues coming in.

But theorizing, even about his own writing, is not an intense interest of his either, and rather than reply to thoughts of this kind he is likely to come up, as he did on another occasion and à propos of very little, with something like: "I'm just reading a book Chamberland gave me; it's by Romain Gary, it's called *Pour Sganarelle*, and he comes out for what he calls a totalitarian novel . . ."

He can depreciate himself nicely, wittily, as when I brought him back from Rome a pocketbook of the verse of Salvatore Quasimodo, with the buildup: "You know? The great left-wing Nobel prizewinner?" Wrinkling his brow at the Italian on the jacket, he replied gently, "I'm afraid my left doesn't stretch that far, my friend." (And accepted the book anyway.)

When I told Renaud I was leaving on that trip to Europe, he took a sheet of foolscap and wrote: André Garand, care of a certain lawyer, such-and-such an address, Paris. A friend, he said. It was not until later that I noticed that *Le Cassé* was dedicated to André Garand, along with Major, and a third name, Michel Laperrière, whom I do not know. And it was not until I spent an afternoon with André Garand that I realized who he was, what I ought to have known about him.

I reached him by taking the métro to the lawyer's address. I emerged in what seemed to me a fairly chic district of the city; the Palais de Chaillot was near the station, and I wandered in, discovering everything at the Théâtre National Populaire sold out for months ahead to lines of students who looked like those you see in the lobby of the Comédie Canadienne when Léo Ferré or Jacques Brel is singing. So I pressed on to my address: on a second floor, an enormous oak door opened and a plump, tousled man in his thirties, wearing a sweater, tight pants, and soft-leather boots stood before me. This was Garand's lawyer, and he wondered whether I sought his legal advice too: "You didn't come over from Canada with the gendarmes close behind, too, did you?" It began to dawn: Garand—*parti pris*—FLQ—exile in France. The lawyer took a note I jotted to Garand, telling him I had a copy of *Le Cassé* if he hadn't seen it, and would like to meet him anyway. He would get it to the gendarme-chased Garand, the lawyer said. During the next twenty-four hours, as I waited for Garand to surface, my memory filled things in. Hadn't there been an André Garand in the Front de Libération Québécois, among the actual caught-and-convicted, and hadn't I once spoken to an André Garand on the telephone when, asked by my boss at the Canadian Press to dig up what I could on likely demonstrations on July 1, Dominion Day, 1965, I'd given *parti pris* a try. Then he was friendly to a strange voice on the phone, but cagey: he couldn't say what might develop in the way of demonstrations, but he'd heard it might center around Lafontaine Park. The mental click took place, André was the FLQer Renaud had roomed with; and a check back to *Le Cassé* revealed this, in the same story that contained the suicidal bit I quoted earlier: "André didn't come. He's always down, it's rotten the way he's always got this long face on. We sometimes go on drunks together. He can't get work anywhere since he threw a molotov cocktail at an armory. They released him, but it was just to screw him up and leave him dangling. Every time he finds a job, the police get him laid off."

I got back to my hotel the next day to find a note in my mailbox from André Garand and a couple I had also tried to reach. They had met at the desk and discovered they were both looking for the same guy. Garand mentioned his address, just off the Boulevard Saint-Germain, near the arty cafés. I took the métro again. I walked down the boulevard and into the courtyard of a big, old apartment block. A thin young man with glasses was leaving with a bundle of laundry under his arm. We had set a rendezvous by phone, I was a bit late, and in our glances we each sensed who the other was. "I have to drop these off at the cleaner's; come along," said Garand.

It was a sunny Paris winter day and I think that's what we talked about. On the way back, after a wait through some laundry-counter bureaucracy, we spoke of what Garand was doing in Paris. "I am beginning to find Paris to my liking," he said. "At first I didn't. Frenchmen I am not crazy about.

"I am writing. A novel. I'm in a hurry to get it ready for a publisher in the United States, but I think I'll ask him for a delay. And there's the problem of living. I'd like to find a job that would offer some intellectual interest, that wouldn't kill me for writing. Do you know what possibilities there would be in the news agencies here for somebody who speaks French and English? I'm looking around, but if I have to punch tickets in the métro, I'll punch tickets in the métro.

"This publisher has so far published books on the Negro movement in the States. When I met him and talked with him about Quebec he was very interested in my story, and told me to show him my manuscript when it was ready. Of course, it would have to be published in English translation, but arrangements have been made for that. I'm not ready yet to let people read any of it, no, but it's coming along."

He suggested a café near his house, and we slid in behind a table: the sun was just starting to sink. *"Un grand crème,"* commanded Garand. "I know the French drink their coffee black, but when you order one of their espressos it's not enough to rinse a tooth, so I order a hot-milk coffee, which comes out about the same size as a cup of coffee in Montreal."

I was not sure how much Garand trusted me. I had dropped by at the Canadian embassy the day before, and it struck me that even that little gesture put me in another world from his. How did he know I wasn't a spy? He raised his eyebrows and opened a broad mouth set in a bony jaw.

"The possibility occurred to me when you wrote me the note and called later on the phone. But I ruled it out. I have found out quite a bit about how the police operate in a case like mine. When I first arrived in Paris I received a call from a French plainclothesman. He was polite, he was confidential, he even seemed sympathetic to Quebec independence. He sat down at my place and explained that French authorities were aware that I was here and under what circumstances, that they would be keeping an eye on me, but that as things now stood I was not doing anything against their rules. They warned me this would not be the case if I became politically active. But even 'politically active' had nuances—simply appearing at a demonstration or writing an article wouldn't be considered that. Speaking at a meeting, organizing a group, would. I don't know how seriously to take this cop. He may just have been doing it to win my confidence, but he'd read a lot about Quebec, I was new in Paris and knew absolutely nobody, and I got some comfort out of his conversation. But you never know what goes on: Ben Barka was kidnapped just around the corner from here, at le Drugstore on Saint-Germain.

"I haven't had any contact with Canadian officials, but my lawyer says that's just what I have to make sure not to do. They know about my departure, they know I'm here. They'd grab me if I got careless and offered them the chance. I could have waited and seen what kind of sentence I would have gotten, but the sentencing was put off and put off, and I had a passport, I decided to catch a plane at Dorval. I've traveled in rural France a little bit since I've been here, but not much. Where would I go if I couldn't stay in France? I've thought maybe Belgium: Brussels is the second French-speaking city over here.

"But tell me about Montreal. How is Jacques, and his new girl? You're lucky, you know, you've just come from Montreal, soon you'll be back there again. Paris looks nice, sure, but look at it this way: I have to think in terms of ten years here. That's how long my lawyer says I'll have to stay to be in the clear. After that the legal threat will be dropped. It's no Quebec for me from now until then. But I've been making a few more acquaintances since that cop called. If only I could get a job it wouldn't be too bad. Do you know Jean Cathelin? He wrote a book called *Révolution au Canada*; a very nice guy—I had a long talk with him."

Garand said he knew a restaurant remarkable for its low prices and edible food. We were back in the world of *Le Cassé*, looking for the Eldorado on St. Catherine for a good meal *et pour pas cher*. As we walked along, Paris lit up all along the Boulevard Saint-Germain; Notre-Dame's two towers loomed up, and I'd stumbled upon another tourist site I'd refused to hunt for. André spoke of French politics:

"It's true the left is better organized in France than in Quebec, has more experience, but the Communist Party here doesn't seem to want to bring the revolution near: it seems to practice an *'attentisme révolutionnaire.'* Take the northern mining town I visited. I talked to a guy up there who said the miners were willing to vote Communist, but only one or two were active in the Party, and none of them believed it was really a revolutionary situation. We in the FLQ may have lacked the fine judgment of the French Marxists in applying action to our local situation, but we did go beyond that kind of stalling action. Had you heard about the Quebec independence movement before we went into action? Were you aware of the revolutionary possibilities in Quebec, of the real demands of the Quebec people? We made them known: even the English journalists admit that before the FLQ people didn't take Quebec seriously. All that changed when the bombs went off. And afterward I joined *parti pris* and began working with them—in the office, on the magazine—because it seems to me that they are making a real effort to study the problem of bringing about that revolutionary situation, of applying Marxism to the Quebec scene, of finding ways of developing to the full the popular support the FLQ awoke."

This kind of talk had always embarrassed me because as a matter of fact I *had* heard most of Quebec's demands and supported them before the FLQ. And I had taken the FLQ for an irrelevant right-wing group at the moment its bombs went off and arrests were made, because it seemed to me that those demands were already being met. It took me some time to admit to myself that bombs could be important in awakening Quebec, could be the starting point of everything in the minds of young men like the *parti pris* group. The importance of the FLQ now seems to me to be to French-Canadian youth: those sections of English Canada able to understand Quebec's situation were already beginning to comprehend; others heard the bombs and joined the backlash.

Garand took me to a French-Canadian student friend's place, where we talked about the student's thesis—on nationalizations by the French government. Socialist small talk which seemed very far from bombs in Westmount mailboxes. And we finished out the evening, Garand and I and the couple Garand had met searching for me at the hotel, by going to Bobino, the Montparnasse music hall where Montreal composer Claude Léveillée was singing his songs:

> I look out on the roofs of Paris,
> Far from my native land . . .

he sang in French, and Garand admitted to me that he'd been to see all the big Quebec variety stars who had played Paris since he'd been there—he knew someone who got him tickets and his list of concerts for the past couple of months put him more up to date on Quebec popular arts than I was, at home in Montreal. To be French but far from home in Paris was the strange everyday fate of André Garand; I doubted that anyone in the hall caught the melancholy irony of Léveillée's song more sharply than he.

My time with Garand—he showed up at a café next door to my place the next night for one more chat—was one of my most warming experiences in Paris: for once I wasn't testing myself against the incalculable reactions of foreigners, but speaking with someone who spoke like friends at home, and whom I was sure, even with my English accent, I reminded of home too. And there was the contact with Montreal: at supper in his little restaurant, Garand had shown me a letter he had received from Renaud. The letter sang; Renaud, I decided, is a born writer, he cannot but write beautifully, even when it is a letter, even *without* joual, without the literary effort, the prospect of publication. It sang of Lafontaine Park and of walks through Montreal streets, of fall, and snow, and of a girl. I knew the girl, and in his reply, which he also showed me, Garand spoke of her as if *he* knew her too: the life of prose had done that for him.

Renaud spoke in the letter of events I'd been present for, and took me back to Montreal and my first contact with him.

I had met Jacques Renaud somewhat as I had met André Garand, without realizing who he was. I was covering the separatist demonstration on Dominion Day, 1965. By nightfall the police had driven demonstrators into the northern part of the city, above the public landmarks they had first gathered around. I found myself on a streetcorner with other reporters, one a man in his early twenties, sportsjacket, tie, notebook; Jacques Renaud of *Métro-Express*, he said. And even though this was a year after *Le Cassé* was published, and he was already Renaud-the-novelist, I didn't remember him. We shared a taxi to an apparent future gathering point for demonstrators, or, at any rate, of paddywagons lined up to resist them. The talk was customary reporters' stuff, but I noticed one unaccustomed bit from Renaud, tossed off in the same everyday tone as the rest: "A couple of years back, when I demonstrated with the guys, we worked it so as not to be dispersed by the police."

The demonstrators were remarkably young: almost as young as the thirteen- and fourteen-year-olds who demonstrated the following year. They seemed to be far apart, Renaud the young demonstrator and Renaud the tabloid journalist. Afterward I made the association I hadn't made at the time—Renaud: *Cassé*—and that provided the link.

The next time I saw Renaud, in the winter of 1965, I was looking for him, but the moment was unpropitious. On Mountain Street in the western part of downtown Montreal is a series of bars and entertainments more chic than the Hut and the Asociación Española (further down the mountain on the same rue de la Montagne are slums as bad as anything in the far east of the city). Walking along the chic part of the street one night, I came upon a quarrel at the door of the most chic of all the Mountain Street spots, a Parisified basement commonly called the Bistro, out of which Jacques Renaud emerged tottering, accompanied by an older man who turned out to be another writer, Pierre Léger. I wanted to talk to Renaud so I stuck with this pair, dragging along the others who were with me. Léger was determined to find a bar where Jacques could sit—he had been expelled from the Bistro for rowdiness, something which requires an extraordinary degree of undiscipline. We ended up in an upstairs club which featured singers and alcoholic drinks, but Léger, cajolingly, called for coffee for Jacques and beer for us. Jacques, he said, was a writer, and he was sick at heart tonight over the state of his country. Jacques was expressing his feelings about the country by crying out, "Bombs! That's what's needed! Bombs, I tell you!" and falling forward onto the table every few minutes. Yes, yes, said the proprietress in her Marseillais accent, she understood; hadn't there been a time when, new in Quebec and in the cabaret business, she'd suffered opprobrium for singing a song no more radical than: "A faithful man is as hard to find as a needle in a haystack . . ."? Even though there had been tremendous progress since those days, when a chap's had too much, he'd best go home and rest up. But she consented to serve the group, and, with only the odd outburst from Renaud, we sat through one show, Léger explaining separatism, literature, joual, and psychology (he is a man of the immediately preceding intellectual generation, separatist but not of the *parti pris* school; modernizer and demystifier, but in things like his essays on the French-Canadian woman in love rather than in the dense Marxist polemics of Renaud's comrades, and he has tried his hand at joual writing only very recently). At the end of the show we worked our way out of the place and began probing to extract from Renaud a clue to where he lived. Jacques was sly: he danced, he did somersaults on the snowy sidewalk, but only gradually let out that he lived a half a block away, on Crescent. We assisted him to the doorstep, and before opening the apartment-house door with his key he shattered a glass panel with a suddenly accurate foot. Once inside his basement apartment he similarly shattered a lamp. We tried to calm him, then said goodnight. But as our taxi pulled away, we saw him burst out of the front door of the building and run down a sidestreet, arms in the air, handsome, big-eyed, red locks to the wind, chanting something we couldn't catch. We let him go.

By the time I next tried to talk with him, he was no longer a newspaperman. The editor of *Métro-Express* had been fired and the staff had quit in solidarity (shortly afterward this tabloid, begun by a liberal French-Canadian millionaire during a long strike at the biggest Montreal daily, *La Presse*, in an attempt to combine cheesecake and progressive politics, closed down). Renaud had moved to an advertising agency. I reached him there, fixed a date with him at his place—he wanted to give me the address, but I assured him I remembered it. I went, he invited me in: the apartment was cozy, a story in the typewriter, a paperback novel folded open on the table. He introduced me to his girlfriend and answered my first question—What was he occupying himself with these days?—cheerfully. The job, writing, the occasional drink, and her. It was a modest résumé, but the more I talked with him, the more I noticed something I think is a constant in the Shouting Signpainters: the concern with life, daily existence, the material, the physical feeling of moments as they go by.

"We French-Canadians are learning a little now," Renaud said in one conversation. "We're starting to eat well, to dress a little better, to learn how to make love, to take an interest in erotic literature and magazines. We have had pornography in French Canada before, but never eroticism." And indeed Renaud is a dandy, a liver of life, even a bit contemptuous of anything—the revolution, for example—which might require him to put material gratifications second. "I'm a bad militant," he says, like his *cassé*. All Renaud's writing is saturated with feelings, warmth or cold, tastes, sexual arousal, textures of walls, furniture, clothing. We are close to the *impure poetry* of that searing Latin American, Pablo Neruad: "The mandates of touch, smell, taste, sight, hearing, the passion for justice, sexual desire, the sea sounding." And Renaud's friend Major, who rejects the designation "Latin" for the Québécois, has nevertheless said it in his *Word in Arms (A Poet's Manifesto):* "I blend my cry with Neruda's . . ."

Knowing Renaud in the late sixties, one felt he must have chosen his suits, ties, vest, sweaters, not so much as symbols, possessions, marks of accomplishment or divorce from the old slum life as for their feel, the pleasure they give to the touch. That, too, was missing in the old life; it simply isn't cool being poor, and Jacques Renaud is no longer broke in cash or in spirit. All this is echoed by Paul Chamberland in his *parti pris* essay on the morals of the revolutionary: "I don't understand the revolutionary who does not take the trouble to make love well," and in a thousand references in his verse to the joy of a cigarette smoked, a room lived in, and a woman loved. The slums kept you ragged and repressed your urges; the ideology which prevailed in the slums was a gray immaterialism which, if it did not in fact *prevent* your masturbating, girl-chasing, lying, and filching, or thinking about doing so, did put the claw of shame into you afterward; if it did not free you from coveting sleek upholstery, sleek automobiles, sleek duds, at least consoled you with the proverb that you were "born for small bread," that French-Canadians don't have any business sense. The revolution invites you to live fully while fighting to make it possible for the whole nation to do so. The assumption of the exploited condition, the ragged life as a flight from suburban boredom, does not exist in the Quebec left as it does among English-speaking youth in revolt. The suburban life from which the young English speakers are in flight is perhaps not as developed in French Canada, and of course the *partipristes* are not by any means the most conspicuous consumers in Montreal. But Renaud's conservative suits, Chamberland and Maheu raising families in the neat backwater of Outremont—coming from the other tradition, I could not dispel an uneasiness about these things.

I met Jacques Renaud now and then throughout my researches on the Shouting Signpainters, most often by chance, as when I came upon him in a bookstore toward the end of my research, looking at luxury albums of bird life to help him picture the fauna mentioned in *another* book he was reading on the Middle East. Renaud: "One must study if one hopes one day to be of use to one's people." It took me a second to decide not to let him get away with this outrage on my *sérieux*, and he laughed when I jabbed him in the ribs.

He was in a tizzy about the Mideast war; Zionism was fundamentally reactionary, that was the trouble; the Jews were always the same, religious fanatics. I was pro-Arab in the war, but I couldn't take this, and I argued prosaically for an understanding between progressive elements in both camps. But I was missing the point: I found myself, over coffee in Murray's (*"Je trouve la cuisine anglaise sobre"*), more and more back in the world of Sartre's *Jew and Anti-Semite*; it wasn't anything particular about Israel that made it blameworthy, it was invested with essential blameworthiness. Lebanon, now there was a country which showed how religions can coexist—but of course there were no Jews. (What *was* beyond the routinely anti-Semitic was a keen interest in the Arabs, but this soured too, at supper later on, when one of that proud people's glories turned out to be their welcoming of such white spreaders of light as Lawrence and—Napoleon!)

All this fitted into a general complaint against myself and the whole left to which I belonged: we were pigheaded about our tastes; some aspects of capitalism were good, some of the old ways were defensible: "I found I couldn't be a militant alongside Marxists. Maheu, for example, is an open-minded man on many subjects, but closed on politics. I was able to work alongside liberals, though, in the RIN."

And throughout it all, I intervene to stress, Renaud was as warm, funny, and charming as ever, and as cultivated and clear-spoken. (The founder of joual literature has one of the most disciplined dictions you will come across in Quebec.) But what I thought I was seeing was the son of the French-Canadian factory-worker fighting not to be swallowed by the new world into which he had moved when he "attained Culture," to hang onto that personality whose vitality, in spite of everything, he had conveyed in *Le Cassé*. "The French-Canadian is a hard worker," he told me, but agreed when I observed that in the factories he nevertheless cuts out a half hour early if he can. "Where, among our writers, is the real enjoyment of life?" he asked, thoroughly enjoying himself. "What about a poem I just read by a guy named Renaud?" I protested, and found myself reciting his last-published verse from *parti pris:*

ME: Unzip the flys of the banks—
HIM: And let the golden coins piss out!

Wasn't there joy in that? Well, he said, true, and "I even eat a good meal when I can, and I've been known to get laid on occasion." He would find life good and his countrymen hearty, by God, colonial exploitation or not, and no intellectual was going to tell him what to think of the Jews just because he'd said something complimentary about his novel.

He told me about his latest writing. He'd quit a job at the CBC as research man for a jazzy public affairs show and was now writing full time, planning a trip to Europe, or maybe to South America to film the guerrilla movements—no longer living on eggs. The last time I'd seen him he'd announced, with the same grave air with which he had expressed his reverence for study in the service of the nation: "I'm starting to write in American. Don't blame me: what else can I do? Quebec isn't independent and I've got talent. Believe me, my friend . . ." Now all that was over. He laughed. "Finished. I'm writing in my old joual again. Did I do something in American? Three long letters. Tremendous! I don't know any English, and when you don't understand a language, the things you can do with it, the new words, it's fantastic." It was Renaud the punster speaking.

(Actually, the last piece of his I had read was in neither joual nor "American" but in French, a funny account of an office worker's dream-war to deploy his coat rack in the center of his office, rather than in a corner. He loses to the cleaning ladies, the infantrywomen of convention. The piece appeared in *Les Lettres nouvelles,* one of the important avant-garde magazines in Paris which in the spring of 1967 gave a number to Canadian writers, oddly taking the placid Confederationist line that Canadian literature existed, was a two-headed creature which spoke in French from one mouth and in English from the other—rejecting, in short, the arguments of the *partipristes*, yet at the same time finding their work the most vital stuff coming out of this monster.)

More specifically, what was he up to? I knew he'd associated himself with a new, thoroughly aestheticist magazine called *quoi*, later with an erotico-aestheticist imitation of the French kitsch *Planète* which went by the name *Sexus*. All of which seemed to leave far distant the *parti pris* quest for an authenticity of nation and class which alone could give an authenticity to artists born of that nation and bound to that class. And I had come upon a press release announcing a recital he was to give at the youth pavilion of the world's fair.

"To music, I hear?"

"Yes—I'm even trying my hand at a few songs. Love poems of mine. I've got a musician friend who helps me with the arrangements and I use old Quebec reels as melodies. You must know this one . . ."

And he tam-te-delamed me a tune entirely unlike what I'd thought would be the musical background of his recital—I'd expected jazz—but true, true to the old French-Canadian vitality he clings to and to the new Quebec rebellion he has embraced, true to the truest Gilles Vigneault, true as Bob Dylan's reaching back to Woody Guthrie's rural whine to tell the story of urbanized America. This truth has never entirely left Jacques Renaud when he has sat down in his room to write, no matter how many false notes, no matter how many reactionary Israelis and hard-working French-Canadians the contradictory tugs on him bring out when he tries to theorize. And it is this truth that takes hold of him when he writes that makes us forgive the clinkers in his conversation.

I mentioned the evening Renaud told me he planned to write in English. For the first part of that evening we were not with him, we simply watched him, a table away at the Asociación Española, singing Vigneault love songs and old hymns in chorus with a *parti pris* crowd. At one point Renaud did a nasal take-off on a sports announcer: "And now we bring you, directly from *parti pris* . . ."

It was at closing time, going over to Ben's for coffee and smoked meats, that we joined him. He was a little drunk, not like that first great drunk encounter, but nicely light-hearted. He sang a couple of ribald reels, talked gaily about nothing. Then he spotted a tall, Asiatic-looking girl at another table. "She's beautiful," he said, with sudden seriousness, and withdrew into a concentration that left the conversation to others. Then, suddenly, he reached for his tie, unknotted it, reached for the expensive and conservative collar that had covered it, ripped it coolly and ostentatiously from his shirt, and set the two before him on the table. He took a notebook from his pocket and began jotting in it—"I've got to do a draft"—then transcribed the drafted poem to the cloth. He reknotted the tie around the collar and carried this offering, with exaggerated shyness, to the girl at her table. The girl looked puzzled, then smiled; her boyfriend laughed sportingly, Renaud contented himself with a word and returned to our table. Nothing more came of it—that I know of—it was simply a perfectly executed Charlie Chaplin performance.

But it seemed to have been the very remoteness of the girl, the very unreality of Renaud's courtship, which gave grace to it, suppressing for the moment the vein of misogyny to which he admits. What to make, though, of his graceless "Women are ignoble" in one of his recent stories, scarcely attributed to his hero as attenuation? The misogyny is a semi-liberation from the family order I have described; but it can only be a semi-liberation, and here Renaud's attitudes are characteristic of the *partipristes'*.

Women writers are prominent in Quebec literature generally, even perhaps dominate it. The novel I continued to consider the greatest French-Canadian novel even into my period of study of the Shouting Signpainters was written by a woman, Gabrielle Roy. Let me put it this way: she is the greatest of the French-Canadian writers; and the *partipristes* the first of the Québécois ones.

Her novel is *Bonheur d'occasion*. It has generally been regarded as a classic by English Canada as well as French. It had an international reach, too, winning the Prix Fémina, published in translation—as *The Tin Flute*—in the United States, and translated into other languages as well. All this in the late 1940's, just after the War.

The War is the background for *The Tin Flute*; it is a picture of life in the Montreal slum of St. Henri when some of the young men are joining the army as a way of amounting to something, others are dodging it (there was no draft for most of the war, but there was propaganda) because they figured they didn't need the army to become something. The heroine, Florentine, is caught between these two types, clinging to the first but drawn to the second. And she is caught in St. Henri, where you move to a new tenement every year, never finding one better than the last, and when you do, and the night you move in you discover why you found it: the trains scream through your sleep. The novel is a fine piece of humane realism. Roy, the educated woman who came east from a French-Canadian upbringing in Manitoba, looks at the life her compatriots live in this, their metropolis, and is saddened.

But if women dominate French-Canadian literature—in a colonized, but literate, society letters take on a motherly function, the kindly eye cast upon the state of the family—there is still no female Shouting Signpainter, no revolutionary woman novelist or poet, nor even an important article-writer, in the *parti pris* group. Why? The alienation of woman, the colonization of sex—for which the French-Canadian mother was avenging herself with her tyrannical ways—is one part of the Quebec malady the *parti pris* demystifiers have left almost unexamined. In the *parti pris* world, woman remains the beloved, the symbol of the land, the one the revolutionary does not neglect to love well.

The most intelligent remarks on the colonization of woman that has taken place within the colonization of Quebec, the closest thing to a *dépassement* of both the colonization and the infantile masculine revolt against its effects, have been provided by Pierre Maheu. The problem was clearly enough posed: "I doubt very much if any but a small proportion of our mothers ever felt an orgasm." Their glory, rather, was in piety and ruling the household. But does this mean these chaste household tyrants must be taken in hand by revolutionary males and molded into women of the world, sensual and undemanding? Maheu is less naïve than that: "But let us not confuse this with matriarchy; it is obvious that women do not dominate Quebec society, were slow to obtain the vote, enjoy no equal-pay legislation, still occupy, in fact, a status of inferiority and effacement. For precisely—it is not in reality but on the level of myth that the mother is exalted."

The future may be where a friend, male, put it during a big argument one night between my wife and a skeptic about feminism. Said the friend, slipping in between the arguers: "When *parti pris* started to create a revolutionary politics in Quebec, they didn't situate themselves with reference to the clerical old guard, they took on *Cité libre,* the progressives of the preceding generation whose progressivism had proved deficient. When are you women going to do the same thing? Instead of harping on the dumbest male prejudices, create, alongside the votes-for-women liberal feminism of Thérèse Casgrain and her friends, who fought their fights in the forties and have since faded into pale pacifism among the suburban housewives, a revolutionary feminism that will go to the heart of the thing?"

The tensions of colonialism are still there, even for the youth who has taken his stand against it. The revolt against woman has created a new tension—"Women are ignoble." The leaving-behind of poverty has cut him off from his community without giving him a new one. At best he has friends, a gathering place, the Asociación. If he wishes to extend his new attitudes to the entire day's activities, to an entire enterprise, to writing, for example, he is up against the dilemma of being sub-Faulkner in "American," sub-Robbe-Grillet in French, or else true to himself in the joual whose most characteristic speakers do not read and whose readers are torn by the same uncertainties—"Quebec isn't independent and I've got talent." For finally there is that nagging political project implicit in writing in the true-to-yourself way, in rejecting the maternal tenderness for the sufferers that comes from drawing back and looking in from the outside, in instead shouting defiance from within that suffering, determined, as a sufferer yourself, to overthrow the order that makes you suffer. The women the shouter encounters are either the rich lesbian or the slave-tyrant slum girl; the foreign woman remains the only way out. The Shouting Signpainter has moved west across the Main, eaten at the Eldorado, then moved on further still, learned the colonizer's language, worked in his offices and begun to drink with him in the more atmospheric spots. But the nation is still back there in the slums, still as he described it in his shoutings, and as long as that is so, he is, if no longer broke, then living on a sort of credit.

Jacques Renaud, who told what it was like to be *cassé*, can buy suits with vests and tear up shirts, lodge in a chic little basement near the Bistro, or on the nice north side of the Mountain, eat three square meals a day, sing Vigneault at the Asociación, accumulate Culture, even embrace the "atheistic communism" which was the forbidden ideology back in the days when misogyny was the forbidden sexual attitude. He can enjoy, conquer, contest. On credit. On the credit extended by a revolution which has not yet liberated his countrymen from the taverns of the east. The unliberated man of

Montreal had been described before Renaud described him—by Gabrielle Roy and others. But he had been perceived from without. With Jacques Renaud, he perceived himself. *Bonheur d'occasion* was Quebec's *Uncle Tom's Cabin*; *Le Cassé* was its *Native Son*.

3
The alphabet of revolution

It is 1966. Paul Chamberland is a small, reddish-haired man of twenty-seven whose appearance combines boyishness and professorial baldness. He wears thick glasses with a single plastic rim across the top and has a slightly walrusy moustache. He speaks quietly and without hesitation in what he considers French, in contrast to the non-French some of his friends have still not broken out of. But it is not the fact that the French-Canadian pronunciation of *cheval* is something approaching *joual* that he sees at the heart of this divergence from French:

"That French-Canadians may always have a different pronunciation does not upset me." (His own accent, like that of most middle-class French-Canadians, eschews the grosser Canadianisms—*baihn*, in one syllable, for *bien; twey* for *toi*—but is far removed from France.) "It is the syntax that is attacked in joual. For example, an expression like *'virage en U'* I find more offensive than an out-and-out anglicism like 'U-turn.' I work at Hydro-Québec—power is one of the few sectors of the economy the Québécois control even without decolonization—and my work there has, well, a purpose. Without exaggerating the possibilities—mostly, it's a living—we can play a role there. In the manuals our office prepares for the agency's staff, we try to establish French forms in their minds: in the case of 'U-turn,' neither the straight borrowing of English words nor the translation from the English, but the original French way of saying it, *demi-tour*."

When did he learn his French? He smiles, but his answer is not a joke:

"Not before I was eighteen, certainly. Every Québécois who speaks French, who really is sure of himself in the language, is in the end an autodidact. All of them. Even those who have been through the best schools available, through the classical system, the lot. Because our schools do not attack the problem of what is happening to French in Quebec. At that age, eighteen, I was studying for the priesthood with the Holy Cross Fathers. The Oratory, Brother André, and all that. My aspirations were in a way not far removed from those I developed later: I imagined myself as a sort of intellectual priest, perhaps writing. I had already been writing poetry for two years, and some of my poems from the period when my inspiration was religious have been published."

He does not take it as a joke either when asked if his Christian faith was as clear in them as his Marxist is in his recent verse:

"When I discarded my first faith, I made sure not to replace it with another. The accusation that we are hastily made-over Catholics, dogmatists of a new dogma, is a common one from our adversaries. I have never quite understood the basis for this. For it is precisely our task to keep our political perceptions from taking on the ossified and comfort-giving aspects of religion. That's the difference. That's why I'm not the same intellectual I would have been if I'd gone ahead with my plan to intellectualize within the structures of the Church. And I think that even when I was studying for the priesthood, I was more a poet than a real devotee of the deity. It was the mysticism of Christianity I liked, not the theological comforts. This may be the reason I never really 'lost the faith'; I don't recall my rejection of Christ as a crisis. You might say the thing just melted away. There was no vehemence."

And it is true that the revolutionary vehemence of his poetry today is not particularly directed against clericalism; the anti-clericalism is taken for granted, it is part of the anti-capitalism. Similarly, the kind of God who was present in his early poems, the Something trembling in the air of the forest or the crowded street, announcing terrible new dimensions to life, still has a place in his angry cries against the social calvary.

So the Holy Cross Fathers presided over the atheization of Paul Chamberland, did not teach him French, and saw even whatever spirituality they churned up in him turn against their order of things. If they fostered any of the old priestly nationalism in him, it too went bad on them:

"I had always, back in those seminary days, been more or less nationalist. Five years ago I belonged to the RIN. Then, after the break, when I was at the University of Montreal studying philosophy, I began to come to socialism as well. I read Marx, and Sartre had a lot to do with it."

The name of Sartre, the world's most famous Marxist *littérateur,* a prince of two anti-clerical churches, the French left and the French language, should have been the occasion for asking Chamberland a question I had sworn to include in my interview: Did Sartre's refusal of the Nobel Prize not make him feel guilty about having accepted, just a few months before, a Quebec government literary prize? Chamberland's prize came from sources surely as hostile and seductive to a revolutionary writer here as Sartre judged the Nobel committee for him? But our conversation was at a touchier, more exploratory level than that, and the question would have to wait.

Chamberland was saying, "I don't want to speak French because I'm proud of it. I want to speak it because it is my language." It was the first flash of the intransigence of his poetry that I had found in him. It did not bother me that the author of violent verse was soft in speech, that he wore thick glasses. He could still be burning inside. But I was dismayed to listen to him retreat, as we ate dishes served up as old-time French-Canadian specialties in a restaurant he had ferreted out in the seedy-nightclub St. Catherine East district, from a line of his long, last-published poem I had put to him: *"Je suis fier de mal écrire."* What he meant there, he said, was that he didn't want to have anything to do with a school of writing which set fineness, correctness, elegance as its standards, which prided itself on not being contaminated, like the daily speech of French-Canadians, with alien and illiterate elements. He was not proud, then, of writing badly? It was a figure of speech, something you said in a poem but wouldn't really back up in a conversation? He answered with an attack on the whole notion of pride in linguistic matters:

"We have had campaigns to preserve French that were based on pride in language. It never worked, because people had nothing to be proud of. What people had was a basic education and upbringing in French, challenged as soon as they tried to live adult lives by the pressure to learn English. It was not an integration of two languages which they were asked to make, which they found going on in their heads, it was a fight between the two. For joual is a decomposition of language, it is not a language. It is a monster."

But French, and certainly English, are also monsters, amalgams of different languages. Could not the elements of two tongues be fitted into one head?

"No, because the French-Canadian knows he is being tugged in two directions. Millions of people speak English without being aware that it is a half-Latin, half-Germanic language, but there is not a French-Canadian who does not know that French and English are two different languages, that the mixture of the two is saleable nowhere, not among the English and not among the French. He knows, the speaker of joual, that he is trying to be two things at once. English, even American English, is integrated; the English-speaker is not drawn in two directions at the same time." Chamberland made a Y-shaped gesture in front of him: "Joual is hydra-headed."

(Hence the French-Canadian myth of that man, perhaps unique in the world, perfectly adapted to the needs of his life: the *parfait bilingue*. Not the good American, the assimilated immigrant who has embraced and mastered the new world culture so you'd hardly notice he wasn't born to it, or even the immigrant who still appends alreadys to his sentences after the eradication of Yiddish, or inverts his word order like the Pennsylvania Dutch, but may be able to make a career of chuckling over it, even impose a bit of it on the collective language, like the ethnically identifiable comics of night clubs and television. Not, either, the instinctive peasant, knowing only his folkloric tongue and needing nothing more. But the two-gun sharpshooter who quickly switches back and forth between two worlds, the schizophrene. One of the languages has got to win. And French is a language that is used to winning, an imperialist language, only number two in the world, but number one in every other situation in which it has come into contact with other languages. In Belgium the speakers of French fall into a minority but continue to dominate, in the Congo and the other old colonies it forces even the anti-colonialist elites to speak their colonizers' language among themselves, in North Africa Arabic is fighting for its life. In Paris a Frenchman wonders what the fight is all about. French a colonized language?

The Alphabet of Revolution

What do you mean? Surely the French-Canadians simply want to go on speaking French as we speak it, with their accent of course, a bit of a patois even, but with the same casual shrug as us? Anglicisms? Over here we have our *buildings* and our *drugstores, mais enfin* . . . Quebec is at one and the same time—this is what the Frenchman cannot get his mind around—the only real French-speaking land among France's old overseas possessions—in neither Africa nor Asia did the colonial languages penetrate any distance into the population, in the West Indies French penetrated but at popular levels became creole, no longer comprehensible to a Frenchman—*and* the only major contact of French with another tongue where French is emerging the loser.)

"But French is a world language and it is Quebec's language, the one spoken every day by the masses of the Quebec population. Even against a still stronger world language, even in the vaunted North American context, it meets the minimum requirements for its survival. In fifteen, in twenty years, when large numbers of Québécois will already be speaking something other than French, the game will be up. If we spoke Danish, the game would be up."

Listening, wondering where the game stood now, there came for me a moment when I began to have difficulty with the program Chamberland seemed to be sketching for French in Quebec. He was describing the French-Canadian workers' deprivation of everything, right down to their language. He was speaking of their lack of consciousness, of organization, of confidence, their lack of the simple good things of the material life. These people were to assume yet another burden, that of repairing a decaying language? Was this not asking something superhuman? "We"—Chamberland often spoke in the plural, since this was a first conversation between an unknown English-speaking journalist and the representative of a French-speaking ideology—"don't ask anything superhuman of anybody. We want the objective conditions to be such that French will survive."

The place of the language in the *parti pris* scheme of liberation was defining itself. The "objective conditions." But what are the objective conditions of a language? Surely nothing less than the entire universe; in practical terms, the whole economy of the country in which it is spoken.

Capitalism in Quebec is English. It came to Quebec first from England, then from English Canada, then from the United States. The U.S. version hired the local English to administer it. ("I think we can say the role of the English-Canadians is that—they are the managers for American imperialism," Chamberland says.) And it opened the factory doors to the unskilled French. It is an abrasive which slowly gnaws away at its workers' language as at their muscles, their self-respect, their diet, their fellow-feeling and unity. It is today the objective condition of joual, tomorrow of proletarian English with a few traces of the ancestral speech. The creation of the objective conditions for the continuation of French in Quebec comes, then, to this: the overthrow of capitalism, its objective destroyer.

But why the overthrow of *all* capitalism, why socialism? Would not the overthrow of *English* capitalism, the installation of a French-speaking possessing class, or even a French-speaking managing class to front for the same old American investments, be enough to create the required climate of linguistic sovereignty? "French," says Chamberland, "is my language." This is descriptive of the present state of things: the most joualized worker, the most facilely bilingual businessman, would be able to share this affirmation with the revolutionary poet. But the businessman sees material possession of the world as within his grasp; only the fact that he has had to trade in his linguistic personality to make his money sours things for him. The writer's interest in buttressing the language is clear enough, too. But the worker? The language of which he is being robbed is his language, he can feel that, but he is not sure that the factory in which he works is his factory; he rather has the impression that it is not his and was not meant to be. Would he not have to develop a similar claim on the material part of his life in order to put socialism on the agenda?

Chamberland's view weaves all these struggles into a whole, refuses the itemization I have suggested. That worker and that businessman might have business with each other under normal circumstances, under different objective conditions; they might have quarrels to settle; they might be calling each other *exploiteur capitaliste* and *communiste athée*, going on strike against each other, clubbing each other on the head and putting up barricades against each other. Or simply hating each other and voting for different political parties. But no. The interplay of these two parts of the one society is frozen. There is a subservience which transcends the issues between the two classes and this is the mutual anglicization—at the expense of your wholeness if, like the businessman, you try to keep your English and French separate, to nurse along your "culture," but be "practical" too; at the expense of your French if you are the worker and cannot pause to worry over the thing. A force from without the society dispossesses them both, the bourgeois of exploitation, the worker of his contestation of that exploitation. The life of the nation does not take place; there is only the life of that nation in relation to another.

I found the view compelling, a delineation of what it is that makes French-Canadians more than just a hard-to-digest ethnic group in the American body. The Greeks in Montreal or New York do not have the potential within their community for the full range of social conflicts; the Puerto Ricans are all, virtually, proletarians. The French-Canadians, both proletarian and would-be bourgeois, would like to get at each other's throats. They cannot, because somebody else is at both their throats. Other nations have been through such clashes, their histories record the settling of accounts between oppressors and oppressed, the coming to consciousness of their proletariats. In Quebec, all that has been congealed under the crust of national resentment. The job is to revive the internal mechanisms, open the working class to combats beyond the old nationalism. The strange element must depart, the life of the nation must begin again. The nation must re-enter history.

The quarrel had been bequeathed to the young intellectuals in Quebec by their elders. We must save the nation from the centralizers, said the old, clerical nationalists. This talk of nation, said the social democrats, is a fascist-flavored evasion of our real problems, which are social. That both accounts were simplistic was sensed by reformed clericals like André Laurendeau and sympathizing socials like Frank Scott (who as a constitutional lawyer took on Duplessis, and as an English-Canadian poet translated Anne Hébert). Then the Fanons and the Memmis, recommended by the Sartres, came into the hands of the Chamberlands out of the crumbling French empire after the Second World War, and the fusion announced itself. In an issue of *Liberté* early in 1963, Chamberland, Major, and Renaud were the youngsters invited by the purely literary rebels of that magazine to state their positions. "Our liberation, finally, will be socialist or it will not be," wrote Chamberland in an article on "The Quebec Intellectual, a Colonized Intellectual." It was as harsh on Catholicism as any freethinking bohemian could ask: "The religious behavior of this people is the subtlest trait of its alienation. No saints, no great sinners. Excess in nothing. Mediocrity and the void." Yet it also scoffed at the individualistic solutions the *Liberté* group offered. Chamberland's use, in one place, of the word *centralizer* betrayed how freshly out of the old-nationalist woods the new writers were, but it was Fanon who was quoted on the sterility of nationalism not deepened by socialism.

In a later conversation, when we were more at ease with each other, Chamberland spoke again of history. "We are a people of amnesiacs," he told me. "Our history, where we come from, we know nothing of this—it's a blank."

But what about *Je me souviens?* What about *Notre maître, le passé?* These harkings-backward were the slogans of Quebec folk-culture. Weren't French-Canadians on the contrary obsessed with their past, narcotized with the exploits of their heroes, their woodsmen, their missionaries, and their Indian-fighters?

"No, not really. For what we remember, what our school books always rehash, and what our teachers pound into our skulls is not history, not even really mythology, it's Punch and Judy—*du guignol.* Take Dollard, defending the Long Sault in the Ottawa River against the Iroquois, take Madeleine de Verchères. This is the stuff of our traditional brainwash. Madeleine de Verchères—a little scene played out nowhere, with no purpose, no continuity, no contribution to anything coming after, no origin in what went before. And, for that matter, we tell ourselves lies about it—we forget to mention the truth about Madeleine, that she was a whore. This is the fact, but my mother, who is after all steeped in the old culture of *Je me souviens* and *Notre maître, le passé,* was scandalized when I told her so."

The role this myth plays in the old ahistoric Quebec ideology is suggested by an article I read much later, while finishing this chapter. The article was in a local imitation of *Reader's Digest,* extracted by the editors from a volume of ahistorical anecdotes by one of the Frères des Ecoles Chrétiennes, a grand old teaching order. It touchingly fictionalizes the Quebec visit of Lord Durham, an aristocratic British reform politician sent to Canada to investigate that last important French-Canadian attempt to break into history, the bourgeois revolt of 1837. Durham belongs to the demonology of French Canada because his report on this uprising depreciated the French in Canada and urged their assimilation by the British colonial regime. The Durham Report has passed on a few famous phrases: "Two nations warring in the bosom of a single state," we are told in our English-Canadian schools, in tune with the liberal Canadian willingness to recognize the French as a "nation," the better to keep them within the same country. French pupils learn that he called them a "people without history." Chamberland would, I judge, agree, saying the colonialist was telling a truth about the colonized that they themselves had not been able to face; but the good brother who wrote the article was, in true impotent-nationalist fashion, outraged: he recounts that the evening Durham wrote his report a French-Canadian servant-girl whose father had fought with the rebels—and who, he stresses, had been well versed in glorious French-Canadian legends by the Ursulines who schooled her—found him asleep over his manuscript, read the insult, and snatched up his plume in a desire to write, not an invocation of her father's history-making activities of a few months before, but this: "Thou liest, Durham!—Madeleine de Verchères." Durham was too much the gentleman to demand who had defaced his manuscript, says Brother Marie-Victorin. Instead, he asked the girl if there was in this wild land someone by the name of Madeleine de Verchères. The girl, equal to the occasion, said the lady in question had been dead a century, recited to him the legend of Madeleine's organizing the defense of a stockade on the St. Lawrence—at Verchères, where her monument, musket in hand, looks out over the river today—against the Iroquois, in the absence of the regular commanders. This tale, the body of the article, is told in the ripest clerical-*guignol* rhetoric, right down to the "hideous masks" of the Indians. Since the Iroquois did and do make wooden masks, I hesitated concluding racism, but a column later the good brother was speaking of "tigers with human faces" and "wild-animal eyes glimmering in the forest," so . . . But Madeleine "held out her pure soul to the Virgin" and beat the redskins. "Very picturesque," says the still-snobbish Durham, who then goes ahead to describe the French-Canadians as a people without history.

The myth has all the required characteristics for a place in clerical ideology. It speaks of a heroism completely defensive, against, not an oppressor, but the tattooed heathen: Madeleine's fort is "a simple palisade around the church and the houses, one of the advance-posts of French civilization on the continent." Nothing is built in the face of oppression, for the oppressors are absent: Jacques Ferron, a grand old man of Quebec anti-colonialism to the *partipristes* of Chamberland's generation, describes how Chénier, the only leader of the 1837 revolt who died in battle, was soft-pedaled by the Church as a candidate for national hero and replaced by Dollard, who fought the Iroquois to defend the French fur routes, not the English to throw off colonialism. Ferron spits on Dollard—the left must deal with the French-Canadians' part in the white plunder of the American Indian before they became themselves victims of conquest (it usually does so by uniting in solidarity with what's left of the Indians in Quebec in the struggle against the present oppressors). And Ferron has done what he can to re-replace Dollard with Chénier: in a play which the Théâtre du Nouveau Monde of Montreal created in a tour of the towns of Quebec in 1968, Ferron has another young girl who has been through the Ursuline convent tell a priest, with the same spark of anger Brother Marie-Victorin's servant-girl showed Durham, that the clergy have always cuddled up to the regime over the heads of the people. "That," mutters the curé, "you certainly did not learn from the Ursulines."

As for Madeleine, she may have been a remarkable person, her exploit a remarkable performance, and also have been the prostitute Chamberland calls her. The point is that the old ideologists didn't want to have anything to do with that kind of complexity, they had no use for history; it was the cleaned-and-polished nuggets of submissive-but-pure behavior from the past that were their stock in trade, a sort of anti-history. And the real Madeleine—heroine *and* whatever else she was—can only emerge from a repossession of Quebec history by Québécois who see a prospect of someday *making* history. For the making of history is a jog to the memory, a shaking-up of the colonial amnesiac; it can sharpen such hazy images as the anti-conscription riots of 1917, bring back such moments of anger as the hockey riot of—was it 1954?—when fans of the revered Canadien Club, because an English-speaking official had suspended the most revered Canadien of all, Maurice Richard, tore up St. Catherine West outside the Forum. It can even inspire a groping for a sense of others' struggles: the condensed book in that same issue of *Digeste Eclair* was *Episodes of the Revolutionary War* by Che Guevara.

This leaves unexplained why an ideologist of the old school chose the anecdote—"Thou liest, Durham"—for a book, why he recalled 1837, why he offered this incitation to rancor against English power. If the Church's line has always been submission, why play with fire in this way? The reason seems to me to be that the Church's line has not been plainly and simply submission to the English order, as the *partipristes* are inclined to say, or plainly and simply hatred for the unbeliever, as the Anglo-Protestant oppressor group is inclined to suspect. But rather a delicate interplay of the two. First, a bit of anti-English propaganda to whip up feelings of apartness from the masters, for without this, with total submission to and unmitigated admiration of the masters encouraged, the French might have found a total embrace of the Anglo-Protestant culture around them attractive, and been lost to the Church, so to speak, on the right. Then, however, the damper on the flames of hate as soon as they risked setting fire to the whole edifice, as soon as the hate sought an expression politically, in revolt, resistance, vandalism. For with that process in motion the Church was in danger of losing its people on the left, when, having hurled themselves against their English economic masters, they decided to throw off their Catholic spiritual mentors as well.

The Church, in this analysis, becomes a mediating force between English capital and French labor, keeping the French just anti-capitalist enough to go on working for the English without proposing to replace them. The hate, anyway, usually turned on those aspects of the English presence that were least oppressive to the French—the liberalism, the sexual permissiveness. As soon as the hatred threatened to touch the oppressive aspects—the conscription of the French as labor or as cannon-fodder—it was the damper of obedience, the word of honor given, the undertaking to be good, property-respecting British-subject Canadians, if the English let you speak French and go to Mass.

Another way of seeing this dichotomy is as a high clergy–low clergy split. Ringuet recounts in his novel *Trente arpents* that in the First World War the bishops declared the French-Canadians duty bound to fight for the Empire, but the curés helped recalcitrants go underground. The man who coined the expression *"Notre maître, le passé"* was a low-ranking priest who, also a historian, won enormous fame as the clerical ideologist who carried the old nationalism closest to the brink of political action. Canon Lionel Groulx can be seen as the intellectual leader of low-clergy nationalism who always just avoided offending high-clergy guarantees to the status quo.

I asked Chamberland if historical awareness among populations had ever gone beyond the anecdotal, the *guignol*.

"In other countries, no, the common folk are not aware of the profundities of historical development; they too remember incidents, heroes, bits and pieces. But we must examine the bits and pieces, find what has been selected from the vast flow of trends and events and retained by the national consciousness. Napoleon, for example, is no doubt a hero, a folkloric, mythic figure whose real historical significance is not fully understood by the Frenchmen who revere him. But while Napoleon was building his legend he was also building France: the chosen hero built what the country in which the hero-worshipper lives has become.

"One of the revolutionary tasks here in Quebec, for us, revolutionary writers, intellectuals, is to rediscover that history which can mean something for the future of Quebec, for the population we would like to see build the future. There is, above all, the insurrection of 1837 to be recouped, that aborted bourgeois revolt which almost, but not quite, brought the Quebec consciousness through the intervening stage between its feudal origins and its capitalist present. If the rebels of '37 had won they would have formed the nucleus of a commercial bourgeoisie, out of which a full-fledged industrial bourgeoisie would logically have grown. We are planning at the éditions to dig up some new materials on 1837, publish documents, studies, which can make our people aware of the stages they went through to get where they are. The fact that these revolutionaries were not fully clairvoyant in our terms, were pro-capitalist, is not the key point: in Cuba, for example, they have given a very important place in the national consciousness to Martí, a figure from the past whose aims were limited in Communist terms but who was a necessary stage, both for the country and for the people who were developing toward a historical consciousness, a background for their socialism."

Chamberland gave two examples of what *parti pris* was doing to give a background to Quebec socialism. One was the publication of the political notebooks of Jean-Marie Nadeau, a Liberal Party intellectual of the fifties who was thinking up the reforms of the sixties before Duplessis fell. The notebooks show him slowly being squeezed out of the party councils as his progressivism bore down on the Liberals' big business financing and their common traits with Duplessis's party, the Union Nationale. *Parti pris* managed to get René Lévesque to write a preface to the book; he may not have been happy that the publisher who unearthed it was *parti pris,* but he did recognize a precursor.

The other project was the translation of *Quebec in Revolt,* a book by Herman Buller, one of those from the English-speaking Montreal Jewish Communist milieu of the 1930's who did make the leap to appreciation of the French-Canadian milieu around him. It recounts the persecution of one Guibord, a member of that turn-of-the-century remnant of the anti-clerical thought mostly snuffed out in 1837, the Institut Canadien. Guibord was for a time denied burial for his ideas.

As for 1837, the *parti pris* mining of this vein took two forms: one skeptical, in the magazine; the other more cheerful, in the books. In one article in *parti pris,* Pierre Maheu speaks of the *patriotes* of 1837 as if their potential as myths or martyrs for a twentieth-century revolution had already been used to the full and shown its shortcomings. "After all," he said, "I sometimes tell myself that what these men sought was to establish capitalism, the very system we're now trying to bring down." (Another, later, *parti pris* piece threw cold water on even this image of Papineau and his colleagues as bourgeois revolutionaries, reading Montesquieu and aspiring to be industrialists. It showed how much they too were soaked through with the old agriculturalist ideology of the clergy.)

But 1837 was a real uprising of the masses against colonialism, and this side of the story is told by Robert-Lionel Séguin in an éditions parti pris booklet, *La Victoire de Saint-Denis.* Séguin is a traditional nationalist historian who has written minute studies of Quebec peasant life even unto *Barns of New France*. In *La Victoire* he tells the story of the battle of St-Denis, where, on a January afternoon in 1838, three hundred farmers with *two* hundred hunting rifles put to rout the regular troops of Her just-enthroned Majesty, Victoria, commanded by a veteran of Waterloo, bogged down like all regular armies facing guerrillas on the guerrillas' home ground. The older farmers, some of them, had learned about war fighting for the British against the Americans in 1812; all had hunted since childhood. The local priest condemned the rebels, but another priest was in the thick of battle comforting them—there's always a *curé de gauche*.

This was a victory without leaders. Papineau had been there earlier but had left town, and Dr. Wolfred Nelson stayed in his house. Repression came down: a governor named Colborne had villages burned to achieve it. Some rebel leaders fled across the U.S. border; twelve were hanged at a spot in east Montreal where there is now a romantic monument to them (and where demonstrations rallied in the sixties). Clericalism revived. From then on, in the words of Michel van Schendel, a Belgian-born Québécois who has written in *parti pris,* "Quebec has been the name of a sickness," the name of a people going through the motions of living, but frozen in the self-image of a century and a half before.

Paul Chamberland was born into a conventional, Catholic French-Canadian family of the Second World War, a period in which urbanization, the accession to a certain amount of comfort, to work and lodging less harsh than the manual labor and slum tenement of the newly urbanized rural Québécois, had not changed the basic reflexes: signs in a male child of a contemplative, interiorized character were the makings of a priest; the only expression for otherworldliness was the cassock and the breviary.

But Chamberland decided his drives were not to other worlds, or were so only in the sense of Eluard's aphorism: "There is another world, but it is in this one." And now when he says "we" or "us," he is not usually referring to the family, the milieu, the universe that is still the universe of the majority of French-Canadians, but to a sub-universe that some young Québécois, for whom the decline of Duplessism is a memory of adolescence, the liberalization of the sixties the climate of adulthood, have opened up within the larger French-Canadian one.

Chamberland often interrupted a conversation on ideas, general principles, to name someone who was "important to us." When he mentioned Herbert Marcuse, I wondered how many others, even in the *parti pris* group, had read this thinker who wrote from—was it England or the United States? Chamberland wasn't sure. (This was before 1968 and the burst of Marcuse publicity; the only work of his you could find in French bookstores was a paperback of *Soviet Marxism*.) But when he said: "Borduas, the *Refus global*, is important to us, you know," I felt the *us* took in more than the most learned of the group. Paul-Emile Borduas was a French-Canadian nonobjective painter of the forties and fifties whose jagged forms are protests in the same way that Charlie Parker's or John Coltrane's horn sounds are protests; they are the jazz of the long darkness of Quebec. Only once did Borduas use words to protest, before he left for Paris for good, and this was *Refus global*, the "total rejection" of French-Canadian culture which he and fellow painters decorated and mimeographed. It was published in 1948, a year before Asbestos; Borduas died in 1959, the year Duplessis died.

In 1966, *parti pris* published an issue called *Refus global pas mort*. It mainly consisted of interviews and samplings from two writers not associated with the revolutionary movement but who *parti pris* felt belonged there. Chamberland interviewed Claude Péloquin, leader of a multi-art movement which took much from the happenings of the English-speaking world. He spoke well of Péloquin's verse. Jan Depocas, who had briefly put out a laïcist-nationalist magazine of his own before joining *parti pris* when it appeared, interviewed Claude Gauvreau, a comrade of Borduas, a writer-painter of his generation, and there were many references to the *Refus global* days in the discussion.

Depocas wrote an introductory piece for the issue in which he noted that many young people to whom Borduas was distant had read *Refus global* in *La Revue Socialiste*, the magazine of left separatism at the beginning of the separatist movement. (This was my case. The original, illustrated edition can be found only in libraries.) It seemed to me to have hurt *parti pris* as much to have failed to rally this pair of rebel poets as it did to be cut off from entire classes of nonartists. Chamberland was later to write that even as a petty-bourgeois intellectual he acted out of self-interest in trying to make the revolution: "For the revolutionary is before anything else a malcontent; whatever his moralizings, he simply doesn't feel at home in existing society, and if he wants change, it's first of all for himself." Péloquin and Gauvreau should see that they needed that change too, he felt, as Borduas had seen, though he had despaired of ever being gratified.

The first issue of *parti pris* included Chamberland's "Poem of the Pre-Revolution":

> O face of fire from which proud and naked peoples forge a reason   a land   a cry of broken bonds
> will you have touched all of Asia   all of Africa and all the tropic Latin slaveries   from shore to shore with flame
> before   you have yanked us from the polar jaws and put into our mole's limbs the fire to be free and wed our injured earth Quebec

The poem's last two words became the title of an anthology advertised in the sixth issue of *parti pris* (for which Chamberland also wrote a long article on "The Contradictions of the Quiet Revolution" and an editorial that said, "Like Saint-Denys Garneau, a poet who lost himself in the swamps of his 'inner life,' and Borduas, who fled to an impossible France, we in turn choose exile—but exile in the future"):

the publishing	*la ville inhumaine*
house of *parti pris*	
will soon present	a novel
its first volume	by laurent girouard

a *parti pris*	*terre québec*
poet publishes	
with Déom	poems
Feb. 6	by paul chamberland

Terre Québec was the book for which Chamberland received the $1000 albatross from the Quebec Ministry of Culture. The time had come when I could ask him if accepting the money did not mark him as perhaps politically heretical, but still okay with the establishment as writer of verse.

"There was no question of refusing, as with Sartre and his Nobel Prize," he told me, "because I'd submitted it. I know that the Minister of Culture, Pierre Laporte, was upset about the jury's choosing my book, but in the end the government didn't intervene—the left would have raised a stink. As it happens, we were pretty broke at the time and it just paid our debts.

"In any case, I don't see a basis for turning down money the establishment sees fit to offer revolutionaries, and if I were, say, to win the Governor-General's Award, I would take it and put the money into some revolutionary fund—into *parti pris,* for example. Sartre's refusal of the Nobel money I regard as one example of an idealism that survives in him, cool-headed revolutionary though he may want to be. Whether Sartre likes it or not, he is a Nobel prizewinner, and the result of his refusal is simply that the money is lost to a left-wing cause."

Immediately after the publication of *Terre Québec* came the blows of the establishment that put the Chamberland family (Paul, Thérèse, and a daughter named Elsa, after Louis Aragon's Elsa Triolet, writer herself and object of a lifetime of love poems by the great French Communist poet Quebec knows from paperbacks and long-playing records) into the bad financial shape he had mentioned. The eleventh issue of the magazine, dated October 1964, announced it this way:

> YOUNG MEN, BRILLIANT,
> SEEK EMPLOYMENT
> paul chamberland, pierre maheu,
> andré major, jean-marc piotte,

staff members of the magazine *parti pris,* have been without employment for some weeks for the most varied of reasons . . .

They are well-bred, well-educated young men, all quite intelligent, all prepared to devote themselves body *and soul* to an eventual employer.

For references, please consult:

> Mr. Pierre-Elliott Trudeau, or Montreal Bureau, Royal Canadian Mounted Police.

For more serious information:

> *parti pris,* 2135 Bellechasse, "A"
> Phone 722-4770

114 *Malcolm Reid*

The wisecrack about the RCMP was probably quite accurate. Chamberland's file with the federal police could date from even before the founding of *parti pris,* since in the early sixties he was frequenting the leftist milieux of the RIN and nationalist milieux of the Quebec section of the federal social democrats, the NDP, that produced the FLQ. What part the RCMP had in the *partipristes'* dismissals from their jobs (the college Chamberland taught at simply did not renew his contract after the first year; no explanation) we won't know until the files of the system are ours to look at.

Winning the prize and finding his job at Hydro-Québec solved the problem for Chamberland, and he worked there, fairly happily and with freedom even to orate at after-work public demonstrations, most of the time from then until he returned to study in Paris. It was during this period that both his verse and his politics intensified, and the same issue of the magazine which carried his writing creed, *To say what I am* ("When I began to write, I was up to my neck in the pink ooze of grace; I drooled literally in ecstasy, holy hallucination: I quite simply *saw* madonnas in whores, holy water in marshes"), also announced the publication, this time with *parti pris*'s own house, of *"l'afficheur hurle, the signpainter screams,* a long poem, vehement and impassioned." The next issue, dealing with the colonial capital of Montreal, contained passages from this work, and shortly thereafter it was on city newsstands as a book. Here is this great shout. Starting with its opening.

I write the circumstance of my life and yours and yours my wife my comrades
I write the poem of a circumstance deadly and inescapable
pardon my familiar tone bear with me through my swamps of silence
I can't talk any more
I don't know what to say
poetry does not exist
except in old illuminated books sweet voices of orchid smell from the vaults where gods are
   born
I'm poor in name and poor in life
I don't know what I'm doing here
how could I speak in the right forms   with the right intonations with the rhymes with the
   conjuring rhythms of things and peoples

I have nothing to say but myself
a truth without poetry myself

The Alphabet of Revolution

this fate I allot myself this death I deal myself
because I will not half-live in this half-land
in this world half-caught in the boneyard of dead worlds
>*(and the idea that comes to me here the image in which I'm burned "in the corrida of the stars" the beautiful image that restores the poem—*
out with it I won't have it it's not mine)
and too bad if I assassinate poetry
what you would call poetry
what for me is a rattle
for I want no more lies
in this present without poetry
for this truth without poetry myself

I live I exist within a daily death
I live my death until I gasp for breath day after day
I live an incurable wound a torn tenderness a love turned into hate
I live I die with a land stabbed in the heart of its harvests and its passions
and my misery is ugly I cannot name it

O you who are closest who come to me in
>my fever and my dereliction O wife in whom
>I move toward my future mine and everyone's you
>who first received my nameless pain that in your hands it speak for all our pains

>>and the task of being born
>>the duty of anger
>>a stray bullet a poured cup

it keeps shining the same dawn-like blood spilled on the soil
the gushing artery of combat across the black night of beginnings
I inhabit a land of spittle of grim mornings and of ugly specks where poets
    kill themselves and women bleed the countryside cracks and rancor
    oozes from the lips of the inhabitants

no no I'm not making it up   I know what I'm saying   I name as best I can
    what it is to die a bit each hour to die politely in abjection and indignity what it is to live like this
to go around and around in the circle of a perpetual November of a poet's
    madness a debrained people's poet
to live through that and to shout it in a single lingering howl for help to rip
    the earth from the bed of the river to the tips of the pines
to live with a cry the only way it can be done

and I hear the rasp of morning at my window
> I hear the world shiver beyond my veins
> I hear men live

but never does a mirror offer me my image
never a sign to read in the snow that banks my heart and freezes it alive in polar paranoias

> who makes this noise
> almost outside the world
> flap of wings crack of leaves
> we have no time to look at faces
> to recognize
> to call out   they pass
> these folk forever absent
> whom we will never know

they offered me faces gazes speeches to speak and I was tempted   names I'd have had titled as red-ensign ambassador to Cyprus envoy to Malaya and Mister Nobel-Pearson to welcome me home   but in my flesh I felt a thousand faces rotting when my lips my cheeks my temples a single non-face moved   the thousand faces around me crushed my eyes to powder

I am a man ashamed to be a man
I am a man from whom manhood is kept
I am a man attacked through his compatriots and who will never perform for other men an act with any sense until he has effaced at last the infamy it is to be a French-Canadian
no the finest sophistry will never unknot the ancestral fault
for I am like a jaundiced regret a diseased shame breaking out on the leg of the day a boil on the body of God
I hear the rumble rising daily from Quebec and it's a bad novel a stupid movie continuous showing in the movie-house America with nobody watching nobody interested any more in comprehending
the torment of my land
its anguished face iced-in with inhibitions slashed with darkness drugged with incense

my country with your drunkard's face your sick man's face your haggard sluggard nigger face your New York pressing girl's wet face
my love for you my small white sin
my quiet desperation   its triviality doesn't matter
will a million horizons gleam for us a million auroras lick the belly of the blast furnaces

The Alphabet of Revolution 117

are we simply the fuel of progress the surplus value chomped without attention by Texaco and General Motors

strange earth which mourns softly beneath my feet distant earth
strange earth lost to its expropriated inhabitants
      expropriated of the world and of its joy
      expropriated of their present and of their future
      expropriated of their living and of their dying
      expropriated of anger and of love

strange earth O tenacious prowlers around the ancient domain O my brothers O blind creatures humiliated in your thirst and in your growth
(ah why was there anything but the long night scream of blood amid the saxophonic neon)
strange mornings world strangely removed from the carnal urges that pointlessly flow from my arms and legs

    gray world
    blackened world
    locked-up world
    land barely out of vague prehistory
    land captive by blood and by bone
    in blood and in bone
    land to my mouth like an unsaid word
    trapped beast in the underbrush of morning
    sister of shame O like to my body stopped servant
    land knotted in roots and instinct
    out of the prenatal blackness out of the savage stupor
    O land to be said   O land to be lived

in this strange lost land I beat my feet on the deserted morning ground the October plowing the ancestral haze
I walk toward you   I brush aside the ripplings of the world for one day to seize your stranger's face which nevertheless resembles mine and brands mine with the brand of existence
in a past beyond childhood you were given to me like bread like blood like name   and I shall release you from the icebergs of nonexistence from the dungeons of glaciation I shall take you like a woman who gives herself in giving life
mistress land
matrix land

silent and magnetic
strange land lost beneath the maze of tracks traced on the crazy dial of exile and unreason

bit by bit the world is crumbling horizons clash and landscapes die revealing through their blood the bare bone of malediction
and it has always been and it has always been
order abundance calm and lies lies
for hate and theft are all that's true
and all that's true is my love for a people ill-loved

I am frail and mad like a man who's going to die any day now any minute

in the mirrors of the small hours I watch my condemned head spin   my small polite death my two-bit agony my underdeveloped hunger my fake opulence my latest-model chrome-plated TVed nirvana

my nowadays they don't respect anything look my undeserving poor look my sneaky servant look my unemployed and spends all his money on liquor look

yes I am incorrigibly mean beat perverse I am dull selfish I am what you wish I am evil I am the evil you have done me I am what you have made of me Dorchester Colborne Durham I am the galley-slave in the barque of America I am the loot of Her Gracious Majesty
I live with death as an intimate as a neighbor woman screeching in your ears day in day out
death is my body's form my destiny's my history's my country's

must we go on now with the long reasonable ruin of every sense   are we not the sombre watchers of the life that isn't there

> in the ruelle Saint-Christophe
> in the ruelle vérité
> is that life's step clattering
> in the shadows sound of madness

the hard sun which hammers down onto the iron roofs of the shacks and slums has the pitiless face of my present
which looks down on me which measures and penetrates me I return the crackle of fall brush   I am November bent under the hoof of the wind
in the ruelle Saint-Christophe is it my life I snatch from the garbage cans and the pavement my life I pursue around the corner   has my vomit become my truth
my truth   that which no diploma refutes not even the gilded diploma of the poem   my truth of undented skulls and latent savageries my truth of

The Alphabet of Revolution

great-grandparents their profound and superb ignorance their obstinate foreheads their ancestral obscurity at one with my own mad wild words
la vérité don't you see I understand nothing of it not a word and I couldn't care less it hurts as the wan smile of the hobo hurts
the dark sun that kills me what hour does it mark for the world
somebody's stopped screaming is this my life is this my blood somebody's stopped shouting at the far end of the lane is this the end of the dull agony of my life

the time is ringing in my brain it smells white like suicide and the endless grin of storefronts presses its lips to my cry
I drip to the ground the dirty water of my years seeps out my life seeps out like a badly phrased question like an unheard wish which refusal fuses into a grimace
the October rain in my hair will erase my head I will no longer have any form but that of the pavement hacked by the tooth of snow

to those who accuse you of blowing the patriotic trumpets you will reply that a shoddy land is your pain and your death
is it my fault that I suffer from a land aborning
from a land occupied
from a pain which is the sweetness of others
from a death that nourishes the life of others
yes I know *real* wounds have the noble extravagance of bad wine they are beautiful they rend the heart and our wounds are gray mute they ring false
is it my fault that we die of half-living that our morosity is the half-truth of our comfort
we are denied even the epitaph of the beheaded the starved the massacred we leave a blank page in history
even to sing our misfortune is false where could I find it a name a music
who will hear our footfalls smothered in the rut of America where we are preceded and already surpassed by the terrible striped death of red-skinned men
in the ruelle Saint-Christophe dies a people never born their history a fairy-tale that ends at the beginning
once upon a time . . . and all there is is the stutter of a tramp who cannot identify his ailment
and who leaves by the rear after a bad joke ashamed of his suffering as of a lie

> in the ruelle Saint-Christophe
> in the ruelle vérité
> is it death that clacks his foot
> in the shadows sound of madness

. . .

oh these sheets of fever that burn my skin and yours stretch them out in the clear kiss of a child's morning
too often my head tumbles like a kite in the tangle of light I dream I dream I can't hear the earth or the cement or the asphalt and the tenderness of days is a vain cloud
child when we know it how we hesitate to leap the abyss of our twentieth birthday   and we say: is it already over life that's all there was to it and all we are is a mechanism for torture we stir the hours that stir us
you've got to love within the chill of the world
you've got to lie down in the bed of dead leaves
don't you

which is no stranger to me
which isn't mortal
which doesn't cross me off the list

come if you don't put your hands on my chest I feel it I'm going to pop like a kettle of boiling ideas
poor lover that I am
have I never anything but a gesture a half-gesture a complaint a sigh
what have we become in the machinery of America in the maneating smasher of the compass-points of life

when you close your arms on my body can you hope to give me for ever and for here and for now to the marvel of your own body don't you see the millions of throbbing parallel lives which tear me to shreds and scatter me across the space of strayed steps of purpled lips of left-behind hands
if only we could escape the icy turnpike life has become but then we would overturn into the chilly fields of nothingness

one day I took you in a forest near a waterfall on a carpet of pine needles and it was on the turned back of golden centuries   we were Tristan and
Isolde minus the elixir the fate minus death
and our mingled lives had the softness of a child's cheeks
ancestors beat in our chests maple-green
we could have discovered fire anew and rain and the world would then have been in our image

do you recall that day your laughter made pearls tremble in the throat of death

. . .

to scorn

said Miron in 1956

. . . *in this world from which god knows I won't escape except to pay my due, and where I've already been jigged, trapped like a rat by all the things of life, fellow men, I yield up willingly to you*

   1. my human condition

   2. I lie down on the ground
   in this world where it seems a better thing
   to be a dog than to be a man

you who were the first to shout the savage aggression the unpackaging of our lives the plunder of the other even unto "the great resinous unconscious" of a people of a soil
you vouch by your body and your consciousness to our misfortune   you testify like a man to the light a man makes in the world when he casts off the absurd pathetic gestures of his agony
our days like garbage on the sidewalks
tossed in a heap from which you extract what you can
scraps to help you live against life like crows against day   owls   catarrhic laughter history's hoboes   discharged men emptied cans

à la claire fontaine in the clear fountain of the Toronto Stock Exchange there flow dollars enough through our fingers love notes for the bosses' lovely lady

brrrrou goudourou xouliminimini crrah vrrah khmè strix
I expected a real language and there came only an octopus to swallow me whole swallow me raw

crisse de câlice de tabarnaque say my people

and they're saying what they've learned no more no less
and it's a draff of rage that dances in their head which whispers in their ear in the tavern evenings
but do they always have to swallow the same stale charity-ball brew to drool with never a hitch unto the last gospel of unrecorded resignation do they have to cuckold themselves with Sunday images with English merchandisers

the day I decided to think beyond the established phantoms to think what it might be to live in this place all I could do was swear was curse what was holy

love placed between my teeth the keys of vengeance
once become true   I am scandalous like a rusty nail in the smooth wall of order

oh I could have been soft as lace but I would have had always to fly to roll on the muscle of a strong earth cascade on the thighs of a mother open to raids of pleasure   Mother Freedom Mother Love Mother tall in the creation of the world

> MEN ONLY.—How to have "SUPERIOR VIRILE POWER" to satisfy the woman of your dreams. Send $1.00 for natural secret. SECRET—P.O. Box 301, Station M, Montréal 4, P. Qué.
> —Classified advertisements, *La Patrie*, Nov. 18, 1964

we'll soon have artificial insemination and men of this place will simply have checked out stuck in an entomologist's textbook Made in U.S.A. ("French-Canadians: Species which existed from 1760 to 19—")

for we're dealing here with a fine race of dogs
of limping uncles of smiling bellies of speakwhite lackeys of two-bit "moderates" who pretty soon will put a people on the auction block of history chanting the love-thy-neighbor of cooperative banditism

may mighty washday mornings come that will rinse the earth of these assassin apostles
and provoke us to a duel for love in the sun of our future

oh give it back yield up the metamorphoses give me back this city to be catapulted with new radiations of happiness

Montreal in the cadence of disaster in the beaming face of a drunk
hey You   step aside You   fucking big brother   anonymous 200 million Anglo-saxons Yankee Canadian hydra shapeless beardless tide with chrome claws Standard Oil General Motors I'm Cuban yanqui no I'm a nigger I wash the floors in a Texas brothel I'm a québécois go ahead and shear me I'm the lamb of God I put on the red ensign for Sunday clothes I starve on thirty a week I'm an inksplotch in the margin of my Bank the Bank of Montreal of Toronto

I'm a Cuban a nigger a white nigger from Quebec fleur-de-lys-decked Canada-Council-sponsored I'm anger in the taverns anger in 200 years of

The Alphabet of Revolution

vomit I don't listen anymore to the sermons of the curés the pastoral-parish-imperishable-values

I don't your-brow-is-crowned-with-go-glo-glorious I've never defended our-hearthstones-and-our-rights no more the luxurious resignation of Their Eminences the Bishops conferring with the cabinet I speakwhite I curse   the lanes of the east end of town are mine and the brothels on the Main

where I put the torch to the whole goddam country with ten cents' worth of moonshine

but he won't step aside but he's got clean hands a clean conscience in the bank of the great American democracy in God we trust but his friends have toothpaste smiles oh you charming French-Canadians but do tell me what makes you so angry unissons nos doo solitoodes why don't we

no he won't step aside we'll show him some fireworks with his dollars and his Canada we'll raid his arsenals with our anger we'll dynamite him our refusal him and his RCMP and his Wagners and his dogs-in-office we'll deminister the big-stick-boys

I write the editorial of terrible future men the editorial of free men   here where the great galaxies of stars neighbor us
the abyss of alcohol we've drunk to the bottom and exposed to the air we're hungry for a sun hot like daily bread
our hunger an ill-got gain
our hunger against everyone . . .
your prefabricated lies for the subtle ghetto wherein we franglicize our ration of life the one you grant us because after all you don't want us to die off us docile actors in a history scripted in advance

your lies we dynamite them
we refuse this *past* where you've nailed us up like sad-eyed elks' heads
you want us civilized we know ourselves barbarous
the winter that's locked in our veins grinds our flesh and it's our place our way of life our poverty *from birth* that horrifies you like the spear of the savage in vestal silks

after we have torn down the idol of the bishops and bankers: the past that clean little corner of eloquent and docile anemias
after we have transgressed the image of ourselves drawn in the statutes of her gracious majesty the Empress of India
after the last constitutional guarantee the last polite formality

>when it's clear that we have nothing
>when the skull is in the dark of madness
>beyond the arrangements and beyond the one-more-attempts to negotiate our lives
>then
>we will penetrate the bitter delight of death
>we are made of bark and resin and plowing
>we're learning the Amerindian anger
>we're learning the ferocity of our roots
>we're delinquent we're criminal
>we're liberated from your laws
>we're Riel and we're Chénier

what I am I will defend with naked fists
man impaled on my cry   this cry will become my morality
man crushed in his inmost motives I retaliate with a burst of recalcitrant poetry
man bought and sold hurled to deaf earth *Quebec* man all around the earth I consent to the ardent fraternity of enslaved bloods
man of muddy visage O newborn one
man of midnight destiny I watch myself bleed through the window of the rich
(but the thunder of the blast furnaces is already brother to the human fuel)
man excluded from the festivals of sunlight where the Idea sleeps with Capital   I assume vertebrally the prohibited millenniums of human rage
man unknown to established languages I shall not stop scribbling the alphabet of revolution

so that table and bread may warm our present moment
and snow and wheat be traded in your smile   woman to chase through your silences the promised lands of blood
so that iron and fire may do the work of peace
and atom and thought help us to share like gods
so that earth and poem find their resemblance on the blazing page of flesh
and Virgil and Karl Marx be published on the vellum of a Reason without seam
so that life and death in the quadrille of the seasons may wed from sowing to reaping
so that here and in other places the dawn of man may rise over reconciled men

die watchman die you men of night
abolished in the first steps of the day

die watchman and erase our 200 years of shame
by the hot grindstone of the aurora birth
matinal may we be on our parental earth
simply solidly brothers in the land of our own arms
land   comrades
if the curvature of the earth beneath our palms escapes us still in this middle of the twentieth century and if the face of things lights up only afar beyond the horizon of our lives
if our hearts are black and secret like the knots of our oaks and if the noises of the universe enter in dreams our wage-bought bodies
comrades   O you stubborn beasts   laughter ripples beneath the bark and the great crackling of the native fire breaks out in the coming memory

O people intact beneath the English erasure

land   comrades
your name   Québec   like a leaping comet in the sleep of our bones   like the gunfire of the wind in the underbrush of our acts
look the heart of the land already bursts our furrows and our streets and our heart replies to its message in the smashing of our habits

Québec your name cadence written on the thickness of need   unanimous clamor piercing the forest of our veins and announcing to the world's face the rim of our day

the time of our humanity

December 63—December 64

    Can a man, after writing that, return to acquiescence? I discuss this with reference to André Major in the next chapter, but I wanted to hear something from Chamberland on it. I asked him if he were a revolutionary for good.
    "Your question is very absolute. Of course, if the revolution ceases to have any sense, one occupies oneself with something else."
    And yet, without the revolution losing its sense, the day-in, day-out difficulty of being an exile in the future is something that has always preoccupied Chamberland, and through his next poem, which appeared over two years after *L'Afficheur hurle*, ran the confession with which it began: *"J'ai peur, terriblement peur."* The poem was called *L'Inavouable*. The reverse side of the *Signpainter*, some would say. It was a long avowal of the unavowable fear that the shouter of yesterday was already half-resigned today. That he was being bought with little comforts:

> I want to lie with my head on the sidewalk holding up the forty-story
>   wall . . . like the tree or grass in the days of the god of my life:
> O newborn state, to create the world each instant (the gesture become
>   commonplace . . .)
> the fifty-thousand-window house is shining like a diamond's faces and
>   telling us of mad tomorrows but him, this man, this fabulous
>   black man (Selma, Watts, Harlem), him in his shacks and
>   slums and cellars barred over by the white man's darkness,
>   he's laughing roaring seizing burning all the pillars of Amer-
>   ica, this man—your subconscious your shame your fear—this
>   man, this fabulous black man, flames and twists and melts the
>   pillars in his hot arms, whitens the entrails of America
> and then this larva life I lead . . .

What has become of the time of our humanity in this larva life within the Hydro skyscraper? The poem encourages itself by reprinting "vehement, impassioned" echoes of the *Signpainter* and by imagining a redemptive murder of "Judge Wernag," that villain who has a few traits in common with Claude Wagner, the terrible-tempered Liberal justice minister during most of the time Chamberland was writing, "for among the 'people without history and without literature' . . . to kill would be at last an EVENT."

All of which may have helped Chamberland kill the Wernag within him, but the real Wagner was still alive and administering and while he worked for the same government, Chamberland had the daily task of living the contradiction between malcontent and lover of life.

Chamberland was concerned about the quality of the restaurant where we went to eat the first time I met him— "There aren't many good ones around here." He liked eating in taverns, but *good* taverns (the Hub, under my apartment and across the street from his office in the Hydro building, passed). These concerns struck me as conventional, serious, grown-up, businesslike alongside the aimlessness in such matters of my English-speaking bohemian and left-wing friends. Chamberland, also, was married. To Thérèse Major, André Major's tiny, stunning sister; André Major is in turn married to Chamberland's sister Marielle. They have one child. (*Terre Québec*: "America blasting outside, you sleep, our child alive in you.") For him, and in general for the Shouting Signpainters, the revolutionary life took place within the food-clothing-and-shelter framework of petty-bourgeois daily life; it was a matter of your views, your political action, your attitudes, not of your trouser knees, meal hours, or household companions. Time was no doubt partly responsible: Chamberland was twenty-seven. But I felt, as he greeted me on the steps of Hydro-Québec beneath the big electric mural that the state corporation, in times of René Lévesquism, had commissioned from Borduas's companion-in-protest Jean-Paul Mousseau, that he'd probably been wearing an overcoat, rather than a short jacket, ever since he felt himself a man rather than a boy, and maybe even the gray fur hat perched on top of his head too.

At a second interview I realized I had spoken for several hours with Chamberland without learning much about him, about his person as opposed to his opinions. I asked him about his family.

"They live on the South Shore, near the plant where my father works. He is a designer with the big linoleum manufacturer, Dominion Oilcloth, which is on the island just across the river from Longueuil, where we lived."

A creative job, then?

"No, in reality, no. The designing he does is strictly within the limits laid down beforehand by the requirements of the company. He lacks even taste."

This bitter tone toward one's family I found only in Chamberland among the Shouting Signpainters. Jacques Renaud and André Major, Laurent Girouard too, hardly seemed closer to their family origins, but their descriptions of the atmosphere at home were detached, even kindly. Chamberland, however, had gone perhaps further, and for longer, toward fulfilling the family-dictated requirements of a son in traditional Quebec; he felt he had been dispossessed of more, and hence felt bitterer when he made the break. He spoke again of his studying to become a priest:

"It seemed the way to fulfill the drives to excellence, devotion, purposefulness that were in me. But as I went along, the fulfillment did not take place as expected, other things were filling my consciousness: writing, nationalism, and eventually social concerns. And that was the way it was when I ceased to believe in God—no crisis, no jolt, just the drifting of that compulsion from my mind, to be replaced by others."

Once at my place I put Bob Dylan's "The Times They Are A-Changin' " on the record player for Chamberland. He had expressed an interest in the American protest poet, but the rustic quality of Dylan's delivery, clear in the American context where social issues entered popular music through the side door of recorded folklore, seemed to make it very remote for him, and he did not follow. Social issues had been in French popular music much longer, and were tied to an urban delivery of a Sinatra kind: a delivery inextricably associated, for the American ear of the time, with emptiness in the material, a delivery which gave my English-speaking friends the same kind of difficulty with the likes of Léo Ferré that Chamberland was having with Dylan. The young Québécois' opening to America was jazz (*L'Afficheur*: "Mingus Coltrane Hamilton"), a music that was of little interest to the English political milieu I knew.

The two milieux were far apart. Yet there was surely a relationship between the angry literature of Quebec and the angry literature of the rest of America, of the English-speaking world, of the whole industrialized West, in the years of *parti pris*. There is surely a common category into which Allen Ginsberg's *Howl* and Paul Chamberland's *hurle* both fall. A common category—and yet a difference. Ginsberg: *"I saw the best minds of* my generation *destroyed by madness."* Chamberland: *"In the ruelle Saint-Christophe dies* a people *never born."*

In a *parti pris* review of a 1964 English-French, Toronto-Montreal anthology of young poets in which he and Paul Chamberland coexisted with Anglo-Canadian writers, André Major had said that the English-Canadian poet is "neither threatened nor revolted by this inferiorization of one nation by another," and hence "juggles, innocent, with the Word." This seemed to me to be true. English-Canadian literature lacked its own central cry and was guilty of a colonial complacency before the French and theirs. Even those things which bridged the two universes were perceived differently: "There are several Sartres," Chamberland said to me, "Sartre the straight philosopher, Sartre the *littérateur,* Sartre the polemicist of the preface to Fanon . . ." And none, I noted, was the Anglo-American Sartre, that aging beatnik who wrote darkly against society and lived on its margin, but whose political role was minimal: signing petitions against a random batch of inhumanities, and, of course—those French—refusing to admit that Communism was just as bad.

"Who's important in young English-Canadian literature?" Chamberland once asked me. "Some of us have had a few contacts—I once went to a party where I met Leonard Cohen. But the contacts can only go so deep. Our situation is so different—the national isolation, the defensive and revolutionary postures we feel driven to take don't seem to make any sense to them. They have a security, emotionally and socially, that we don't have. Other loyalties. Cohen is sure of himself in the English language, the big Anglo-American cultural stream is his outlet. His identification."

"There is also his Jewishness," I suggested. There is a Montreal-Jewish pre-eminence in Anglo-Canadian letters. The young poet Leonard Cohen, the novelist Mordecai Richler, the older poet Irving Layton—they summarize the past three generations of Canadian writing. This has generally been taken to be merely a local version of the prominence of Jewish writers in the United States in recent years, but I think there is a particular Canadian aspect to it. The tradition of the Montreal Jews is particularly suited to representing us: they are English-speaking, close to the Anglo-American mainstream, yet they are close, too, to our problem group in Canada, have lived alongside the French since childhood; and they have a radical tradition which lessens our uneasiness in the presence of this problem.

English-speaking: Jews were for the most part neither English nor French on arrival; they assimilated to the economically dominant—and also the most liberal—group, rather than to the clericalist majority. In speaking English they spoke the language of America, and were in some ways closer to the English-speaking cultural mainstream than other Anglo-Canadians: one of Mordecai Richler's stories describes a Montreal Jewish intellectual's pilgrimages to New York, and Richler has lived most of his adult life in London. "Put it in the hands of my generation," Cohen says on the jacket of a volume of verse. Layton had his time with the beats in New York, later his time in Rome, for which in a volume of *his* verse he thanks the Canada Council, which understands that a poet needs cigars and wine.

Montreal: In the French metropolis, alongside the strange Canadian minority, the Jews could convey to the English-Canadian reader the French bohemianism of one Montreal, the French obscurantism of another. Allusions to the Latin-Catholic culture which surrounded them in childhood are in all three of the writers I have named: Cohen calls a poem "Alexander Trocchi, Public Junkie, Priez Pour Nous"; Richler gives a poor hero a French-Canadian girlfriend from the slums of the Laurentian village where his wealthy Jews have their summer cottages; Layton imagines the constricted feelings of the bearded Jewish prophets on pedestals in a cathedral.

The radical tradition: The Jews' own sufferings gave them a feel for that other poor religious people, the French; their long militancy in the Communist Party and other left-wing movements placed them on the side of liberation of the French working people. The same sufferings and the same radicalism made them disdainful of much about that poor religious working people, of their anti-intellectual, sometimes anti-Semitic, tribalism. And all this helped the English-Canadian reader enjoy the fleeting evocation of French Canada without the bad conscience that might otherwise accompany it—for this was no arrogant Anglo voice speaking, it was the voice of urbane internationalism. The radicalism, also, was by now muted: in Layton it was a passion of youth cooled with age; in Richler, something around the house from another time; in Cohen a figure of speech. The only Montreal Jewish writer I am aware of having fully assumed a solidarity with French-Canadians that the radical tradition implies is Herman Buller, author of the novels *One Man Alone* and *Quebec in Revolt*. His solidarity is of the order of that of the Jewish trade unionists who gave their lives to the Quebec workers' struggle, but his writing has a certain amateurism about it and he has never been as accepted by the English-Canadian intelligentsia.

They summarize us, the Montreal Jewish writers. Canadian, yes, a little uneasy about our French-speaking colony, but mostly anxious to shake off dull Canadianness and flee to universality. We feel our own historico-geographical situation as nowhere-in-particular, we want to go where it's at—San Francisco, Selma, even—if we are from elsewhere—Montreal. Leonard Cohen lived in Montreal, knew the city's colonialist section, English-speaking and (even for Jews) Protestant-school-attending, Greenwich-Village-style-coffeehouse-supporting. Knew, too, that there was a colonized section, to the east, even if he didn't know it by that name. There had been a time—Richler writes of it, Layton drew his early socialism from it—when the Jews lived in a poor area downtown, hard by the French-Canadian slums. No more. It was wealth and suburbia Leonard Cohen was leaving when, having published a first book universalistically called *Let Us Compare Mythologies* at Protestant-colonial McGill University, he left for overseas, for a Greek isle, there to evoke American junkie writers read, bohemian loves lived, and the Big Problems, the Bomb, problems suggested by his title from this period: *Flowers for Hitler*. More recently he has reached the larger Anglo-American audience, singing, on record, songs in the purest Lennon-Dylan vein. The relation between his part of Montreal and the French slums was never one that engaged him, sucked him into a life of shouting, signpainting, or even reacting to the shouts from the other side. What engaged him was America, Europe, talking to My Generation, joining the Robert Graveses and the Lawrence Durrells in their sunny, non-national Parnassi. So it was with his compatriots.

There is something tragic in our quest for universal engagements when we haven't come to grips with a situation in which we are ourselves implicated, and I thought I saw a case of the tragedy in a young Montreal Jewish poet I knew from that same Protestant-colonial McGill, and met again while working on this book. His name is Henry Moscovitch, and he was capable of writing this, in that 1964 anthology in which Chamberland and Major appeared with the young Anglo-Canadians:

EX-SOCIALIST
for K.A.
You too will grow old, you sigh.
Your joy will also flutter,
gasp and finally die
as mine did.
(across the wifey's smile?)
. . .

Never—I grew my talons young;
am no idealist; no illusions
for those that clench

> the world—they will not change.
> My laughter springs
> from your rotted guts and theirs
> —an eternal well.

I asked Henry Moscovitch if he knew Chamberland or his work. "Yeah," he said, "I've read some of his stuff. A very political sort of thing . . ."

Chamberland liked the idea of poetry made mass medium by singing on record, and spoke of this development in Quebec.

"Vigneault sings the country—in both senses, the rural areas and the nation. But Claude Léveillée captures the life I've known better —Montreal, the city, the neighborhood. He's not the only one. I'm waiting for a record I've heard is coming out soon: Pauline Julien sings Raymond Lévesque." He smiled in anticipation of this meeting of the sexy middle-aged singer and the sad-funny tunes of the very-proletarian-Montreal composer, previously rendered only by his own hoarse voice and mandolin:

> When my time came to go to work,
> I got a job, I didn't shirk,
> I took my chan-ce.
> They paid us dirt, so we walked out—
> And straight into a flatfoot's clout . . .
> La belle provihn-ihn-ce!

The *belle province* motto Lévesque was ironic about is out of fashion in these post-Duplessis days, but the misery he speaks of is not obsolete. Chamberland, somewhere else in the same conversation:

"We can go too far in emphasizing the North American standard of living Quebec is absorbed into, and in seeking the marks of colonization only in the language, the psychology, the cultural areas of Quebec life. We're colonized in a material way too—in every economic area our standards are lower than in the surrounding country, especially in Ontario: unemployment, ratio of secondary to extractive industry, everything." (Maheu had covered this ground in an article on Montreal in *parti pris:* "The most striking figure is that on infant mortality caused by the child's condition at birth rather than by the surroundings afterward—it is a difference of 145 percent between French and English, and indicates our—I'll say it—colonized physiology! Demographers wonder why; most conclude it is the poorer diet and medical care of the French-Canadian mother during pregnancy.")

Chamberland had brought a batch of *parti pris* mail up to my place; he began opening it. "A letter from a university out west; they want to publish a poem of mine in a magazine."

"*Du biculturalisme, eh?*" I specified. It was a sneer. The Canadian federal term for racial coexistence was held by the *partipristes* in about the esteem Maheu had suggested in that same article on Montreal: "There are two Montreals, one in the east, poor, French, the native quarter; the other in the west, rich English, part of it calling itself 'The Town.' This is known as biculturalism."

Yes, Chamberland replied to my taunt, but a bit as if he hadn't intended to be that harsh. As if he'd have been inclined to give the student editors out west the benefit of the doubt. And the poem they wanted.

At a poetry evening at the University of Montreal I watched Chamberland debate, with similar tolerance, a non-admirer, a student editor who himself wrote verse. He reproached Chamberland, and the rest of the *parti pris* group—indeed, most other young poets of Quebec—with, in a word, laziness. Instead of grumbling about colonialism, he said, the young should sit down at their desks and put in the hours of searching, exploring, working, and reworking that are needed to produce world masterpieces. Chamberland's verse totally lacked technical newness or contestation: it was conventional language used to push revolutionary political ideas.

Chamberland stood smoking a cigarette, one hand on his hip, his cigarette hand gesturing lightly now and then. Thérèse watched tensely. I caught a few of his responses.

"I don't give a damn about talent, any more than the surrealists cared about talent. It's not a matter of genius shining through, it's a matter of circumstances coming about in which valid writing can be done. Colonialism isn't one of such circumstances: masterpieces don't tend to issue forth from colonized communities."

The critic quoted James Joyce: the colonization of Ireland had not dimmed his luminosity.

"Joyce wrote in the language of the oppressor. You can't separate the work from the social surroundings, they touch each other; I just try to admit that truth when I write, to see to what degree I am what the facts around me make me."

The evening's program gave the decision to the social-surroundings argument: it began with readings by professional actors with delicious voices of poems by purely aesthetic poets of the pre-*parti pris* era in Quebec. Things warmed up with Chamberland and Gaston Miron, whose 1956 cry of pain Chamberland had quoted in *L'Afficheur,* reading their own work: Chamberland calmly and Miron with agony, but both sharing intense social consciousness in their lyrics. And it came aflame, the evening, with a young poet, all trim haircut, eyeglasses, and business suit as he approached the lectern, delivering his poems on sure, wild, bebop airs with generous scat-singing, stuttering, playing-around with the written texts, and gesture:

> I debaptize you, I exorcise
> your ear, mouth, heart, mind, readying you for the flood from my eye,
> and I die
> upright, cruciform, like the Place Ville-Marie
> [arms out and dead]

His name was Raoul Duguay, and he brought down the house. He comes, as one of his choruses told it, from

> Abitibi
> Abitibiabitibi
> Abitibiabitibiabitibi
> Abitibiabitibiabitibiabitibi

and he had looked up Gaston Miron soon after getting into town; the legend of the older poet's encouragement of younger ones had reached him even in the northwestern corner of Quebec. The jazz on which his delivery was based had not, however; it was after hitting Montreal that he began to develop his style of delivery. His stuff was backwoods and big-town and American and separatist all at once, and the actor who had read Alain Grandbois exquisitely just before could not help exclaiming: *"Formidable, ce gars-là!"*

The university poetry-listeners gathered in the U of M social center agreed, and not the least of their reasons was that they agreed with Chamberland that poetry had something to do with the goings-on out there beyond the desk where the poet toils at his images. (And Raoul Duguay was to become Quebec literature columnist for *parti pris*.)

Chamberland, and indeed all the Shouting Signpainters, are careful not to advance gross claims for the explosive power of their, or any, art.

"It is Trotsky, I think, who has said the most intelligent things about it among the Marxists," Chamberland says, and Trotsky's precept was, "In the beginning was the deed; the word followed, as its phonetic shadow."

The *partipristes* shared with the previous generation the extolling of the earth of the oppressed nation, the *Terre Québec*. What to make of this dwelling, by city-bred Marxist writers, on the soil, the land, as a big value in their revolt? Especially since *parti pris* has no use for the back-to-the-soil mythology of the old nationalists, which had *already* been demolished by the *citélibristes* when *parti pris* hit the scene. Even some of the newer manifestations of the same thing have been pilloried by *parti pris:* "What are you going to do with men who need to look at a hydroelectric dam to believe their nation exists?" they wrote after the *littérateurs* of *Liberté* published an issue on what a boost they got contemplating the state-built Manicouagan project in the far northeast.

In the case of Chamberland, the soil was there before the Marxism: *Génèses* is full of trees, lakes, and fields, usually with gods or God concealed somewhere among them; and the pastoral bits in *L'Afficheur* are in exactly the style of the early poems: "I would abolish mirrors in a land that looked on me with love." They are simply rarer and have the effect of release from the harsher images of the city as charnel-house of colonialism: "Once I took you on a carpet of pine needles . . ."

And this nature-as-relief, I think, is simply that constant of American literature, getting away from it all. Often, very often, an urban Quebec literary hero will take off for a cabin in the woods to think things over; the woods will be blanketed with snow, this will help soothe the malaise. *Parti pris* heroes are not exempt. But in their case there is the additional motive of wanting to know the land that is to be liberated, wanting to get out of that Montreal where the revolutionaries gather, yes, but where the colonial order is most depressingly implanted; to get to know a few of the outland Québécois who just might be the future guerrillas of St-Denis. They always come back.

And then there is the erotic aspect of the thing, the land as woman, woman as the land. Here there is a confusion of a worrisome order. The land, national territory or not, is after all a thing with which dialogue must necessarily be unequal. One really has to swallow the agriculturalist ideal whole to see it otherwise. The land must be upgraded and animated by heavy doses of myth, and woman much simplified and abstracted by the fortunes of sexual conquest, to make them blend, and the operation risks the kind of *malentendu* invited by a well-meaning talk on English state radio which *parti pris* reproduced to praise the Québécois commentator who'd given it. The speaker told his listeners that for the young poets in Quebec (he is one), "Quebec is a woman just conquered, and passion is at its most intense." He quoted *L'Afficheur* to show this. Aha, the English are going to say, it's sexual repression that was eating them, and more pills, less priests, and a few mixed schools and sex manuals will fix them up. "I'm glad you're standing tall," as a Confederationist folksong cooked up for Ian and Sylvia by a biculturalist friend in Toronto puts it. But this counter-poetry doesn't meet the problem, and real poets like Chamberland should know better than to encourage it. (The clash between the Catholic-repressed stereotype of the French and the Latin-lover one doesn't, of course, bother the Anglo.)

That there is a sexual aspect to the liberation movement is obvious, that the ability to meet woman without remorse can have something to do with political adulthood is certain. The two have come at the same moment, with the toppling of the single old ideology which barred them both, and the writers have expressed what it is to feel the two elations at once. But to make the claim on the land and the claim on woman one is to ask for a jolt when the autonomous claims of woman—of women, particularized and conscious—make themselves felt. The neurosis the land-woman illusion encloses is visible in Renaud's *Cassé*, where the woman, Berthe, who has attained the kind of full life the man himself craves—material security, surrounding cultural apparatus—is seen as necessarily cold. Sex is something one can seize from woman by being better placed than her; given the opportunity, she would castrate anew, as she did in the old order, where she was anointed the center of the household.

France is the chief source for counter-images when the Québécois are fighting off the images imposed by their English-speaking neighbors on their own continent. But no sooner do French dictates threaten to envelop them than they are fighting back with their Americanness. I told Chamberland I was leaving for a short visit to Paris. He began speaking of the Ben Barka case.

"You haven't heard? Ben Barka is the leader of the opposition in Morocco, a socialist; he was kidnapped in the middle of Paris while on a visit there, with French cops all around, and nothing was done. The thing is a delight to the royal regime in Morocco and an embarrassment to de Gaulle: it seems France was only too glad to cooperate."

In Paris, André Garand had spoken of Ben Bella in the same tone, and had difficulty feeling warm toward even opposition culture in the French metropolis (in the sense of *métropole,* or home base of a colonial empire). I came back feeling even my enthusiasm for Paris was a bit of an Anglo-Saxon privilege. But I could not help speaking to Chamberland of a linguistic theory I'd brought with me.

France, I said, is a correct, rationally structured country—at any rate, Paris is such a city. Oh, I found myself saying over there, so a city *can* be built right, there can be harmony even in capitalism. America teaches you the opposite. Commerce required that this building go up here—who cared if it fit in with the next. A land of shacks, cities of collage. Each merchant's sign or window striving for rightness, but the streetful of competitors fatally wrong. And French is a correct, rationally structured language, as careful about its conjunctions as an architect about his beams. This is surely no simple reflection of Paris; for the countryside made French, too, and most of its grammaticality is simply Latin, and shared, for example, with Italian. And Rome, I was able to verify on the same trip, is in some ways (its reversed neon signs, its repairs from the war that Paris never had to make) more patched-together than the Americas. But could the rationality of the building of Paris not have *brought out* the rationality of the language, emphasized it, made it dominant? English, American, is a Germanic language. It goes for collage. Notions are combined by tacking-together, their precise relation left to the intuition of the hearer: folk-rock. English, of course, is Latin too, but the haphazardness of the unrolling of capitalism across the continent brought out, emphasized, made dominant the haphazard aspects of the language. And developed the Dos Passoses and Dylans who write in strings of images, with scarcely any grammatical ordering. Had French been called upon to participate in such a process, would its resources for haphazardness have been developed beyond what orderly France saw fit to do? Might they yet be, by the Shouting Signpainters? Renaud, reader of *Manhattan Transfer*, describes Montreal in strings of unstructured images. Chamberland, straining for the mélange of elements that was the old Quebec ideology, comes up with *"les pastorales-annales-valeurs-éternelles."* More than anglicization, this, I told him, by now warmed up; germanization.

"Perhaps," he conceded.

The caricature of Paul Chamberland as a timid, priestly bourgeois strayed among the revolutionary wolves had some currency even inside the movements he has worked in. Before attending a meeting of the Mouvement de Libération Populaire, created by *parti pris*, I had listened to another member describe Chamberland as "no doubt a good poet" but a problem for the group because—an odd complaint in the nervous North American left—he was still working out his own complexes. At the meeting Chamberland did not participate prominently, but at one point in the discussion of a text to be adopted he suggested a word change, and the chairman asked Jean-Marc Piotte if he accepted the amendment to his phrase. "Yes," Piotte said with a slight sigh and smile before continuing his remarks on the politics of the text; as if to say, no doubt the suggested word is better, but the difference is on a level of nuance I haven't quite reached. There is a physical resemblance between Piotte and Chamberland which makes the characterization of Piotte as a tough—true, he did go in for black leather jackets as opposed to Chamberland's sports coats—and Chamberland as a mouse even odder. On another occasion a Parti Socialiste staff worker told of Chamberland's showing up to do party work during an election campaign: "Yes, Paul

Chamberland, the poet. We found him some paper work to do in the office."

I have to conclude that the poetry is the key thing, and that if a man less robust than Muhammad Ali ventures to write verse he is bound to receive the sickly aesthete typing from his fellows. The same man, however, is one of the main thinkers of the movement, and during the period of my conversation with him he had in the works an article which was obviously important to him, which he felt would count in the evolution of socialist independentism in Quebec, but which he described with such diffidence I did not take it as seriously as I should have.

"It is an article against some of the ideas which have persisted in our group after their applicability has ceased—the idea, for example, that we must regret there is not more poverty, misery, oppression, open repression in our streets because these are necessary to bring about the revolution. The idea that the revolution must come to us, that conditions must meet our requirements. An idea that existed within the FLQ to a considerable extent. We have ex-militants of the FLQ in our ranks and a certain conflict of attitudes has grown up. Between, let us say, the intellectuals and the activists. The text I have written tries to find its way through these problems. It is a text against regretting that things are as they are, against activism, against fanaticism."

I had resisted this contrasting of the fanatical terrorist and the cool intellectual, it smacked too much of the Anglo-liberal's contrasting of the sane minds of *Cité libre* and the wild kids of *parti pris,* of the notion that reason went with submission to the oppressions of the world, that revolution was the dream of the impractical. *Parti pris* was magazine, publishing house, *and* political movement at the time, the magazine had taken on the air of an organ for something broader, and I felt that this very diversification of activities, this combination of reflective, theoretical work with action, and indeed the subtlety, nuance, analysis of the reflection alongside its anger and turbulence were sufficient answer to the charge of fanaticism. That Chamberland himself, his writings, his style, his calm intelligence, all present in even the most violent passages of *L'Afficheur*, the most impatient of his polemics, far from proving he and *parti pris* had lost their heads, amply made the case that the anger was justified by the Quebec condition and clearly went beyond anger to the other modes of a full humanity. I feared the article would appear a confession.

When the article appeared it provoked a similar reaction—from the right. The enemies of *parti pris* thought they saw in it a retreat from positions first held, a betrayal of the spirit of the movement—which, of course, delighted them.

I, on the contrary, felt good when I finally read it, felt it was a review of the problem that was splendidly true to all that *parti pris* had been, both on the side of anger and on the side of sensitivity. I bought the magazine at the University of Montreal newsstand: "the revolutionary and his morality," read the jacket, "special articles by paul chamberland and mario dumais." I flipped it open at my desk before my lecture began. I had just time to savor a bit of Chamberland irony: in the midst of his discussion he paused to say, "Well, before we get lost on the summits of Sinai . . ."

Later I read the whole text. We are oppressed, it said, but not bloodily. We must rise up against this oppression, not halfway but totally, but we must do so in a way appropriate to the form the oppression takes. And that means a refusal of moderation, reformism, a drib and a drab of social welfare legislation, and, for the rest, tolerating capitalism. It also means retaining the tools of rich daily life, of humaneness even while we are still beneath the oppression of capitalism:

> If I wished to find a striking example of what I mean by this praxis for revolutionary behavior, I would say: where we think and act politics, we ought always be moving at the same time toward that which is not political. It's the same thing in art, in one's profession, everywhere. The moment I am about to yield to a fanatical theorization of life, I again make it my duty to turn myself from the depths of my consciousness to some "humble task" of the desperately apolitical day-to-day world; I repair a table, I repaint a chair. The drift of this praxis is always the negation of what it is at any given moment. This by criticism, irony, play, the refusal to take oneself altogether seriously. I don't understand the revolutionary who neglects to make love well.
>
> I'll try to define this praxis more clearly. This will have to be a bit like a lesson. He's rehashing his Red Classics, some will say. But God almighty, do I have to blush for inviting people to tune in on the symphony of thought from Hegel to Marx to Lenin?

So, as a good scholastic should, I divide the praxis into three parts (for purposes of explanation only, I hope it's clear):

The first is paying attention to concrete reality. I know, I know, I'm putting my finger between the bark and the trunk. As soon as I say "concrete reality," I'm up to my neck in the abstract. This can rapidly turn into pure, pigheaded theology. But the things I want to say are just a few. By paying attention, I mean trying to see things without any preconceived intellectual props. A near-impossible thing to do. But we have no choice. If we want, that is, to avoid all mystifications, especially those which speak in left-wing tongues. Paying attention. Perceiving. And make no mistake, I mean completely giving oneself to the world of dazzling outward appearances—a drink or two may do no harm here. See things, and above all, see oneself, one's condition. But I don't mean any kind of introspection, I mean looking around at what aquarium you're swimming in, tracking down its habits and tics, the places and the times you feel good, the things that please you and those that don't, the schedules you're glad to adhere to and the ones that piss you off, the needs, the fears, the dreams. This exercise, when well conducted, when it's not just a sort of mental masturbation, takes us into the various regions of society, of a city, of its construction and its living and breathing. We can see the places and times that mean a lot or have no meaning for us. See what men and women are all about, what institutions, plans and changes they go through to become what they are. Here in Quebec, North America, 1965, in neocapitalism, consuming refrigerators, cars, and TV stars. This exercise of perception, I would make it a constant shaking-up of all our pet conceptualizations, especially if we think they are leftist ones. For the aim is to reshape them, reshape them to fit the moving flow of our daily life. We are fortunate to be able to reshuffle our bag of certainties.

But how not to get paralyzed in this gawking at the facts of life? Let me say that that's not what I'm recommending, that I have no use for the anti-ideological ideology of the guy who doesn't-want-to-get-involved, sees-things-for-what-they-are-and-doesn't-have-any-illusions. Hence the second part of the praxis: theory. A reflecting that goes right back to the basics. And I don't mean some sort of eternal truths, laws of nature: Marxist "truths" don't mean a thing unless we make them up over and over again as the occasion dictates, and this is true of scientific hypotheses too, and indeed of any intellectual material. And I did say "goes back"—which is what the word "abstract" means—we go back from the day-in-day-out looking at things carrying the general truths we have gotten from it. And that being the case, I see no reason for being shy about the number of intuitions, models, and rules we come up with. As long, that is, as the concern for the concrete is always there as the guiding passion. No revolution can do without its algebra and its utopia.

Well, before we get lost on the summits of Sinai, let's get together our logbooks and our duffle bags. Abstract thought is sound only if it's both a climb and a descent. What, by the way, are elsewhere called strategy and tactics.

The descent is the third part of the praxis: its practical moment, the moment of action. And action is plainly and simply the acts I commit, as individual, as party member, as member of a society. These acts, or rather the burden of perception and reflection I invest them with—their direction. You can't call an action anything that isn't, somehow, ultimately, a changing of individual and social reality according to an orientation that reaches into the humblest flesh of daily needs and the maddest shadows of future dreams. Efficiency? A ruse that the sweet dream has up its sleeve, to *make it so,* to make them real, these ghosts that keep us going. But humble or grandiose, not a single one of the intuitions, utopias, models is worth a damn if it doesn't work. Truth in this business lies in realization—once again, the *real content* of our certainties and institutions is the behavior, acts, results, the material existence they have. Theory and practice are both nothing unless they are entangled the one in the other.

I want to conclude this dissertation on the praxis by saying that it's not just political action. Whether we like it or not, politics, in practice (and what other kind is there?), is a specialization. A special specialization, yes, because it is the whole set of decisions which is at the point of the revolution. But, soaked in its own purposes (what Paul-Marie Lapointe calls "tactics"), it risks going mad, forgetting what it's all about: making possible all that is possible to man; it risks devaluing the rest of human life for its own glory. Then it's a fanaticism, a dogma, a terrorism blowing itself up.

The praxis is politics (theory, practice) AND other acts. All tied together. The praxis rescues politics from terrorism by always recalling the obvious, the daily needs that make it necessary, and rescues daily things from nonsense and dispersal. I believe it's hard to make all these things hold together—*raison de plus* for trying hard.

The revolution is more than revolutionary politics, taking and holding power. It is the endless transforming of every human conduct, activity, and need. The praxis is the thoughtful and passionate drive that bundles them together and also tells them apart. In this sense, it is the "permanent revolution."

You will forgive my air of priest or "theoretician." At least I didn't align my words with any of the assurance of the man who knows what conclusion he's coming to. I may be less valorous than others, but I cannot yet persuade myself I always act according to my revolutionary standard. Hats off to those who can.

And now, forget all this; read *L'Automne à Pékin* or *L'Ecume des jours*. Boris Vian is an exemplary man, one of the few who knew how to live with gravity and passion and sometimes playfulness, and hence a man whose style was revolutionary.

On this recommendation I read *L'Automne à Pékin*, which, appropriately enough, does not take place in autumn and is not set in Peking. (It was, and this may have something to do with it or may not, written around the time Mao Tse-tung was advancing on Peking.) The revolutionary point of Vian's amiable nonsense was unclear to me; there was kindliness amid discomfort, generosity amid absurdity, and lots of fun. Vian was a French jack-of-all-arts who would have liked to make over the world, and who found, in capitalist Paris after the capitalist Liberation, that he could at most make over a basement on the Boulevard Saint-Germain into a jazz club; hence a voice for days of revolutionary discouragement.

And this was what one comradely critic of Chamberland's dissertation found in it: the idealism of the loser. "Paul Chamberland writes 'The Revolutionary Individual,'" wrote Jean-Marc Piotte in a note a few *parti pris*'s later, "Pierre Vadeboncoeur publishes *L'Autorité du peuple*. The first wants to live in a way that will radically transform his life; in the situation-individual interplay, he stresses the individual. The second wants to return man to the human. But anyone who really sought to achieve one or the other of these moral codes in his daily life would do well to reserve a room at the Prévost Institute. For these codes are *utopian*. . . . And the fact that two men of the left publish utopian manifestoes so close together testifies to the pessimism of the Quebec left. Utopia is born in moments felt to be unsurpassable." (This disagreement resolved itself in the magazine with an accord between Piotte and Chamberland on the wisdom of some remarks on the matter by another defeated revolutionary: the Italian Antonio Gramsci.)

But was *parti pris* abandoning positions it had held? Was Chamberland, by quoting as an epigraph to his article Boris Vian's "What interests me is not the happiness of all, but that of each," by warning against intellectual terrorism, stepping back from his vision of a people about to revolt? From his 1964 "Measure is criminal, prudence assassinates," from "We live under colonialism, but a colonialism *terribly* [I underline] sugared and disguised"? Was it a retreat to say, as *parti pris* now seemed to be saying, that Quebec's standard of living was neocapitalist and not Third World? To publish an article by a linguist, Gilles des Marchais, which assured *parti pris* readers that "as long as the syntax, the morphology, for old words and new—we know, for example, that a borrowed English verb drops its *-ed* and *-ing* and puts on French clothes—remain intact, we are still dealing with the same language"?

The Laval University newspaper *Le Carabin* thought so. This student journal was in a right-wing phase, after moments of *partiprisme*. It spoke of "The Mamma's Boy Philosophers." Chamberland answered it on the same note in which he had replied to Piotte: "I content myself with a notification. That it is perhaps early for drawing conclusions. For if revolutionary morality, if certain points of self-criticism are under discussion, let it be known that it is in view of a revolution we have every intention, and should afford ourselves every means, moral and political, of *making*."

And when I went to that University of Montreal poetry reading to hear him do his thing for the students of Quebec, still pondering the choice of their alliances, the old violence of language and calm of voice were still there:

I am mad
you haven't seen my crazy face
I'm mad to live and mad to die
I have the rage of all that escapes me and all that
    I cannot escape . . .

And when, a few months later, he packed his family aboard a steamship in Montreal harbor, the same boat his comradely critic Piotte was taking, and for the same reason, bound for Paris, and studies, and haranguing the French leftists of *Lettres nouvelles* on the fictitiousness of Canadian literature, and the Arab anti-colonialists of *Jeune Afrique* on their connections to the Quebec struggle, and joining

André Garand in that strange strangeness of the French-speaking North American in Paris—in that maddening fall of 1966 I have every reason to assume Paul Chamberland was still balanced on that same praxis of calm madness.

4
A man of letters

André Major is perhaps the greatest talent among the Shouting Signpainters, the most *enjoyable*. His stories particularly have an ease, an immediacy of the guy at the next table in the Chinese restaurant, of the street you will probably step into when you step out your door. If that door is in the east end of Montreal, hovering somewhere outside it will be the green, riveted spans of the Jacques Cartier Bridge going across to the South Shore. Listen to what happened "Just Last Week Not Far from the Bridge":

Nine o'clock or thereabouts, a night in April.

The alleys exhale their evil odor. Well, it could be worse, that's the wives' honest opinion. As for the husbands', don't ask, they're burpingly consuming their beer, asses firmly planted on the last step of the staircase. Soon, heavy with beer and wear, they'll place their asses alongside their wives', the mattress will squeal, the baby will awake to cry his stretch.

Bands of youths drift here and there, with boredom on their foreheads. A clang of tumbling ashcans! There's got to be some fun, eh? And a grocery window shatters. Lamoureux Provisions. The harm's done, might as well get something out of it, grab an Export and a case of Molson. Hey, life still has its moments, eh?

"Scram, *les boys*. Here come the dogs!"

Sonny is the last to run, it's to prove he's not scared. A leader can do anything but show fear. It's a principle.

For the guys, theft is not a crime. All that matters is doing something while they're young, occupying their hands. And there's no work. Unemployment. A cancer.

Work isn't all that hot, but at least it absorbs you, wears you out, at the end of the day you haven't got it in you to bum around. A working people is a healthy people. But with us, with all the unemployment around, well . . . Whole days to kill, hands empty, heart empty. And being poor on top of it. Finally comes the anger.

So it's nine o'clock, or almost. Nine P.M., and Claire is letting Gaston feel her up. They've tucked themselves behind the door of the shed. It smells of rotten wood, and rotten wood, when it's wet, let me tell you . . . Gaston's hand is nervous, stiff. Claire bites her lip (upper? lower? dunno). "You're hurting me, Tonton, not so hard!" "Yer awful squirmy," he answers, pressing her breast under his moist palm. He slides his hand under her bright red sweater that he doesn't like, finds, stroke of luck, what he's looking for, and busies himself with one thing and another, notably with passing his free (his lucky) hand between Claire's thighs. She twists and untwists herself with the pleasure she is surprised to feel (no one ever told her about that, never oh no never).

And the poverty is forgotten, and the weeks that never end, and the dirty dreams you get to having when you're alone. What they're doing is the movies, the real thing. Feeling yourself isn't the same, somebody else's hand is so much better . . .

When she opens her eyes, a bit of moon is coming through the cracks of the door.

Chez Bob, the corner restaurant, the jukebox never stops. Dime after dime, the kids take in the tunes.

"I don't like the way you twist," Rose says to Jean-Pierre, chewing his Export. Rose nibbles the straw in the last drops of her Pepsi. And all the while their feet tap the floor. You could say the rhythm is in their blood, music lovers.

He promised to marry her if she does what he wants. Wants to teach her the secrets of life. But she's afraid. That's how her sister ended up in a family way. She's tempted, yeah, but there's the risk. "If you check out after, I'd be sitting pretty, eh?"

But Jean-Pierre swears, honest to god, that it'd be the church if only she'd give him his bit.

Couples, crazy, wild, take turns on the dance space. Fire in the ass and nothing stops us once we're started. As long as there's music, we'll twist and shake in the million gestures of exorcism of the demon that possesses us.

"Lemme have a quarter, willya Sonny? I'll pay ya back next week."

"As' somebody else. I already lentcha too much, y'never paid me back."

. . . And now Claire has stretched out on the ratfloor and her arms hold him tightly against her. No danger she's going to leave. They're breathing dust, their nostrils and mouths are full of it. Couldn't give a shit, they've found the thing and they forget about the rest, everything.

Tonton and Claire will go to the restaurant afterward, and Sonny will dislike the look of contentment on Tonton's face, and smash his Coke, and Claire will leave, and in the fight little Gaston will surprise even himself by laying Sonny low. Elated by his double victory, he will take his first initiative against his father: returning to their slum, he will find the old man bawling out the old lady once again. He will tell him to leave her alone, will shove an ironing board in his stomach when he lurches forward, and will run for the street.

A sixteen-year-old kid raises suspicions. Can they arrest you? Reform school? Lord Jesus but it isn't funny!

He feels this swirling inside . . . In front of the house where Claire lives he whistles, hopes she'll show her face. Nothing. Twice nothing. Lonely as a garbage can. Nobody in sight. No question of going home again. At the end of the alley, a truck. He looks for a butt in his pocket. Nothing, dammit! He heads down the alley, slips in behind the wheel of the truck, and, nose against the windshield, he stares out, out at the cruel metal of the Jacques Cartier Bridge, at the moon behind. A big cat is doing his round of the garbage.

All this happened just last week, not far from the Bridge.

That story was dated January 1964, but wasn't published until a year later. What was André Major thinking about when he put it on paper? *Parti pris* was then new, Major was active in it. The January 1964 issue contains nothing of his, but the February issue has his review of *Poésie/Poetry 64*, that bilingual, poetry-for-poetry's-sake anthology in which he and Chamberland were represented.

I am asked to speak of an anthology in which I myself participated. So you'll have to take my critique for what it is, a *parti pris*. And no one will be surprised if I accord more importance to the political meaning of this effort than to its poetic interest.

Poésie/Poetry belongs to the enterprise of mystification to which the federalists summon young writers. Here we prove, they say, with illustrations at the ready, that Canada-from-coast-to-coast is a good and great harmony of two great cultures coexisting in equality, parallelism, respect (like Gordon and Baptiste). . . .

Fighting poets (and I am one of them) denounce this trap, which is a worse alienation of their creativity than even the old cultural reclusion. We are called to cultural competition; it is the better to steal our essential dynamisms. Culturally, it's known, the *canadians* consider us their equals; when it comes to political sovereignty, nope.

That's why *Poésie/Poetry* is a lie, and it is good that some of its contributors contributed in a thoroughly negative way. Their poems are a contestation of the existing order, the one we're asked to accept because the odd bilingual book is brought out. When politics seeks to corrupt literature, the crassness is not long in betraying itself.

Militant, then, but more against the denial of "political sovereignty" than against the poverty, the weeks that never end, that were eating at his characters *pas loin du pont*. And that last bit about politics corrupting literature: the next page in that same *parti pris* happened to give another glimpse of Major in those early days of 1964. The writer was Jean-Marc Piotte:

> Major isn't always an easy guy to get along with. When he has found a book he judges interesting, he wants to share the discovery with all his friends. Any means is good. His latest was reading me all the good parts, which came to half the book, and lengthening them with comments of his own. And this went on until I'd promised to read his book. My head is hard, but his is harder. That night, after two-and-a-half hours, I agreed to read Pierre Vadeboncoeur's *La Ligne du risque*, restraining with difficulty my urge to boot him in the pants.
>
> Three weeks later, I was at last reading this latest discovery of Major. In a single night. It knocked me out. I looked at the walls, hypnotized, wondering where to begin.
>
> A man was crying out to me to live what I was. Funny! I'd never lived by my guts. I'd listened to my conscience, which listened to others.
>
> I began listening to my needs, my instincts. Acting my desires, never mind the circumstances. I experimented joys. Drink to the bottom. Make love to exhaustion. Say "fuck off" to the fuckers-up. I was living at last, and my thoughts found infinite spaces. I was living at last. I was thinking at last.

Vadeboncoeur is a Catholic, but a hater of that Catholicism which calls for the "cultural reclusion" Major said he preferred to assimilation. So it was not likely Major would be a traditional nationalist, a Latin puritan. And he is a socialist, a hater of the Catholicism which calls for repressing the urge to claim one's due, submitting to the given social order. But then, the *Poésie/Poetry* piece indicated that even a demand for "political sovereignty" can pass for a contestation of the "existing order."

I met André Major at the end of 1965. The short story collection had been published with the *parti pris* symbol on the cover just a few months before, but by this time Major was no longer a *partipriste* and he spoke only for himself when he tried to evoke for me his notions of how one must go about being a writer.

"We don't have a tradition of the man of letters here," he said. "The man who, in France, lives by his pen, and if not by his literary works alone, then by literary journalism in connection with it. We are closer to the American tradition of the writer who has done every job in the book."

Yet Major himself is, at twenty-five, precisely a man of letters, precisely a man who lives by the pen, by writing, by reading and writing about what he reads. He left the *parti pris* group in an ideological quarrel and took up work as a literary journalist, first as arts editor of the huge circulation, deadly dull weekly tabloid *Le Petit Journal*, then as theater and book critic for *Le Devoir*.

His articles in the two papers, one mass and one elite, both middle-of-the-road, tended toward the bookishly universalist, toward reproaching the literary left in oblique terms for sectarianism, for prejudice against priest-writers, for mingling love with politics in poetry, love which should be oh-so-sublimely for-its-own-sake. As art should be for its.

"They said I had a synthetic style rather than an analytic one," he says of his former comrades. And indeed, his is a mind in which diverse elements are made to lie down together. He began to outline to me the plot of his next novel, something I found the writers I interviewed surprisingly willing to do. (Surprisingly and maybe misleadingly, if it is anything like that other *parti pris* habit of endowing oneself beforehand with a whole future *oeuvre*. Renaud's *Cassé* announced as "in preparation" a tale to be called *Un os d'or pour une garce—A Gold Bone for a Bitch*; that is not the title of his forthcoming novel. Chamberland promised in *L'Afficheur* a volume of prose and verse called *Le Vrai et le faux*, and an essay on himself and his comrades called *Les Ecrivains se vengent*; instead he published *L'Inavouable*. And Major—Major's first book announced his second and four others, his second announced the four plus a fifth: *Les Enfants de chienne*, *Transports en commun*, and *Les Francs-tireurs de la Catherine*, three volumes of a *roman-fleuve*; essays, to be called *Au Fil du couteau*; and poems, *Les Injures salutaires*. None has yet appeared.)

In the novel Major outlined to me there were, among other elements, a Christ figure returned to earth via Dorval Airport as a beatnik revolutionary hunted by the cops. There was a betrayal, even, and a crucifixion of sorts. Yet Major denied it was a Christian novel; it puzzled him that I should say I found it Christian of him to put Christ among the beatniks, against the authorities; he thought it daringly anti-Christian to so bummify the deity. The cops, after all, were Christian, the system was Christian; the back-to-fundamentals myth seemed foreign to his idea of Christianity in a Catholic situation, whereas it seemed to me, in my Protestant world, a cliché of neo-Christian art.

One suspects that it was this reaching for the folk traditions of French Canada when seeking roots for the revolution that had alienated Major from *parti pris*. The magazine was itself concerned with finding the sources for anti-colonial revolt to draw on, but it sought them in anything that was not Catholic, not mystical, not ideological in the Quebec of the past; in the *dis*obediences of Quebec workers and peasants to the clerical order, not in their fascination with its symbolism.

"I argued that it is credit, finance companies, that prevent the French-Canadians from making a revolution," Major told me. "As long as they can get by with loans from finance companies, buying themselves the things they want in the way of the rich life without even being able to afford them, then they will never realize their exploitation. But they"—always the *they* of estrangement when referring to the *partipristes*—"said these were right-wing arguments."

It sounded to me like social credit, and I asked Major if he were a *créditiste*. He said no, with some puzzlement it seemed, but without shock. As if it had never occurred to him that such a line of reasoning, with its willingness nevertheless to contemplate revolution, could be thought right-wing in quite *that* way. But he didn't rule out the possibility that social credit might have an element to offer his world scheme.

The mystical and allegorical seem little present in what Major has published so far. It is rather their narrowness of range, their concentration on a few things André Major has seen and done, felt and known other people to feel, that gives them their strength. (I found this in many a Shouting Signpainter: the desire, once he'd gotten down the brutal stuff he had to get down, to free himself to flights of fancy.)

Le Cabochon was begun as a serial for *Vie étudiante*, a classical-college student newspaper published by Jeunesse Etudiante Catholique. Three or four chapters were published, then the staff of the paper quit in a dispute over discipline. The authorities said that the staffers' dabbling in Marxist politics was the reason, and *parti pris* commented: "We knew that Major was collaborating with a Catholic paper. We weren't afraid of being contaminated." The irony becomes double in light of the later break.

Parti pris felt the incident showed the panic of the old clerical establishment when faced with an ideology more dynamic, more able to meet the demands of questioning youth than their own. This belief that all youth would find its way to *parti pris* had once been shared by Major, but no more.

"I used to think—when I was a doctrinaire Marxist, that is—that *parti pris* represented the whole younger generation. Of course, I knew that it really didn't, but it seemed to me that it had to be in that direction that things were going. Since I've ceased to be doctrinaire I've changed my mind. I'm a reader for Jacques Hébert—Les Editions du Jour—I have some manuscripts in my briefcase right now. And I've discovered a whole class of young writers, some good, who are trying all kinds of ways, science fiction, fantasy, everything. Some of them have said to me, when I mentioned that I was reading their work and was amazed to learn they were doing these things, 'I was afraid to tell you, I thought you'd consider me a writer who was abdicating his responsibilities.' That's what the label *'parti pris'* did."

Le Cabochon represented an idealism of a kind perfectly easily shared by *parti pris* and Jeunesse Etudiante Catholique, and one wonders why neither in the end felt properly represented by it. Or perhaps its "synthesis" of elements was once again the very reason for its unacceptability. It is the story of a working-class boy like Tonton, but a brainy one, being sent through the inevitable bourgeois classical college by a family just barely getting by financially. He is out of place, a "cabbage-head" with funny ideas and doubts that make him unable to get with it as a member of the "future elite." He quits the college, checks into an ordinary high school, finds himself spoiled for that company too, because his comrades there are unquestioning doers of good or bad deeds and he has been poisoned with a questioning intellectualism. (Major's precocious autobiography, *Mémoires d'un jeune canoque*, published by another magazine after he left *parti pris*, indicates that the story is not his—he had parted with his classical education simply to educate himself. One thinks of Jacques Renaud, who tried an out-of-town seminary for a couple of years before returning to his east Montreal secondary school.) Major's character quits school altogether, has to do without the support of even his girlfriend, a traditional plunge-in-and-do-the-job-with-an-accepting-heart figure. He rents a room on a slum street, fills notebook after notebook with his thoughts, and finally has to make his flight from school, job, submission-preaching woman, and society a physical one, with a hitchhike through the Laurentians. This ends in unconsciousness by the roadside and return by police car. There is a restrained upbeat ending with the beginnings of communication between rebel son and laborer father.

The real climax, though, is the letter the *cabochon* leaves his girl before heading for the mountains, a manifesto announcing, perhaps, spiritual revival, or perhaps revolution:

> Evening, and he writes. A farewell letter. "My dear Lise . . ." No. He crosses it out and takes another sheet. "My Lise . . ." He looks at these words, crosses them out. New sheet. "Dear Lise . . ." There, that's simpler. "Dear Lise, I hesitated a long time before taking my pen, but here I am, since I have to, telling you about the decision I felt I must take"—out with "felt I must take"—"which I have taken. You will no doubt ask what kind of a devil I have in me that makes me act so foolish; I expect this, since for you living is adapting to society. For me, though, it seems to be the opposite, and I'm coming to believe this more and more: that to assert yourself and develop an aptitude for freedom you have to resist the demands and conventions of society and even reject them completely. How can I explain? Look around you: our social misery, our moral misery, our leaders . . . Mediocre, all of them. No free men in our country. We have no history, but a series of defeats; penned in and weak, we haven't got the will to resist, to be-

come men. Will we always be narrow-minded, contented servants? Those are vital questions, Lise, I'd like it if you would take them seriously. Because they concern you, too. You're going to say that you love me, that I should love you, simply and without complicating things, with all my heart and without looking at what is happening around me. Organizing recreation sessions for youngsters, you consider an escape from egotism. But aren't those recreation sessions perhaps just a way of seeing no further than our own parish? To amuse youngsters who are growing up when our country can't even give them work? When the government of our country doesn't even belong to us?

"Can you understand my anger? Can you comprehend that I don't aspire, not me, to a plain little happy life like the one you suggest? If I were not attached to you, I wouldn't bother even to write. But I need you, and I'd like you to accept me as I am, cabbage-head and all. All I want is to understand the people who live around me. I spent two months with bakery employees, I discovered something I'll tell about some day, because my intention is to write. You see that I am beginning to narrow down what it is I want from life.

"I'm leaving, Lise. Tomorrow or the day after. For the country. For two reasons: I have lost my job at the bakery, and also I want to know rural people, live with them, not only out of interest, but chiefly because I like the idea of their kind of life. I like changing places, seeing new people, adopting new habits. I may come back with the idea of being a reporter, or a sociologist, who knows? Once I've found what I want, I'm sure I'll recover my desire to study. For the moment, forgive me for running away this way, but I have to get away from this city, move around, breathe new air. I'll write again to you, I'll tell you what I've seen. Kisses, if you still love me? Antoine."

This is mild stuff, "a novel for teenagers"—Major insistently stuck by the advertising band attached to it in the bookstores, even after its suppression by the JEC gave it an aura of something hotter. His author's note: "Those who seek anything else will be disappointed; for dirty prose, I refer them to *La Chair de poule*, which will be coming out in January." Not that *Le Cabochon* was a compromise: "That was limited to the language," he told me. "I didn't have my characters swear."

The difference between this and, say, *Bonheur d'occasion*, a more brutal and mature evocation of poverty, is that the earlier novel merely broke the heart and pleaded for some sort of compassion;

whereas Antoine will not come back a sociologist, he will come back a socialist. This is the portrait of the adolescent who, as a young man, will be a *partipriste;* Major, if he wants to show youth taking other paths, will have to write another novel—this one dates from the days of his faith that all-roads-lead-to-revolution. The *parti pris* insignia on the jacket is an essential part of *Le Cabochon,* whether the author now likes it or not. (And the novel will continue to deliver this message to Quebec adolescents for some time yet: Montreal Catholic school boards, confirming finally Major's insistence on the innocence of the novel, have ordered a special printing from *parti pris* to hand out at graduation ceremonies.)

In *La Chair de poule,* the tales of the goosepimpled of the world, the choices are rawer. In one, a young writer—first person—has to choose between the *petite vie tranquille,* job and no writing, and writing, shacked up with his girl, but no money, and contraception somehow or other, no kids. (When I met him, Major's job on the *Petit Journal* had solved that one for him. He lived in Varennes, a town just across the St. Lawrence from Montreal, with his wife Marielle, his child, and in-laws. We had to get together in one of his old downtown taverns on his weekly manuscript-carting visit to St. Catherine Street and surroundings.)

A girl in the frock factory—we're in another story in *La Chair de poule*—has to choose between continuing to look out for the polite young man, the Jewish owner's son, who turns out to be interested only in one-night stands, and judiciously letting herself be felt up by the regular French guys at the snack bar, one of whom might eventually ask her to marry him.

I had worked a day in a factory almost exactly like the one Major describes where Lise sorts underwear into *"small, médium, lardge."* I packed boxes of machine-knitted booties for shipment to five-and-dime stores. My fellow workers were almost all French-Canadians, residents of the unskilled workers' districts to the east. My bosses were a young Italian who had learned to speak English but not French, and, above him, a young English-speaking Jew with relatives in New York and customers across Canada. The pattern is familiar enough in Quebec. Jacques Renaud tells of it in his family, and on Visitation Street in the heart of the east you can see it closer to its labor market: there you see Jack Miller, Inc., Mfr. of Ladies' &

156 *Malcolm Reid*

Children's Lingerie, with the same brick exterior, the same narrow front office, and, through the upstairs windows, the same mechanical looms, the same tier upon tier of metal stock shelves.

The European Jews who came to Montreal in the same waves of Jewish immigration which hit the eastern United States and the rest of Canada in the early part of the century learned English and built their commerce and their public life, as the others did, in English, with French an occasional extra capability. This seemed normal to them; the French were Catholic and closed; the English, the comfortable minority, were Protestant and willing to open their school system to Jews without theological quibbling. There were those relatives in New York, Toronto, Winnipeg.

Above all, capitalism functioned in English in Quebec, big capitalism; those who wished to participate in its lower and distributive levels naturally learned the language of the big boys. Even those who challenged capitalism in socialist politics in immigrant central Montreal in the 1930's did so, if not in Yiddish, then in English, the language spoken in Ottawa. The French, not immigrants but an "ethnic group" that bore the same historical relationship to the Quebec English as the Indians to the New England Puritans, were to be hired, employed, taught enough to keep the machines going; even feared when one's politics were too far left for their clergy and their anger at their own impotence sought Jewish windows to break.

The French-Canadians I worked with were not in a window-breaking mood that day, but signs of their impotence in the universe that surrounded them were as visible as ever. They knew what language young Dominic had worked his way to foreman's level in, they saw the labels on the bootie cartons, the descriptions for English-speaking Woolworth managers, and I knew from a few months put in as stock boy in a Woolworth's in poor, French, east end Ottawa that there the situation was often the same as in the Montreal plant —English on top, French spoken among the girls. Indeed, the English on the labels controlled their whole approach to the stuff of their daily labor: what they were packing could only be *booties, kiddie sets, sweaters, jackets:* it came into existence only in English terms. The *"small, médium, lardge"* of Major's Lise. It was all made on English machines, sent to English customers, categorized in English categories.

I listened to a cheerful middle-aged man stack knitteds by colors: *"Passe-moi six pink, veux-tu?"* (Baby clothes, of course, come overwhelmingly in that color and *bleu*.) I wondered if *pink* had displaced *rose* in his consciousness, or if it was only a category at work, not yet a generally applicable word. (Chamberland had told me of tests in which joual-speaking French-Canadians were shown slides of objects and asked to name them: they came up with French words—which apparently they had learned and retained. It's simply that in life, context after context suggested to them that *truck* was more appropriate for the moment than *camion*.) I looked around for something to test this with, and found Dominic at the other end of the storage room. I pointed to his shirt: *"Quelle couleur, d'après vous, la chemise de Dominic?"*

He looked up from a box of booties, the employee, and, a bit puzzled, replied: *"C'est du—pink."* With a little upturn of the voice, as if: "Yeah, it's the same color as the booties, so I don't see why the same word shouldn't apply." And he turned again to his work, work that pays (me, anyway) $1 an hour, or $50 a week. (In Major's story, Lise's friend Monique, who has gotten her the job, tells her: "To start off, you won't have a big salary. Between twenty-five and thirty a week, but don't get discouraged, just tell yourself plenty of girls'd like to be in your place.")

I asked a pretty teenager who was sorting socks to name me the same color among those she was handling: *"Ça, c'est rose—pink."* A bit younger, a bit newer on the job, a bit less caught up in the process, and the French was closer to the surface, but ready to cede its place under the first stress, after the first year.

I ate lunch in an Italian restaurant with the assistant manager, a friend, and listened a bit sullenly as he talked to me in terms of the left-wing opinions we shared of the difficulty of raising wages in the competitive garment industry. He'd gotten fired from jobs in the States for trying to organize the workers, and he'd finally left the country out of pacifist objections to its war machine, so he wasn't against a better deal for these people, but you had to remember that most of these small companies were on the brink of going under, and that would only take away their jobs altogether. I went home numb from that day of work, wanting only to get drunk. Too tired to wonder how representative what I had seen was, too tired to formulate the elegant judgment that in the same sense that for Lenin communism was the soviets plus electricity, colonialism was *pink*, was *lardge, médium, small*—plus the kind of material life you can buy yourself for twenty-five to fifty a week. My English accent at least had spared me the experience told me by a French-Canadian friend after a similar spare-cash day at that shop. The workers, listening to his speech, that of a high-school educated Québécois who had never been to Europe, asked him, "Hey, you an Algerian?"

Major is the Shouting Signpainter whose appearance is closest to what has always struck me as the French-Canadian type: lean, dark hair, fairly pale skin. His brown eyes and straight, brushed-back hair also take something from the Indian ancestry he claims.

"My father was a schoolteacher at the Louis Hébert school in Rosemount, but for most of my childhood we lived nearer the river, in a working-class section like the one I described in *Le Cabochon*."

Fingering his glass of draft beer on the arborite tabletop, leaning back in his chair and speaking gently, with a smile that never quite left the corner of his lips, Major tenderly evoked his father. His belted black-leather coat was slung over one of the empty chairs in this tavern, one of the garishly but grandly decorated ones west of the slums, usually at least half full of clerks and others who have business on *la Catherine*.

It was his mother, however, who made a linguistic purist of him: "In our homes in Quebec, we call everything *'une patente'*—you know the mark on commercial products, 'patent 1955'? But my mother insisted that we apply the precise term to every article—no *patentes;* a chair, an iron, an ironing-board. This is curious—or perhaps it is explicable—because my mother was English-speaking, had lived in the United States and learned her French late in life."

His view on joual as a written language is the conventional one among the joual writers: it cannot really do the job, its value is one of scandal, of shock, of documenting colonialism. "A joual literature which would be heard, and not read, might be a possibility."

"Vigneault?"

"Yes, Vigneault is that in a sense. But as soon as you write it down—and even in *La Chair de poule*, I never went all out at writing joual, but simply used it in places for special purposes—you run into problems, both for the writer and for the reader. The writer doesn't know how to spell his words: there is no system for mingling two sets of spelling rules, even if English and French use the same alphabet. I was in close touch with Renaud at the time he was writing *Le Cassé*, he brought me his manuscript. Renaud is lazy: he had spelled all the English words *à l'anglaise*—*chesterfield* with a *ch-*, and so on. I prodded him into gallicizing his spellings, making chesterfield *tchesteurfilde*. But when *Le Cassé* is put before a prospective reader who speaks much as its characters speak, Jacques turns out to have been right, to have had the right instinct about the right spelling for *chesterfield*. I have tried to interest some of my relatives and in-laws, guys of about my own age, in the joual writers. These are workers, ordinary guys. They weren't hostile, but weren't very interested, either. They didn't get the French spellings—the words were meaningless. 'Oh, you mean *chesterfield?*' they would say. For them that was the only way to spell it: not merely the sound, but the whole English reality had imposed itself on their consciousness."

He is similarly resigned about imposing true French terms in speech where anglicisms have taken root among French-Canadians. "I ask for *de la monnaie*, and the bus conductor doesn't get it. So I've given up and I ask for *du change*."

This distaste-for-flair-for-joual is plain in the stories in *La Chair*. The very title is a homage to the richness of popular language, and "chicken flesh" is exactly what Major has when his arrested comrade fails to show up for a Montreal mountaintop rendezvous. But that same story has some false-ringing overworked joualisms to show how terrible this scourge on the language is:

> C'est vrai, t'as perdu ton travail, ta djobbe je devrais dire. Use their words, it shows them the wound they've dealt you. Comment ils t'ont magané. No smoking and no parking, we don't speak french. I'm sorry, boy, you must speak english, no work for you . . . Province of Quebec, town of Montreal, deuxième ville française du monde siyoupla, parka-veniou . . . French pea soup . . . Time is money—l'argent est anglais! You must accepter c't'e patente-là, oké, si tu veux arriver à quèque chose dans vie, c'est moé qui t'le dis!

In *Le Beau Pétard* the joual comes easier, truer, more lovingly:

Dans une demi-heure, la semaine sera finie. Finie. Et puis ce sera la fin de semaine. Le ouiquenne dont il faudra profiter. Deux jours de liberté. Essayer d'être heureuse. J'sais pas c'qu'y pense de moi, Djémé . . . Les dernières minutes passent, lentes et creuses, et toujours pas de Djémé. Puis la sonnerie: cinq heures trente. Course folle vers la liberté, la mauvaise odeur de la rue St-Laurent. Djémé l'attrape au passage: "Pas si vite, la belle Lise!" Elle en a le souffle coupé. Son coeur frappe contre sa poitrine. Il sourit. Mondieu! Faut que j'dise quèche chose . . .

The description of the end of the factory week, the flight to the Main, the heartbeat in the chest when the boss's boy Jimmy calls out to wait a minute, all could be understood by a French-speaking person anywhere. And yet there is the perfect just-slightly-distorted *Djémé*, the gallicization of weekend into *ouiquenne*, so nice it was worth including even if the anglicism is more characteristic of France than of Quebec, where it's usually *fin de semaine*. And the utterly Quebec contractions: *c'qu'y* for *ce qu'il*, pronounced exactly like *ski*. All this is much more in the spirit of Renaud's joual, where there is never any laying it on thick, never any of the sarcasm of the joual hater. When asked whether *Le Cassé* could be understood in Paris or Gabon, Renaud, rather than launch into a speech on the scandal of it all, the horror of the state of the language and the urgency of uplift, is likely to be almost defensive: "*Es-tu capable de comprendre tout* Mort à crédit?"

(So I tried, and I wasn't, but I did comprehend why the late Louis-Ferdinand Céline is one of the favorite writers of Renaud, Major, the whole gang, despite his reactionary politics, despite his hopelessness. Like them, he tells what the streets are like, like them he likes human beings but doesn't like admitting it, like them he feels free to use the language of the streets to do all this, in narrative as well as dialogue; the admission of Paris argot to the universal canon opens the door the crack necessary for other sub-Frenches to enter.)

And even Major breaks down and admits it: "There are some Quebec realities we can't convey other than in joual. I tried to tell a Frenchman what *slutch* was." (It's *slush*, which joual gives a *-t-* sound.) "We tried to eliminate the word, find something French for it. *Neige fondante?* But no, it's more than melting snow; you'd have to say melting snow mixed with mud and other debris. So we surrendered. *Slutch.*" (And at least Major was never so insecure before his language to have done what Jacques Renaud did in a M. Jourdain moment before he decided to give joual to literature: take e-nun-cia-shun lessons at one of the numerous improve-yourself-and-get-ahead schools around Montreal for the neurotic *colonisé*.)

For in Quebec, literate culture is preserved in halls where linguistic purity is a trumpeted concern, even if it must be both a farce (the petty-bourgeois elites who are in charge of classical education being themselves joualized at levels their surroundings do not permit them to recognize) and a masquerade in a land where the language is ravaged by capitalist realities just over the academy walls. Major's father, the proletarian teacher with the petty-bourgeois aspirations for his son, sent André to a series of colleges, like the *cabochon* of the novel, and it was there that both the man of letters and the iconoclast began to emerge. Major's first published *oeuvre*, an amusingly tiny effort printed on a single sheet of cardboard about the size of a postcard folded to yield four pages, or, if you wish, a front and back cover (published "chez l'auteur" it says ponderously, with his family's address, and his at the time, April 1961; but the rebel bookseller Henri Tranquille, in whose shop I bought this work for its published price of ".05," admits to having had a hand in its production), was a requisitory against Major's college mentors for:

1. Neglecting all critical development of students in things doctrinal. A neglect become an intellectual murder, a paying vice.
2. Making insignificant phrasemakers of our writers, theologians of our philosophers, apologists in bad faith of our historians, little girls expired from zeal of our saints.
3. Exploiting a perhaps false naïveté for the sake of an indoctrination which could be refused only on pain of excommunication.
4. Collaborating in the conservation of a shameful national mythology. Examples: the St-Jean-Baptiste Day sheep, the cult of unquestioned authority, etc.
5. Setting up a totalitarianism which ruled out all individual freedom.
6. Legalizing the cohabitation of the spiritual and the temporal; the only offspring could be a bastard race. But the two lovers had their fun . . .
7. Falsifying the simplest notions of liberty, truth, life.
8. Monopolizing thought in the service of orthodoxy. And this in the purest fascist-dictatorship style.
9. Imposing Catholicism on French-Canadians without their reasoned consent.

10. Denying the right to insubordination before oppression, which in our case is theocratic. . . .

Not yet *partiprisme*, but it will be noted that unlike much individualist and libertarian-Catholic thought, it does not balance off fascism and communism as the equal rapes of the person that the two extremes of conventional politics produce. Quebec theocracy is compared with that of *fascist* dictatorships. Major was clearly situating himself on the left. For such outbursts (this one seems to have been one issue of a miniperiodical called *Liberté étudiante*) Major was eventually expelled from the Collège des Etudistes on Rosemount Boulevard, and the rest of his education was self-administered.

It was no less classical for that. "Major has a command of culture, *mon vieux* . . ." said a young unpublished poet I came upon in a search for the successor generation to the *parti pris* writers, and he completed the sentence with a gesture of the hand which seemed to speak of something too vast to express.

The presence of a strong line of political exploration in the European literature of his language is an unavoidable influence on a young French-Canadian writer, even if his social context makes the political odysseys of twentieth-century Frenchmen hard for him to digest.

"I am coming back now to my early favorites among writers," Major told me. "Malraux . . ." And the then French minister of culture is as good an example of the problem as any. On reading *La Condition humaine* and *L'Espoir*, Major could not fail to appreciate the political point of these epics of the Chinese and Spanish revolutions, the sympathy Malraux had for their militants and his broad endorsement of the Communist Party they fought in. He has testified to part of this since leaving *parti pris*, in his generally anti-Marxist *Mémoires d'un jeune canoque*:

> It was at this point that there appeared that sign from on high, that gift of the gods: the pocket-sized paperback book. . . . Everything began with *La Condition humaine*. Along about Easter, I think it was, the college invited us, rather pressingly, to undertake a closed retreat. And it was at Joliette, between pious walls adrip with repentance, that I came to know the ecstasy of Revolution. . . . Here [in Tchen] was a man who, possessed by a great idea, carried it through to its necessary conclusion . . .

On the one hand this kind of revelation led the French-Canadian college student into the political problems raised by these novels of the twenties and thirties: socialism, freedom, violence, terror, the oppression of nations by other nations and of classes by other classes within the same nation; Camus, Sartre, the literature of the decolonization of Africa. In January 1962, a few months after discovering the revolution and leaving college, a few weeks after his one-after-the-other first two booklets of poetry, *Le Froid se meurt* and *Holocause à 2 voix* (dedications to the old rebels Gilles Leclerc, Gilbert Langevin, Gaston Miron; lines like "I grasp at all that lives," "My people is Pilate/Those who dare are locked away/And they plead innocent to this blood," "TO LIVE WE MUST ARM"), but still a full year before the FLQ, before *parti pris,* he wrote a letter answering the *citélibristes'* call for the voices of the young:

> Being for both independence and secularism, we reject both separatists who don't talk about clericalism and secularists who are against separatism (as for our choice of independence, it suffices to say we share the views of Mr. Marcel Chaput, *Pourquoi je suis séparatiste,* Editions du Jour). Our problem is two-headed! Our liberation will take place at all levels, inside and outside. It goes without saying that independence for us implies a socialist government. We are not believers, but we still hope this liberation will bring a religious reform, a spirituality which has always been missing here. In the *cité libre* we hope to build, all will breathe, none will suffocate.

He described the group he spoke for. Twenty to twenty-five, politico-poetic, unemployed and tolerated by their families. But not tolerated by the clerical watchdogs, and feeling no solidarity in this fight with the Catholic left, the forty-year-olds at *Cité libre.* Not hateful, either—"Our verse used to scream, now it constructs." Socialist, yes, but unblushing in endorsing the contentless separatism of Chaput. And the *citélibristes* received all this with a modicum of cordiality: the FLQ was yet to come, *parti pris* was yet to howl. The young separatists didn't seem to be altogether fascist, and *Cité libre* itself had not yet gotten up its full anti-nationalist steam: its ambiguity was visible in the inclusion of an editorial by Gérard Pelletier, finger-wagging at the young, in the front of the same issue of *Cité libre* in which Major's letter appeared, as well as an angry article against the French suppression of Algerian nationalism at the back. But things moved fast.

That spring *Cité libre* came out with its famous anti-separatist special, including Trudeau's characterization of the separatists as comparable to the men of letters on the French right for whom the Nation meant down with the Jews, up with the army. Quebec wasn't Algeria, was the refrain, Quebec wasn't Africa. And that fall Major wrote this account of his encounter with Algeria, with Africa, with *Les Damnés de la terre*:

> I won't review Frantz Fanon's book, *The Wretched of the Earth*. What I will try to do is take its essential ideas and show, by a rigorous dialectic, in how many ways the situation they sprang from resembles ours. I shall obviously take account of the basic differences too. It is the essay's *principles* which I shall apply to our struggle. That struggle, like the one Fanon describes, is in the name of two values: nation and class. It is a NATIONAL REVOLUTION because it involves the oppression of one nation by another, and a socialist one because it involves the oppression of one class by another. "If it triumphs, it will be socialist, this national revolution," Jean-Paul Sartre says in his preface. "If it is braked, if the colonized elite takes over, the new state will be sovereign in form, in imperialist hands in reality." That nicely summarizes what the colonized are fighting for. . . . Elsewhere in that preface Sartre says: "The real culture is the revolution; it is created at white heat," and I think our intellectuals, the young ones, have discovered that— culture is no isolated growth, it doesn't exist of itself, it mingles and grows with the nation around it.

The magazine this time was *La Revue socialiste*, the political mentor of Major's circle was now Raoul Roy, and the various metals which would be poured into *parti pris* had almost reached their white heat. So had the anger. Another signature in that issue was that of Pierre Schneider: he argued for a self-determination-for-Quebec stand by the New Party, a social-democratic growth which had come to the province from English Canada and the trade-union movement. But the stand would not be adopted. The next spring the first bombs would explode in Montreal, and the next summer Pierre Schneider would be among the score of faces in the papers the day the FLQ was broken up. He, like Tchen, had carried his idea to its necessary conclusion.

But if all this was one of the places to which the contact with Malraux had led André Major, it had also led him to a consideration of the evolution of Malraux himself: his rejection of the revolution, his turning to pure aestheticism, his rallying to capitalism as the protector of the human personality. Also, even back in his prewar days, his fascination with individual heroism, his finding it even in his Communists. "We need a revolutionary elite," read one of the subtitles to Major's piece on *The Wretched of the Earth*. It did not seem very well supported by the text that followed, maybe Major didn't write it, but its inclusion suggested that the same young men who had gathered around *La Revue socialiste*, who had emptied the bookstores of Fanon's book and would take up the half-price offer announced by the magazine, liked at certain moments to think of themselves in that light too. And there was, despite Ottawa and its English-speaking political sway, and the need for a NATIONAL REVOLUTION in capitals, despite the east end of Montreal and the cancer of unemployment and all the material oppression that cried out for at least a socialist one in small letters, despite joual and theocracy and the whole cultural deterioration that drove a young intellectual to feel a special need for a revolution all his own—despite all that, *Cité libre* did have its point, there was that undeniable Western consumer society, the same as the one which had emerged in France in the period of Malraux's conversion to the status quo. There was, alas, the incomprehension of the revolution by the millions of working-class French-Canadians to whom Major would have liked to transmit it, as Kyo transmitted it to the Shanghai coolies.

Thus Major and his comrades had to try to digest Malraux without having lived through the times and experiences which had formed the man, without even being able to draw on some handed-down experience of this European and to some extent Anglo-American radicalization of the between-wars period. For at the time when young Frenchmen and Americans were gobbling up news of the progress of the revolution in China and signing up to help Spain fight Franco, young French-Canadians—unless they were living completely outside their own national tradition, in English Canada, Europe, or the English-dominated Communist Party that operated in Quebec in those days—were "buying" little Chinese souls at school, paying the price the missionary orders said it took to save one heathen, praying for the triumph of *Christ-Roi* in Spain, and breaking those Jewish storekeepers' windows when nationalism needed a violent expression. Not something likely to bring them close to the militant Jews of the Montreal left. And all this applied very largely to the future *citélibristes* and left Catholics, too. The Spanish war jolted a few of their consciences, but their big awakening came with Asbestos in 1949.

A clear demonstration of how the prewar years were prehistory for progressivism in Quebec is the contrast between the response to Malraux's visit to Montreal in 1937, when he spoke for the Spanish Loyalists, and that to his return in 1963 as an emissary of de Gaulle. In 1937 he was received by an English-speaking social-democratic milieu of Loyalist sympathizers—my mother always tells me an anecdote about how he thrilled one of the young literary couples of this milieu by forgetting his gloves in their apartment. The French press found him an unwelcome red-tinged *maudit français* (the term, the French-Canadian rustic's for a Frenchman, may not have been used, but the rustic's contempt was there). The French-speaking elite spared the Prix Goncourt only the roughest aspects of the reception another pro-Loyalist visitor, a Basque priest, received in those years, when a meeting the abbé was to speak at was broken up by University of Montreal students and militants.

In 1963, a Quebec in full quiet revolution, well sprinkled with separatism and Francophilia, received the statesman-*littérateur* with open arms and was delighted with his call to the Québécois to build the future with France. Quebec had moved to the left, Malraux to the right, and the two found themselves in each other's embrace. Except for the youngsters who had discovered the revolution in *La Condition humaine* and had taken themselves for Tchens; they, or most of them, received their prison sentences the day Malraux stepped off the plane at Dorval and I do not believe he made a public reference to them during his entire stay. No matter, the English press by now saw almost as great a menace in Malraux as they later discerned in his boss, that old Catholic soldier who in 1967 made his pitch to French-Canadian nationalism even more explicitly.

The parents and the political mentors of young English-speaking left militants can tell their charges about those great adventures of the thirties, and the kids, though perhaps they cannot read it in the original French, can fit *L'Espoir* into a rough historical context. This may even lead them to reject it as dated while the young Québécois embraces it whole. If the young Quebec militant's father had anything to do with the Malraux of the thirties, it was probably as a profascist demonstrator, and he cannot pass on a notion of earlier revolutionary milieux. This makes it hard for the young Quebec reader of *L'Espoir* not to take it as either a literal, immediately applicable political document, or a disembodied piece of art, beautiful, eternal, and unrelated to present society. Of course, the difficulty can be overcome with further reading, but it is not inconsiderable, and it is one big reason for why there is no close alliance between the young English-speakers on the left in and around the two English universities in Montreal and the national left that has taken shape among Quebec youth.

"It looks to me like this is one part of America where old left ideas are more applicable, and I don't quite fit in," says one friend of mine from the English milieu. Though he comes from a fundamentalist family in Alberta, he feels he has been through the leftism of the thirties; he cannot take the Leninist literature of those days as literally as he finds Quebec leftists taking it, and for him pot, rock'n'roll, and communal living are as integral to what makes him a revolutionary as are the opinions he holds. The French seem to him to be one stage behind. But he dutifully slugs through the American translation of Sartre's *Being and Nothingness* to find out what they have on their minds.

So it is with another friend, the son of a Montreal-Jewish merchant whose circle was Communist in the thirties. "I'd like to get closer to the French left, but . . . Independence for Quebec, okay, I'll buy it, but I can't feel it, I can't really be a hard-core separatist myself. I'm not French and it's not my baby." He knows that French-Canadian nationalism can be and has been something conservative, anti-Semitic, and he finds it hard to put it up there among his priorities.

In Paris, on that visit during which I spoke to André Garand, I heard of the idea of the "actual consciousness" and the "possible consciousness" of the audience of a work of art, which I think applies here. I learned of it from a young Frenchman who applied it specifically to French Canada. (He had taken it from Lucien Goldmann, the French Marxist literary sociologist, who in turn took much from Georg Lukács, the Hungarian *éminence gris* of Communist cultural life, already man of letters and man of state in 1919 when Hungary had its brief first period of Communism.) Garand had contrasted the FLQ, which *dared,* and the French left, which had long since settled into waiting and seeing. On the métro from the Sorbonne to my home quarter a few nights before I'd listened to a similar view from the other side, from Michel Bernard, a shy assistant to Goldmann in some of his political courses and author of a book on Quebec, *Le Québec change de visage.* I'd met him in the crowd as a group of students on strike turned him and Goldmann away from a lecture date at the Ecole des Hautes Etudes Pratiques, an elite night school at the University of Paris. We'd had coffee, Bernard had offered me a copy of his book, had added that it did not take account of the *parti pris* development, which had not taken place at the time of his visit to Quebec. He found the *partipristes* sound in their general views, a bit rigid in adapting to their local situation, but valuable, very valuable.

"They are, of course, way in advance of the average consciousness of people in Quebec. But as a spearhead they are very representative. It's like the internal conflicts of Saint-Denys Garneau: they seemed personal, but they expressed the asphyxia of the entire city population of Quebec. There were, around 1959, voices like Roland Giguère, Gatien Lapointe, Gaston Miron, men ten years ahead of their countrymen, but precursors, prophets. We see this in *parti pris,* in its poets. Everything, for a certain time, is going to move in that direction. The screen of the Church risks blocking part of the trend, but the Church's ability to hold things back is declining. The *parti pris* writers may have to modify their violence, may not be able to realize their full intent. But their books—somebody had to write them, even if *Cité libre* was going to cry totalitarianism, fascism. There's this thing called *actual* and *possible consciousness.* The poet, the intellectual, his function is to become conscious of what seems to be on the way, things that are to be. If he wrongly anticipates, he will speak to deaf ears. But if he is in the current of history, he will help reveal the collective future to the mass of people.

"In general, I think it is the poets who are playing this role in Quebec; the novel seems to me to be behind. But yes, I've read Renaud's book. And enjoyed it, laughed a great deal, remembered things I'd heard in taverns in Quebec, things Renaud had gotten down exactly. But it has a limit, it's an act of combat more than of literature. It can't be understood by most people over here, and won't be readily understood in Quebec in twenty years. But it may not die for all that; I learned many things from reading *Le Cassé*, and the Québécois may wish to do the same in the future, just as we continue to study the *Chanson de Roland* even if its French is no longer ours. What was perhaps missing was an insertion of the sub-proletarian Québécois in the scheme of a *Québec libre*, what it all means to this man without education, without any kind of culture if it's not religious."

And he went on to talk about himself, about the intellectual in France. He envied the *partipristes:*

"In France we have an overproduction of intelligence. I write the occasional article for *Le Monde*. It is an excellent paper, but when you write for *Le Monde* you always know that if you don't, there are other writers just as good as you, just as intelligent, as well-trained, left wing like you, who will write them. Am I a Marxist in the *parti pris* sense? Am I a Marxist at all? I consider myself so, but I do not feel that it excludes me from a Christian view either, and I would diverge with them there: they have thrown out the positive values of Christianity along with the alienations. But they find themselves in a situation where they can explore, they can launch new ideas, apply untried ideas to the world. Here in France there is a highly developed left critique of the society which is established, confident, and there is a profound and continuing exploitation of man which goes on at the same time: it is a deadlock, and a French intellectual always wonders about the usefulness of his work. No such doubts in Quebec."

An eclectic like Major, it would seem. But no. Even the mixing of left culture with Christianity is not the same thing for the European and the just-out-of-theocracy Québécois. When I told Bernard that Major was now writing for *L'Action nationale,* the magazine of the crypto-separatists of the Canon Groulx school, dismay came over his face. "What on earth is he doing with that bunch?" he asked.

A Quebec literary success which illustrated Bernard's thesis was that of Hubert Aquin's *Prochain épisode,* a novel which had come out before my trip, but which neither of us had yet read. In *La Chair de poule,* André Major had included a story called *"Mental test pour toute la gang,"* in which the narrator tried to come to terms with the arrest of a comrade for possession of a gun. The comrade is fairly obviously

Hubert Aquin, and *Prochain épisode* was his telling of the same drama. It outsold all other French-Canadian books in 1964–1965, was identified by the haughty, cool-to-separatism critic Jean Ethier-Blais in *Le Devoir* as the Great Novel At Last, and fascinated the federalist English press with its picture of a moody separatist brilliantly writing away in a prison mental ward. It was published in Quebec by the leading apolitical bourgeois house of Montreal, the Cercle du Livre de France, and was published a year later in France by Robert Laffont.

But more formidable for me than the critics' reception were the reactions of the writers I esteemed. Major coolly told me his opinion: "For me, it is the best Quebec novel ever." Renaud, opening it up at my apartment one evening and reading aloud its opening sentence, "Cuba sinks in flames in the center of Lake Leman and I descend to the heart of things," declared it *"génial"* and tucked it into the belt of his trenchcoat to take it home for further communion.

Yet when I did read it I was unable to be greatly moved, and I wonder if this was not because it was too clearly made to be found great, a work of genius, a mystical object whose glow is instantly communicated and cannot be explained. Because, in a word, I was not French-Canadian, not separatist in the guts. The book is a separatist secret agent's account of an episode in Switzerland in which he fails to knock off the Swiss counter-agent he is assigned to neutralize and even seems—it is a stream-of-consciousness mixture of reverie and narrative—to lose his blonde loved one to him.

Now a certain amount of information about Aquin was known to me and everyone else, and I like everyone else did not hesitate to make a fairly complete identification between the narrator and the author. Aquin is a thirtyish Montreal intellectual who joined the first, politically dead-center, wave of separatism, tried to do his bit to hoist the Québécois to equality with their Anglo-Saxon betters by playing the Anglo-Saxons' own game as a St. James Street stockbroker's assistant, but failed his apprenticeship at this unaccustomed trade and slid back to the native domains of literature (in *Liberté*), broadcasting (CBC), and underground politics (he was held several months after his arrest in 1964 for the "mental test" of Major's title, then finally completely cleared). His real-life adventures continued after the novel came out, with his expulsion from the Switzerland he so poetically described in the book. The Swiss apparently feared he was up to some real undercover politics on a later sojourn on Lake Leman; it seems he was mostly up to writing a second novel.

These facts were, I suppose, enough to clinch the French-Canadian novel reader's good disposition. Mine no. Major had said it in his praise of the book: "Aquin is saying, 'The French-Canadian alienation is not some worker, physically miserable, some lumpenproletarian scarcely surviving from day to day; the French-Canadian alienation is me, with all those problems perhaps solved, but with the fundamental one still there, because my country is colonized.' " I could not share this search for the *essence* of colonization, the elusive something that was unbearable to a French-Canadian, even to one free of the material oppression, even to a French-Canadian who is comfortable. No doubt—and the Maheus were there as proof—the well-off member of a group that is by and large oppressed suffers certain pains and inferiorities which spring from his situation, his belonging, as Maheu the pre-FLQ diarist put it, to "the wrong group." But these pains could be analyzed, were not mystical; attributing them to the outraged essence of *québécicité*, that resides in even the privileged colonial I found impossible to take, and hence every sumptuous Swiss meal, every sublime Swiss alp that Aquin provided himself in *Prochain épisode* only served, for me, to remove him from the real exploitation of Quebec, to make him a spoiled and petulant *prince-nègre* blaming his emotional shambles on the colonialists.

For me the real atrocity of the colonization of Quebec would always have to be its physical, material, bread-and-butter aspects— and psychological ones, too, but workaday psychological. The Québécois who did not feel the pinch in this elemental way joined the anti-colonial struggle by relating himself to these daily atrocities, not by dissociating himself from them. The refusal to see it that way, the insistence that there is, apart from class and wages and housing and linguistic humiliation, some essentially Québécois suffering in every member of the nation which must be redeemed by national independence was, of course, the substance of the views of the neither-left-nor-right-but-simply-separatist movement, the RIN. The RIN had been Aquin's party, and *Prochain épisode* was, I conclude, and the sales figures would seem to concur, the RIN novel.

I value Hubert Aquin for something else. Not for being the Ian

Fleming of Quebec liberation but for being its phrase-maker, perhaps its Oscar Wilde. In articles in *Liberté* and *parti pris* (for despite belonging to the RIN tradition of plain-and-simple separatism, he has frequented the *partipristes* and is, it must by now be plain, esteemed by them), he has found again and again the ironic expression which precisely captured a facet of the Quebec malaise. He has spoken of the "cultural fatigue" of French Canada, is compensating for its nullity in the big money world by a tremendous artiness, a disproportionate output of words, pictures, melodies, and other pearls beyond price which masters generally consider excellent forms of expression for slaves. He has ironized upon the Québécois' expertise in "the art of defeat" and he has noted that in all the editorialists' and speechmakers' metaphors of marriage, cohabitation, and copulation in their descriptions of the French-English thing within Canada, *the English are always the men and the French are always the women*.

But if Aquin is able thus to demolish the inventors of one sexualization of a political question, Michel Bernard found in *Prochain épisode*, when he read it a year later, an Aquin-invented sexual metaphor for politics. Bernard wrote his analysis for *parti pris* when the book was published in Paris. The hero, he felt, is the revolutionary, the Swiss villain his colonialist enemy, and the woman his country, whom he seeks to liberate, but who has a fatal tendency to offer herself up as "prostitute to the bourgeoisie." The revolutionary, a bourgeois himself, feels more in common with the enemy than with his people. The whole is the "facing-up to an impotence." What Bernard did not say was that this very personifying of the nation—meaning the people, the "laboring classes" on whom Chamberland places his hopes for revolution, whom Renaud and Major painted in their east end setting—as a love-object which can be only mistress or whore, is a perfect representation of the emptiness of separatism as a total doctrine. An emptiness which is a fully adequate reason for the impotence of the "revolutionary." To this sort of revolutionary the population of the nation to be liberated is an object to be manipulated (or lost to a better manipulator). The thought does not occur to him that she is a being whose autonomous motives, wants, and view of herself exist, indeed can be the only guides for the man who seeks her liberation. That her "prostitution" is her attempt to live as decently as possible, that only the perspective of a better life will win her to the revolution. That her fidelity must be earned by the revolutionary's commitment to her, that the merging of his strivings with hers is his only hope of overcoming his "impotence." And to undertake that merging, the revolutionary must somehow be in touch with the folks back home in the slums; he can run missions to Geneva, he can even drink Fendant du Valais, but it all must have something to do with the *cassés* in the *ruelle Saint-Christophe,* with the girls in the garment plants. It's not up to them not to be whores: it's up to him to offer something better.

Perhaps it is because, as my English-speaking friends feel, *parti pris* is stretching the "possible consciousness" of Quebec readers too far that the groups' works have not had the same success as Aquin's novel, which might be said to have gone just far enough to take the bulk of Quebec readers' "actual consciousness" with him. Major himself appears to be a casualty of this tension between real and potential consciousness. Indeed Aquin and the entire young pure-separatist movement show clearly one possible result of the exposure of a group to a body of thought some of whose important aspects are beyond its actual consciousness.

"It is difficult to make the revolution in a country where . . ." RIN leader Pierre Bourgault used to begin answers to questions at public meetings. He'd show no hesitation about taking over the vocabulary of Kyo, of Communism, of the national liberation movements of parts of the world where they are unambiguously class conscious. Similarly, Aquin happily evokes Cuba at the opening of *Prochain épisode,* and young intellectuals and separatists who have no ambition beyond the political sovereignty of Quebec, apart from Ottawa, will refer briskly to the literature of Communist militancy in Europe, place themselves within its world, speak of militants, the masses, party discipline, the established order, collaborators. This vocabulary has been swallowed whole, none of the political stages through which its authors in Europe went were necessary. Quebec may still need its Balzacs and its Zolas, simply to catalogue the social conditions, to chronicle the physical facts of life in the province; this does not prevent young readers from leaping forward to their contemporaries among French writers for whom this cataloguing is something already done, something taken for granted; for whom the first, simple socialist reply to those conditions and facts is also something uttered, believed in, put to certain tests, adopted in its basic aspects by a large part of the population. And who see their job, hence, as exploring questions which go beyond the recital of facts and the proposal of solutions; who wonder about points that would remain in suspense even were socialism to come about, who contest aspects of capitalism which are left unchallenged by the anti-capitalist mass movements which exist in their society. Nor are young writers restrained from leaping to *produce* such works. It is because of this lack of historical homework that the kind of Robbe-Grillet Quebec can produce when it takes to competing with the real Robbe-Grillet is just what Laurent Girouard said it would be: "sub-sub-Robbe-Grillet."

But of course this is pedantic. It cannot be on Quebec's agenda to go through all the phases of France's (or English Canada's, or any other country's) development in some obedient-pupil fashion, and writers who took on the job of being the French-Canadian Balzacs and Zolas, hoping somehow to catch up on the older land on its own itinerary, would be as screwed-up as the sub-Robbe-Grillets.

It is here that Fanonism, a look at Quebec in the light of the Third World, has something to offer Quebec writers seeking their way between these two dumbnesses. Springing from struggles roughly contemporary with Quebec's own present awakening (the postwar decolonization of Africa, Asia, and Latin America), emphasizing the starting-from-zero which these societies had to undertake, the prehistoric blankness of the past which colonial oppression had imposed upon them, doing this to give value to negritude, Islam, Bolívar, whatever gleamed through the blankness as usable native tradition, Fanonism spares the young Quebec writer both unauthenticities. It spares him self-scorn for lacking the diplomas which Balzac, Zola, the Revolution of *Quatre-vingt-treize* and the Congrès de Tours of 1920 gave France; spares him also the ignorant dream that without them the Québécois can leap right into the same bags as are occupied by the Sartres, the Robbe-Grillets, even the Malrauxes of the older land. He can take up his own struggle where he finds it, not trying to skip it, not carbon-copying some previous and distant one.

But there is a catch. It is this: though Quebec shares with the Third World a certain blank prehistory before its decolonization got underway, in material life it has gone through most of the changes of the Western world. A young French-Canadian socialist can find few compatriots of his parents' generation who can tell him of rubbing elbows with the Loyalist Malraux in 1937 or of demonstrating for Sacco and Vanzetti before that—although some can tell him of labor battles in the forties—but almost all can tell him, just as an Anglo-Saxon youth's elder could, of having it tough in the Depression and of things getting better in the fifties; of unemployment in the thirties and TV sets in the boom years. Hence, in a sense, Quebec has lived through the same events as its English-speaking neighbors, without having lived the same spiritual itinerary. It's hard for a young revolutionary to work this out.

One of the youths who has gotten most sadly entangled in this jungle, I could not help beginning to feel, was André Major. He had hastened into a movement that, perhaps by intellectual shortcuts, had found a revolutionary solution to the Quebec problem. There, as a Shouting Signpainter, he had presented himself, for purposes of the analysis of the fairly advanced capitalist society he lived in, as a Marxist, but for purposes of placing himself historically, as a just-awakened colonial who had no intellectual history because his nation's domination by a foreign occupant had frozen all intellectual dynamics around a few defensive nationalist fetishes. But then the haste began to be felt, the shortcuts proved to have been too easy, difficulties of analysis came up, the masses didn't move quickly into the battle positions *parti pris* had drawn up for them, and Major fled, simply wrote off this engagement as a mistake. Instead he adopted a series of other expedients: As a writer he would be a pure artist, not a pamphleteer. Politically, he would retain only an unconfusing separatism, interpreting that socialist literature he still respected loosely enough so the idealism, militancy, and discipline it described as pertaining to the struggle against class and capital could be applied to any struggle at all. Intellectually, no need to go back on his agnosticism, his individualism: enough space had opened up in the new Quebec even while it remained simply the French province of Canada, enough tolerance had been breathed even into the Church, for both to be viable now. But perhaps for him these were not merely expedients, but a true solution; perhaps, as an American New Left friend put it, enough mobilities had opened up in the province-that-

176 *Malcolm Reid*

is, and the republic-that-is-to-be, for French-Canadian intellectuals to be freed of any dependence on a proletarian push for their fulfillment.

Major got himself a job as a literary editor with an apolitical paper. Its being apolitical didn't bother him—that's what he thought literature should be. The only problem was its being a mass circulation journal: that made it hard to write about something like literature, not the masses' cup of tea. But as time went on I watched Major solving such problems in ways that saddened me. From the mass *Petit Journal* he moved to the elite *Devoir*. No more worrying about whether your audience was understanding you: at *Le Devoir* you know your readers read books, you can count on their being choosy in the mass arts.

Still, little magazines had their place, and shortly after I interviewed him Major began publishing an autobiography in *L'Action nationale,* the organ of the old, Catholic nationalists; his tone was without *hargne,* still with much of his *Chair de poule* evocation of past scenes and moods; indulgent, snobbish, seeing nobility in his old comrades at *parti pris* (Piotte he'd met in a scout troop, they'd been good scouts together, Piotte the chief and Major the brave, and they'd been good tavern-talkers together at a later stage, Piotte the Marx and Major the Engels), though of course he'd grown out of their political simplicities—much as he saw nobility in Malraux's Communist heroes by abstracting them from their cause. And he edited the magazine's literary section, gallantly seeing talent in some left-wing poets and initiating his priest-and-professional readership to the unlikely joys of jazz.

Snobbish and urbane, too, were his reviews of shows and books in *Le Devoir*: he was shocked as a good humanist should be by apologetics for the Vietnam war which crept in among the TV actualities, appreciative of what was fine and aesthetic in books from left or right, paternalistic about the beginnings of high-class pornography in French Canada.

I saw him again at a play; he was friendly, interested in my book, modest about his own; I couldn't work up any anger. I asked him what he thought of the play, a conventional treatment of the FLQ in which the terrorists were portrayed as linguistically resentful youths and the conflict was not between class-oriented and strictly nationalistic tendencies within the movement (as in fact it fairly obviously was), but between the movement as a whole and an outside critic who went no further than to find it immoral to take life.

"I don't think it comes across," Major said, but I heard only the simple nationalist in him speaking, wishing the soundness of the linguistic grievances and the unacceptability of the sacredness-of-life argument had come through more clearly. He also told me he was living in Montreal now, separated from his wife, and I felt the wound.

Then came the cruelest blow: coming upon his by-line in *Aujourd'hui-Québec*. This was a stodgy imitation of *Time* magazine published by the extreme-right clerical reaction in Quebec and distributed, the liberal press had revealed, largely through the collaboration of religious orders and parish priests in rural dioceses. On looking a bit closer, it turned out the piece was one the magazine had lifted from *Le Devoir,* as it often did when its own output of secret documents on Moscow plots to corrupt Quebec youth through such agents as *parti pris* and "Georges Schoester" (a strangely Jewish misspelling of the Belgian Georges Schoeters' name) was low. But it was Major who had put himself in a position where *Aujourd'hui-Québec* was pleased to pirate him. Yes, the story is that *Aujourd'hui-Québec* had a liberalizing change of heart just before its demise. But Major's piece did not need this to rate: it was a complacent eulogy to Canon Groulx, who had just died, and was exactly the patriotism-and-literariness I now despaired of ever seeing cease to flow from his pen.

Then I heard something good: *"La Semaine dernière pas loin du pont"* had been made into a movie, a short by a fledgling director even younger than Major, and it was to be shown at the Montreal Film Festival. I called Major to beg tickets. The same friendliness, the same expansiveness as that afternoon in the St. Regis Tavern:

"The remarkable thing about the film is that it's the first time in a Quebec film that the characters swear naturally. Bergeron shot it with nonactors recruited in the district, *pas loin du pont,* and he's given the whole thing a very nice naturalness. I'm at work on other writing besides my work at *Le Devoir,* including another film. For this one I wrote the scenario—I didn't do anything on the *Pont*—but this one I created as a filmscript. It's been shot for Radio-Canada, they're going to show it in color, even. It's called *Sweet Savage.* I wanted to call it *Damn Savage,* but they said no, people might take it wrong, even though I meant it ironically; after all, I'm one myself. It's about an Indian who lives off the reservation, in a big city, in Montreal, but doesn't feel at home there, feels estranged by the city. He decides to flee to the country and moves into a cabin with a solitary old man, another Indian. But he discovers that he's not at home there either, that there really is no place he feels at home. And that's how it ends, simply the dilemma of a man the world has no place to offer."

I cheered up. He hadn't disowned his *parti pris* story of the goose pimpled, and he seemed to be writing further explorations in the same vein. Maybe, I thought, my man was himself a savage not at home in the old convent-walled world or the new politicized one either, maybe he was making writing his home by still, without reference to ideology, telling the bleakness of Quebec life the way his true eye saw it to be.

But no, this was too good. When finally I saw the film it had somehow careened away from the good stuff Major had outlined to me. The Indian was no Indian, his Indian ancestry was not a cross to bear, had become a mere picturesque detail, and he was played by an actor utterly French-Canadian in looks and style. Even Major, leather coat and all, would have given more flash of raven eye to the role. And his malaise was intellectual; he was, of course, *an* intellectual, a very 1967 French-Canadian intellectual, living with an art student girlfriend in an old, gabled house downtown, wearing handicrafted scarves from the boutiques, his hair brushed down over his brow, his eyes glowering at the portrait of Nelligan that was the center of his cluttered decor. (Nelligan is as grave a case of the Quebec *mal de vivre* as one could seek: a "universal" poet of the turn of the century who wrote of his Catholic faith and his love of his mother in a language shaped by the *poètes maudits* of Europe, and sank into demented muteness after a single, adolescent burst of verse. A sort of uncorrupted Rimbaud.) He was working as a reporter at *La Presse,* diverting himself at the coffeehouse Le Patriote, and tormented. Tormented by—oh, it's hard to say, some gnawing dissatisfaction with urban life, desire-to-write-versus-need-to-eat, the unauthenticity of his subway-catching job, a sentimentality about the woods and the north, where he flees to be with his recluse Indian (but also Frenchified) grandfather. Yet he is unable, even when he kicks over the traces, to write those poems, to say those great suppressed things the city wouldn't let him. Somehow there is a certainty that as things are, writing, creating, any kind of growing is doomed to a snuffing-out in the Nelligan manner. The ending is upbeat, but the whole is an exercise in that self-contemplation, that soul-searching in the bathroom mirror that was the stuff of pre-*parti pris* Quebec literature. It is *Prochain épisode* and its song of alienation from the motherland, it is *Le Chat dans le sac* and its toying with social protest while withdrawing from society.

The resemblance to the last-named film, which caused a small scandal when Gilles Groulx brought it out under the National Film Board imprint, is striking. Look, they said in the English magazines, Groulx is assigned, or gets approval for, a film about troubled youth, and he takes the Canadian government's dough and makes a film about a separatist, in which his approval of separatism is not even veiled. But in the end it was the Film Board that was right, the scandal-searchers wrong. For to the young man of *Le Chat,* separatism, *partiprisme,* was merely the mode his malaise took on; it did not really help him, as he gazed through the window of his northwoods retreat at the end of the film, to situate or understand himself, to understand why a sensitive soul, wanting to write, craving to contribute, should feel thus frustrated in the Montreal of the sixties. He is puzzled. He is paralyzed. And he is no danger to the Canadian unity the Film Board exists to fortify.

In the case of Groulx—and even of Aquin—the spectator who feels the problem has not been tackled can nevertheless give marks for honesty. The pro-separatist *cinéaste* and the almost-terrorist novelist may not comprehend their own and their younger brothers' malaise any better than that, but they are at least stating clearly feelings they have felt or observed, wondering what gives rise to them in so many young petty bourgeois in Quebec today. But the theme of the young petty-bourgeois intellectual, bohemian, or artist, contemplative or introspective, one who cannot beat the grinding urban world around him, has attracted writers who do comprehend. Chamberland, almost exactly a year before, had contributed a script to the same TV series that did Major's *Doux Sauvage.* Called *Par delà de tout,* it was a sculptor's story, and it was the same campy-apartment, sportscar-and-coffeehouse, escape-to-the-wilds scene. This is Chamberland's scene, and he has not beaten it either. But where Aquin's, Groulx's—and Major's—heroes in their quest confronted only their own souls, Chamberland's sculptor confronts the Minister of Culture at a gallery opening, smashes his glass and calls him a fake, and then explains why to a friend in a waterfront luncheonette: "They use our work to buy themselves prestige!" In other words, the metaphysical anguish of the sculptor has something to do with the material relations of those who can buy prestige like they buy everything else, and those who must sell to them. Just how to crack it, Chamberland's sculptor doesn't know, outside a drunken dream of hacking up the gallery-goers in a huge, toothed mechanical sculpture, and the closing clinch (the same one Major gives his man) with the dream girl. Chamberland's character is just a little further out of himself and into the world than Aquin's traveler or Groulx's adolescent.

But is Major's *Sauvage* one of this breed? One of the mystified who have not yet discovered an enemy in the real world? No. No, because you cannot go back into the Eden of social ignorance, of obsessed introspection, once you have made your way out of it. Major knows, as surely as Chamberland does, about the Ministers of Culture, and about their bosses the Prime Ministers, and about theirs, the industrialists. And below, about the thousands who work unrelievedly for every one who breaks out in poetry, even goes poetically mad like a latter-day Nelligan. He told about them in angry articles in a magazine called *parti pris* once; he wrote a novel called *Le Cabochon*, and a story called *"La Semaine dernière pas loin du pont"*; he knows.

He knows, too, how hard those realities are to budge, how far beyond the strength of one writer they are, how uncertain the fortunes of the writer who nevertheless takes his pen to be a sword against them must be. It is not André Major's understanding which must be examined when wondering why he turned away from his knowledge, it is his courage.

Near the end of his film, when, to the credit of the author's lucidity, the hero is discovering he can't live away from the crushing city either, Major has the hero confess: "It's not blood that flows in my veins any more, it's ink." All of André Major is there. And yet it was André Major himself who best corrected that kind of confusion of liquids, that kind of denial of the materiality of life in favor of the unsullied spirit, in a beautiful poem dedicated "to Paul Chamberland":

> EN TON CRI TOUS LES CRIS
> you gave yourself to the cult of the orange and its pleasures
> you lived playing the dark game of the eaters
> too young you had your desires melted into a pretty ring
> which held you captive
>
> . . .
>
> too young you heard them say: your evil blood
> too young you heard: your human frailty
> you saw the blood lost the time stolen
>
> and the grimy men lose the fine skin of their youth
> and the club for taming them
> and the holy water kneeling them in defeat
> and death taking them nowhere
>
> . . .
>
> all the while your steps struggling to be free of the paralysis of shame
> all the while the blood issuing up from your love
> at last you drank the blood of hate and were born to your desire
>
> you recognized in your cry all the cries of the earth

5
Wanting men to know what I have known...

The Shouting Signpainters identified the main current in the Quebec past as conservative, Catholic, and capitulationist, and rejected it. But they came from somewhere, these interrupters of the main current. They attracted others to their way of seeing things. And they led Quebec literature somewhere. This chapter will be about some who preceded, some who followed, and some *partipristes* and semi-*partipristes* not spoken of at length before.

Somewhere, as they grew and wrote their way from childhood to *parti pris,* the Shouting Signpainters came in contact with a tradition unlike the French-Canadian mainstream; a tradition that was communal, anti-clerical, disputatious. It came to them from outside, of course, from Europe. Renaud has mentioned Céline, and Major Malraux. One could trace the roots of *parti pris* back through French literature or find its roots in American literature; it is in both.

But as I talked with the Shouting Signpainters I began to hear names, Quebec names, that were from a region of Quebec life that was not itself in that main current; names that many, or not so many, years before the *partipristes* had found a way of being at odds with Quebec from within Quebec. I have reported on some of these names as I reported on the *partipristes* who evoked them. Girouard mentioned Albert Laberge, Gilles Leclerc, Gérard Bessette. Chamberland spoke of Borduas. Influences from a distance, mostly, getting to their countrymen through books, much as did the Frenchmen or *colonisés* who got to them, the Fanons, the Memmis, the Sartres.

One name kept coming up, though, that wasn't represented by

any volume making the rounds; it was mentioned in others' books. Gilles Leclerc had dedicated *Journal d'un inquisiteur* to the man, and Chamberland had brought him right into *L'Afficheur hurle*. André Garand had known him in Montreal, and talked about him in Paris, and then, on André's advice, I bought Jacques Berque's book of reflections on decolonization, and found him at the top of a chapter. The name is Gaston Miron, and at the time I was inquiring into *parti pris,* its origins and extensions, Miron had not published any book. He was all legend, all companion, all conversationalist and comrade.

"It's hard to say why," Garand had said. "Perhaps Miron is a myth-fancier. But he recites. I remember times when Gaston recited whole sections from *La Batèche* for us, just like that, sitting across a table like we are now. I remember whole afternoons we spent together, talking, talking. Try to get Gaston to recite for you if you meet him when you go back."

Gaston had been translated into Arabic, Garand told me, and perhaps he was referring to the passage quoted in Berque's book:

> moi je gis muré dans la boîte crânienne
> dépoetisé dans ma langue et mon appartenance
> déphasé et decentré de ma coincidence

The lines, almost medical in their description of a suffering mind, are from a fragment Miron called the finale to his *Monologues de l'aliénation délirante,* and they occur in a passage I would translate this way:

> Around me is the opulent city,
> mighty St. Catherine, the street that charges
> through an Arabian Night of neon light
> while I, I live in a prison brain
> stripped of my poetry, my language, and my homeland
> askew and adrift from my place of belonging
> I rummage my memory and search my flesh
> for the cries that will render a nationless reality.
>
> I go down to the cringing part of town
> where the air they breathe is pestilential
> and find here my truth, my life constructed
> off the scrap and junk of History—and this I claim, this I assume

> and drift among its swirl of dead-end streets
> refusing a personal salvation; a deserter,
> identifying myself as one of the humiliated
> and wanting men to know what I have known.

When this passage appeared in the literary magazine *Liberté* in 1963, a few months before the first issue of *parti pris,* it was followed by the dates 1955–1959, meaning it was composed in the last four years of the life of Duplessis. Thus it predated the separatist movement and the FLQ and the socialist-separatist integration of *parti pris,* it preceded the naming of the condition of Quebec as colonial, and if it contains a hint that the cringing part of town may explode, that others may assume its humiliation, then it anticipates. But it wasn't published until 1963, in a number of that secularist, liberal magazine which also contained a concerned article on the FLQ by Fernand Ouellette. (The FLQ, this Quebec emulation of the Algerian rebels, had arrived to trouble the consciences of French-Canadian intellectuals, its bombs and the death one had caused had raised the question of means among those who had proposed changes, and Ouellette, Algerian sympathizer though he considered himself, said no to violence.)

Other North American poets had written of the alienation of the cities, but most of them were Americans—in the sense of U.S. citizens—and for them using the English language to describe the feeling was to triumph over it, and the city enriched the language with its new neon words. But for Miron, the Québécois is "the sub-man, the suffering grimace of the Cro-Magnon," the less-than-American, and the city subtracts from his language, alienates in the simple geographical sense of rendering him an alien, a foreigner. (Joual, if it is the result of the colonization of Quebec and its working people, is, it has always seemed to me, *also* what American English is: the meeting of an old language with a new continent. But treasuring it for this positive fact about it, still visible through the sad colonial circumstances in which it took place, had never appealed to writers up to Miron's generation. It was not until the *partipristes* that some signs of embracing and affirming joual were seen among writers, and even they saw in it, so they *said* anyway, the frailty of French in America, not its resilience.) Miron does not even command the language imposed upon him, the sub-man is not even equipped to *give in* to the alienating forces. English is the language of most of the signs on St.

Catherine Street, but when the poet tries to integrate some English into his poem to represent the French-Canadian as the thing, the object, of his English-speaking employer, his choice of expressions has a false sound:

> l'homme du cheap way, l'homme du cheap work
> le damned Canuk

Miron cannot seize the precise tone of the boss as he speaks of his worker, but he senses it is hostile. These descriptions of the colonized Québécois, sub-man, cheap labor, damned Canuck, are from the few fragments of Miron's unpublished masterpiece, *La Batèche*, which *Liberté* printed in that issue. The anglicisms he put in the mouth of his English employer may not ring true to an English-speaking ear (*Canuck* is not favored as an abusive term for the French-Canadian by the English, who do not grant the French speaker the exclusive title to Canadianness he has traditionally claimed), but to the French speaker they suffice to convey the sort of thing he has heard hurled at him. Thus Major drew on Miron to call his autobiography *Mémoires d'un jeune canoque*. Miron's own title I have not been able to find a translation for. *The Curse? The Goddam?* (*Batèche*: from *baptême*, baptism, a sacrament and therefore a swear word in French Canada.)

I wanted to meet Gaston Miron and asked Chamberland to help me. He suggested a three-way conversation and I was pleased with the idea, but he didn't call back. I arranged, shortly afterward, to attend a meeting of the Mouvement de Libération Populaire, the political movement that grew out of *parti pris*, in which both Chamberland and Miron were active. It was an important meeting because the members were to discuss a plan for solving the problems of survival the group was having then—1966—by merging with another group, the Parti Socialiste du Québec. I found Chamberland, but not Miron.

Miron, however, arrived in the middle of the discussion. The vote to negotiate into the PSQ had been taken and the talk was of the conditions to be set. Miron the clown came into play. Gawky, looking perhaps older than his mid-thirties because of a middle-aged formality about his grooming—black hair slicked back flat and conservative, one string falling loose, horn-rimmed glasses, blue suit. He leaned awkwardly against the tables at the back of the dingy hall not far from the door he had entered, squeezing through the crowd, swinging his arm up to put a question. His questions were at the same time silly and shrewd. Was there a historical precedent for a revolutionary party going into a nonrevolutionary one? Was this fusion pure and simple or a federation?

"I ask these things—you know, deep down, I'm really sort of for it—I'm just asking to give you more arguments." Laughter.

"Gaston knows the precedents," another partisan of the PSQ merger told me later, referring principally to the Bolshevik presence within the Russian Social Democrats. The thing was that some less erudite MLP members were still skeptical: "He just wanted to make the discussion as complete as possible."

Chamberland and I did not manage to pin down Miron for more than a few minutes that night, and what I will tell of him is based on a scattering of occasions when I was able to halt him briefly. At the time he could have been described as the world's most famous unpublished writer. He had published only a few poems and parts of poems in a few newspapers and magazines. (This is no longer true—in 1970 he published a volume of his verse.) His fame was made of many things: of the English editor's reference in the preface to *Poésie/Poetry 64* ("I take it Montreal is Gaston Miron to the French Canadians"), of the praise of a Vancouver professor compiling his history of French-Canadian literature for Paris publication ("His *La Braise et l'humus*, that poem of unhappy love, would be enough to give him his permanent place"), of a young *parti pris*-oriented academic named Jacques Brault drawing what seemed like all the young writers of Montreal except Miron himself to a high-ceilinged University of Montreal hall for a lecture on "Miron the Magnificent."

"In the 1950's many of us were interested in politics," he told me on one occasion, "but this rarely showed in our poetry. Myself, Yves Préfontaine, others, perhaps implied some political meanings in our love poems. And Gilles Hénault, for example, was once in charge of the whole Sudbury section of the Communist Party. But it was not until the young ones came along that literature itself became a political act." (Miron himself, as we have seen, had come close to writing-as-politics, but had not published until just before the young ones appeared.) He went on: "They say we've tacked our leftism on, as an afterthought, that all we're really interested in is independence, nationalism. In fact, it really happened the other way around for many of us: our first concern was social. I myself ran for the social-democratic party, the Canadian CCF, in Outremont in 1957 and 1958, and rolled up a good vote, too, for a Quebec riding: about 1,900 in each case. But as time went on I found it harder and harder to contain my social demands within a pan-Canadian framework in which I found no understanding, none, for the particular character of the struggle in French Canada. It was the disappointment in this attempt, the lack of comprehension in the English-Canadian socialist milieu, that made me see that Quebec must break out of this national repression to move toward socialism on its own path."

Miron fingered his Western sandwich in the "Canadian cuisine" restaurant—i.e., American snack bar—just down the street from the Librairie Déom, the bookstore and occasional publishing house on St. Denis Street in eastern downtown Montreal where Miron long made his headquarters, the base for his own publishing house, Les Editions de l'Hexagone. Under its imprint the main Quebec poets of his generation have been published, the ones he mentioned as hinting at politics but not openly practicing it in their work. Now Miron was into his favorite themes, the ones he harps on when he gets up behind a microphone at a bar on St. Catherine Street or in a resort in the Laurentians.

"We have to mine the national past for the themes, the traits that have marked us. These can be negative, destructive; we have to face them. French-Canadians have always, for example, been given to nostalgia, to living in a dreamworld woven from the past. The logger in his camp will sing"—and here he, softly, truly, over his sandwich, sang—"Oh, the days are long from morn to night/And my girl she forgets to write." The bit was folklore, but later that year a Radio-Canada newscast producer who wrote songs and sang on the side took the same theme and made it into a piece of modern folklore, a ballad sung by a worker at the huge Manicouagan hydroelectric project in northeastern Quebec, that big technical accomplishment of the Lesage regime, whereby a French-speaking state rivalled Anglo-Saxon private technology and provided the French-Canadian petty bourgeoisie with a symbol as well as a source of power. The worker to his girl:

> Si tu savais comme on s'ennuie
> A la Manic

> Tu m'écrirais bien plus souvent
> A la Mani—couagan.

Sung by its author, Georges Dor, to a heart-rending cabin accompaniment, this was a mighty hit on Quebec juke boxes.

Miron told of receiving a call from representatives of the same state technological class that built and saw itself reflected in the Manicouagan dam, planners now for the coming Montreal world's fair:

" 'Mr. Miron,' they said, 'we'd like to ask your permission for something. In designing the Quebec pavilion at the fair we planned to inscribe in certain places on its walls extracts from Quebec poets and we wanted to include one from your work.' I told them: 'No. You've exploited, scorned, excluded poets, spat on them, allowed them to starve in your midst, Chamberland, me, others, you've violated every vision of nation and of community we have projected. And then, when you are putting on your show, you want to adorn it with our phrases. No sir. Never.' "

He was less categorical about Expo as an international meeting place, however. "I may finally publish this year. Not because I want to any more than I have, not because I think the time is any more appropriate, but there is to be an international conference of writers at Expo and it will be difficult for them to invite me if I haven't published. Quebec writers must talk to their fellows in other countries, in other contexts, must try to explain, win support." This internationalism he believed in even when it didn't produce much—when, as he told me another time, "they got up a meeting for me and a few others with some English-Canadian poets, a Toronto group. Raymond Souster and Jay Macpherson, among others. We couldn't get through to them. Not a ray: 'But can you not express yourselves freely within a Canadian framework?' It kept coming back."

When I told him I was off for a summer's trip to Latin America, he said he had an address for me. A poet in one of the Latin countries who had translated him down there. The address was in Managua, Nicaragua, and when I called on the poet in question, he turned out to be a young student-instructor in history at the country's national university, partly invalid and living with his middle-class family in a small house near one of the grandiose stadia the Somozas, Nicaragua's lineage of dictators, had built in Managua. He was working on a Miron extract published in *parti pris,* on a copy left with him by an Argentine friend who had been to Montreal. The plan was to publish in a university literary magazine, but his French was weak, he had become bogged down on Miron's lines

> Le non-poème
> ce sont les conditions subies sans espoir
> de la quotidienne altérité

(hard for me too, but it means: "The non-poem/is the lot, accepted in hopelessness/of "—and this was the part that stopped the Nicaraguan—"daily differentness") and the project had been delayed: now it seemed unlikely that the magazine would be bringing out another issue.

Still, he was interested in Miron—"Is he a young man, Gaston Miron?"—in Quebec—"To us you are North American, not part of the underdeveloped world"—and in *parti pris*—"Why so much anti-clericalism in the magazine?" My questions for him were about the politico-cultural situation in Nicaragua, an attempt to discover just how rare was a marriage of the left and the artistic avant-garde. I asked about the election campaign that we'd plainly seen was on (one of the Somozas was making a comeback and riots followed his success some months later—I have never learned if my friend was among the leftist students imprisoned as a result).

"All the posters you've seen are for bourgeois parties. None of the revolutionary tendencies has money, or access to the press, or any of the traditional publicity techniques. Nor has a guerrilla method ever taken root in Nicaragua. Our revolutionary martyr, Sandino, attempted to develop a guerrilla base but he was wiped out by the Somozas, just as attempt after attempt to get a foothold outside of Managua, among the peasants, has been wiped out. We now have, us students, what we call a Sandinista Front—some labor elements are with us, and we work by demonstrations, pamphlets.

"Writers? Our best writers are reactionaries. Literature is not closely tied to the revolutionary movement. There is a small group of young writers who are also Marxists, but I can give you an idea of them by saying, quite unpretentiously, that I am the best known. We are not strong."

In Colombia, when we arrived, a controversy was being carried on between the Communist Party weekly and Gonzalo Arango, a talented young short story writer who had just refused a Cuban invitation to attend a big writers' meeting in Havana: "I'm not interested in dancing the Communist cha-cha-cha." But here perhaps (I wasn't able to track down Arango) we were in the presence of something different from the mere control of cultural life by the establishment described to me in Nicaragua. For Arango had been recommended to me by a Colombian friend who is a solid pro-Castro revolutionary; even the Communists took care in criticizing his refusal to visit Havana by saying, "Our Gonzalo may be a great literary talent, but . . ." and Arango, as he represents himself in his writings, is anti-bourgeois, contemptuous of capitalism, guru in fact to a whole youth movement in Bogota whose representatives in the bars asked us eagerly: "What do you have up in Canada? Beatniks? Existentialists? Here we're Nadaistas." *Nadaismo,* a local being-and-nothingness subculture whose name is not its only evocation of Dadaism, seems to be an arrested revolt, a start toward the politicization of bohemia which could move left despite the anti-Cuban testiness of its founder: such an evolution seems to have taken place within the North American beat enclaves of the fifties. So Colombia was beginning to appear a middle term on this scale of political involvement for the arts, with Mexico, with its long-standing revolutionary domination of intellectual, if not other, life, the far-left one.

I didn't find the occasion to give Miron a detailed account of the progress of his Nicaraguan translation. He is the kind of man who will stop and talk with you for hours on any number of chance occasions, but who never seems able to set aside an hour for a planned meeting. Indeed, the pictures I have of Miron are mostly ones of a man in a hurry, distraught, disorganized, shouting some judgment on literature or politics across a distant table at the Asociación Española, coat over his arm; or trying to flag a taxi in downtown Montreal at a busy hour; or stacking newly arrived volumes at Déom; or extracting the anti-colonial ramifications from a play by Aimé Césaire in the lobby of the Place des Arts at the intermission of a French-African troupe's performance.

It is conventional on the left in Montreal to see Miron as a tragic figure, the genius beaten down, intellectually, sentimentally, materially, by a harsh environment unheeding of his gentleness and sensitivity. The problem of the isolation of intellectual revolutionaries from the working class, even when their origins are in it, is raised, and it is mentioned that Miron, for one, was for a time a common laborer in the soft-drink trucking industry. "It destroyed Miron more than it accomplished anything else," will be the disabused comment. Miron himself encourages all this by such remarks as his riposte to the Quebec pavilion's request for rights to a couplet, by his entire style, both when he is bewailing his colonial lot and when he is laughing at himself, which he does often. He will tell the story of a lecture at which a teenaged girl came to speak to him afterward, chaperoned by her mother: "She told me, 'Mr. Miron, you have a poet's hands!'" And with a Chaplinesque gawk at his outstretched paws, he will break into his old-man's cackle of laughter.

Or at a recital at the University of Montreal, he will begin by announcing, those same paws clenching and unclenching before him: "In the 1950's, I recognized the fundamental truth about myself: *I am alienated!*" And swing into his verse, chanting automatically, eyes closed, without reference to the papers he shuffled nervously onto the lectern before beginning:

> You, my love, you stand up straight now
> We love with a strength as great as that which sunders us
> The rancid smell of falling metal interests
> You know I can return and be by you
> it's not the blood, the anarchy or war
> and yet I fight, I swear to you, I fight
> for I am in danger of myself to you
> and both of us of ourselves unto others
> the poets of these days are sentries to the world

Or:

> I write myself under the riot act
> I want to bleed upon you from my wounds
> I write, I write to make a fool of myself
> to make myself the court jester of everybody's court
> a volunteer on the auction-block of scorn

I find something tragic in Miron that is not simply the abuse that a revolutionary poet undergoes in a capitalist, colonized world. It is that such a figure, after a long familiarity with his status, can slide so easily into the role of court jester, can become frozen in his pose of scorned oppositionist. One example is the simple-minded separatism he manifested one day when he delightedly pulled from a bookstore shelf the newly published book by the wife of a French-Canadian industrialist, a paper manufacturer much smaller than the paper giants who rule the Quebec bush, but on the rise (the book, it was noted inside, was even printed on some of the output of her husband's mills), in which she describes a tour of Canada and chats with members of her own class in English Canada who are unwilling to accept her in their club. It had driven her to the edge of separatist pique. That a revolutionary could delight in such babbling from the rising native uppercrust dismayed me.

Also dismaying were some of Miron's published writings of the late 1960's, when he for once enjoyed a mass audience. Since working for Coke destroys you, you've got to take what intellectual work the establishment offers, and Miron wrote a book review column for the French edition of Canada's big family magazine, *Maclean's*. The columns reached ordinary readers at the edges of the province, the people of the *"terre de Québec, Mère Courage"* one of his lines finds pregnant with revolt, and yet it was completely conventional, conveying to them nothing of what is most important to him. It was not that Miron betrayed himself, told it like it wasn't; it was simply that in the month-in, month-out drone of admiration for the beauty of this book, the talent of that, not a word of the unbeautiful world beyond books came through. On a new Cuban novel appearing in French: "A new kind of writing, where eras, men, and languages mingle, lands, bloods, and voices mix, to give the 'Cubanism' of today." Yes, Gaston, but they had to bring down Coca-Cola to do it. Your reader in Abitibi has a right to hear this from you.

(And toward the end of the sixties, something like this feeling about Miron-the-ill-loved was stirring among the Shouting Signpainters themselves. The literary event of the year, said Maheu in a literary column he'd begun in *parti pris*, was Miron's nonappearance on the bookstands again in 1968, and the time had come to tell him enough is enough. Tell him good! "For the time has come to go beyond your—our—unhappiness. To persist in pursuing it, now that Quebec has found its name, that the colonized are building themselves a land, would be a kind of complacency. It is time to publish, because it is time to move on to other things. And if I permit myself to say all this, it is because your own *Love and Militancy* announces 'the luminous land of my being—offered with the taste of newness.' I know this Miron-the-luminous is possible. And I think Miron-the-happy would give us all a taste for finding a self-in-happiness in a Quebec of our own.")

While Gaston Miron linked with the younger writers who had combined writing and politics mostly through the politics—by joining their independentist-socialist movement—the novelist who was the clearest precursor of the Shouting Signpainters, Jean-Jules Richard, linked through the writing. It was éditions parti pris which brought him out of a long silence. And so, in 1966, while I was reading Aquin's *Prochain épisode* in search of parallels to *partiprisme*, I also found myself reading Richard's *Journal d'un hobo* in search of advance signals.

I already knew Richard as the author of *Le Feu dans l'amiante*, another generation's ballad of liberation, which told how the fire caught in the asbestos mines of the Eastern Townships in 1949 and warmed the French-Canadian miners to insurrection against their American bosses. The book was sloppily written and published by the author with little proofreading, and ends cynically with this exchange between the overseers: "The strike is over? They've won?" "That's what we're going to let them believe." But it traced the freeing of a few colonized souls, and before Richard had it printed at his own expense to gather dust in bookshop stock rooms, it had been serialized in *Combat*, the newspaper of the Communist Party in Quebec. Literature had thus become a political act for one writer as early as the 1950's, even to the half-embarrassing, half-amusing inclusion of a laudatory cameo of Gérard Pelletier, who consecrated *Le Devoir*'s reputation as a friend of labor by reporting the Asbestos strike from the strike towns in 1949, but who has since decided that the workers' cause is best served by the federal Liberal Party and has thus become, for *parti pris*, a *bête noire*.

I knew a few other things about Richard. Before Asbestos he had fought with the Canadian army in Europe and had published, more regularly, a collection of stories and a novel, *Ville rouge* and *Neuf jours de haine,* which had given him the reputation, in the dark old days, of being a sexy writer.

The novel which Richard now published with *parti pris* was called *Journal d'un hobo*. The old Richard, the Richard who wore CANADA on his shoulder in Italy, is very much present. (Has anyone remarked that there has been no French-Canadian novel of the Second World War except his? The big novel about the French-Canadians in Normandy, Armand Lanoux's *Quand la mer se retire,* is by a Frenchman; in *Bonheur d'occasion* the war is offstage, something the men in the heroine's life flee from or to.) This is the same Richard for whom the meaningful political commitment was hands across the country to the English-Canadian working class in the Canadian Communist Party. In general, a Canadian Richard, a coast-to-coast Richard. In the *Journal* we see him in the Depression, bumming across the country on the tops of boxcars. Calling himself by the anglicanism *hobo,* not even, as preferred in joual, *bomme* or *trimpe*.

Richard spent eight years writing the book; its conception dates from well before the *parti pris* identification of the French-Canadian ailment as colonial and it is a picaresque tapestry of all the Canadian provinces, from the Maritimes where the narrator is born, to British Columbia, Vancouver, the west coast. All this, and Southern Ontario, and Winnipeg, is sung with as much gusto as any English voice for national unity. The narrator goes across what is obviously his country without ever giving a thought to crossing the U.S. border. The book, one imagines, could do very well in English translation if issued from Toronto, but would not stand a chance out of New York. And yet the narrator is a personality of a bizarre ambiguity which may be read as a grotesque allegory on French-Canadian alienation. The character is what Paul Chamberland calls joual: a monster. A sexual monster, with both male and female genitals, a two-way sex life based on inborn anatomy.

The author imbues this bisexuality with a mystique, translates it into linguistic terms, using IL in capitals to designate his masculine aspect, ELLE his feminine, and giving the character the tic of an old-French form for I was: *j'étions,* or *I were*. The child, born to an Acadian fisherman, is approved by the local sorcerer—and here the flamboyant anti-clericalism of *Le Feu dans l'amiante* is back—as "the perfect being," God's realization of the best of both sexes in one. The effect is farcical until you remember where you've heard it all before—in the rationale of bilingualism propounded occasionally by the English biculturalist, more often by the bilingual French-Canadian himself, and exemplarily by the *bonne-ententiste* priest: the *parfait bilingue* is a better man than the unilingual, he is more complete, he is superior, even if he has added his second language in an attempt to catch up with a man who has amassed more worldly things than he in one language. There is an almost universal French-Canadian resentment of the English-speaking person who tries to turn the tables: few French-Canadians can abide hearing French spoken with an accent; the faintest hint of English will bring out whatever English the listener has. Cosmopolitanism, the delicacy about reminding the foreigner integrating your ranks that he still has a certain way to go, is alien to French-Canadianism, to a colonized people. Even a Québécois with enough self-confidence in his language to allow you to try your hand at it without feeling something is being taken from him is likely to engage you in a conversation about what in the world persuaded you to get involved with *our* language? Every French-Canadian is convinced that French is a splendidly difficult language—this is true among the most *joualisés*—and that English, by comparison, is easy. And that this is somehow the reason for the language patterns around him; that there may be ill will among the English who don't learn French, but there is above all a shrinking-away from the onerous task of mastering French. Indeed, in Montreal the facts seem to go far to bear this vision out: all but a handful of Italians (and even Italians have recently fought to have their children's primary school become an English, rather than a French, one) among neo-Canadians learn English rather than French, and all but a handful of French-Canadians put together some sort of English so that they communicate with the Anglo-Saxons in *their* tongue, and with Chinese restaurateurs and Greek merchants in a language foreign to both. Faced with that kind of defeat for the language you would speak if you spoke only one, the belief that you are superior for speaking two becomes necessary for surviving the humiliation. Nobody else needs or wants my language, the *colonisé* vaguely feels, but at least that makes it my private possession. When the English-speaker attempts to break that pattern, the French-Canadian reacts with, "You've got everything else and you want to take *that* from me too?"

These language problems get a fair amount of direct discussion in *Journal d'un hobo*, as when the hero's women (he is most often male) are living together: "Pastel began to learn English. Why did Bijou not learn French? It wasn't necessary." The closest Richard comes to making the language-sex analogy explicit, however, is this:

> There was man-father. The sorcerer would have liked him to be the father of men, but he was among the legions of the normal, and like them he died before his time, at sea. There was woman-mother and her rough affection. She did not have the luck to be the mother of men, she was normal. A rare being was engendered by them. He hauled at the fishing nets and made cakes. Love was normal in him. He made it as others breathe, without thinking about it. Without realizing it. But love is not meant for normal beings; they are too primitive. They hate and are always on the point of killing. Some are rough-hewn, others monstrous, born by chance, near misses, failures, black and heavy like lead, bitter as incense, made not to be completed.

Love, then, is not for the normal being, rough and black, born by chance, who is the colonized Québécois? I do not know whether Richard consciously meant this, whether this chant that all things are given only to the super-endowed, the twin-cultured, is satire, myth, or the subconscious of the author speaking, and I do not think that it matters. I was curious, though, and I would have liked to put this and other questions to him. But I could not. Gérald Godin, Laurent Girouard's successor as head of éditions parti pris, gave me a number but whenever I tried it, night or day, Mr. Richard was at work. At last the voice which informed me of this suggested: "I don't think Mr. Richard is interested in those things." This referred to my request for an interview for a book I was writing. Was the voice Richard's? I don't know, but I accepted its remark as the last word I was likely to get on the private life of this man who had kept his projects under wraps for eight years and pronounced himself in parables.

The climax of the *Journal* is a historical event from that store of left-wing lore to which I have suggested English-Canadian radical youth has access through parents or less direct processes of historical continuity, but which is generally closed to French-speaking revolutionaries. It is the march of the unemployed on Ottawa in 1931. The narrator undertakes it from Vancouver, and the Montreal group which is to join the marchers from the west, the army of the hoboes, "remained prisoner, three thousand men locked in their island. And the talks have become a fiasco. English fair play is exhausted, and though eight western representatives are allowed to approach parliament, elsewhere in the capital it's the hunt for hoboes that is on: out!" This is the Richard who could write in his magazine *Place publique* in 1952, when almost all public debate in Quebec centered around autonomy for the French province: "It is the workers who hold the mandate of the people for peace, in the face of war and of imperialism."

What is upsetting about the *Journal d'un hobo* is its quality of fantasy, Richard's need, still, after Asbestos, after *Bonheur d'occasion*, after joual, after *parti pris*, to put the problem grotesquely, to use the freak hero, to surround him with fanciful props and write halfway between the conscious description of events and a dream world. Richard has no trouble with joual: he writes even his straight French passages of narration in a staccato style reminiscent of joual's sentence pattern, and he can sketch a raucous barn-dance evening on a Quebec farm or a hunt for an open car on a freight train with a few strokes. He even seems unwilling to sustain a sentence through any complication of grammar, to prefer to paint in daubs, as in speech. Why then, this need to be removed from the world, to dehumanize, to steep in magic? We are back with Anne Hébert's never-never *Chambres de bois,* but on the rooftops and gutters of Winnipeg, where we should be hearing about real people and feeling real events. Why, if we are at last watching writers, the old and young, demystify life through literature, the gimmick?

Raoul Roy doesn't especially fancy himself as an appreciator of literature, doesn't think the arts have much to do with politics, and doesn't seem to frequent the Mirons, the Leclercs, the Richards. But he is one mentor who introduced the *partipristes* to the specific political ideas—decolonization, independence, and socialism—they brought into the Quebec debate, and made clear how necessary they were to each other. I went to his apartment on Amherst Street to talk to him about it. ("Yes, yes," he'd told me on the phone, "I founded the socialist independence movement, the movement that gave birth to *parti pris*. Certainly I consider myself implicated in their activity.")

Amherst is in the heart of the French east, one of its decaying secondary business streets. Roy's lodgings are a typical east end dwelling on the second floor: newspapers on the linoleum floor and stovepipe up the often-repainted plaster ceiling in the kitchen, old-fashioned rug, old-fashioned chairs, and old-fashioned glass-fronted bookshelf in the living room. But Roy has the Foreign Languages Publishing House complete works of Lenin in the bookcase and Mexican souvenirs, which strike an oddly non-bohemian-but-not-proletarian tone, on the walls. He received me in slippers and green plaid shirt, a lean man with neat gray hair, gray moustache, gray eyebrows behind plastic-rimmed glasses, and soon, too soon, we were into the sectarian points that divide him from other socialist separatists. For *parti pris,* paternalism:

"The *parti pris* group have often fallen into the error of insisting endlessly on their denunciations of the clergy, their anti-religious views, which can only alienate the bulk of the Quebec population. They have cut themselves off from those groups—the workers on the one hand, the new, technocrat class, the petty bourgeoisie, on the other—which have to be bound together in order to achieve independence. For us that is the first necessity. But I see that in their latest issue they are coming around to this understanding, are ceasing to insist on the old socialist arguments that alienate moderate elements that might be won to the cause of independence. For there are two kinds of socialism: the old proletarian kind that the Communist parties have preached in Europe, and a socialism of decolonization, more flexible, meant to construct a country."

Was he, then, for joining the RIN, the independence-first, economic-discussions-afterward movement? No, because, "The RIN has always been so timid, so petty bourgeois a group, I've never been able to bring myself to enter it. I've maintained good relations with it, though, right from Marcel Chaput's time." Chaput was the most middle-of-the-road of middle-of-the-roaders; Bourgault, the leader at the time, preferred to exude at least a faint pink coloring.

For Pierre Vallières and the FLQ Roy had nothing but scorn, for they had committed the sin of driving away the moderates. He did not comment on the first FLQ, several of whose members had been initiated in anti-colonial thought by his own early sixties study groups, but the Vallières wave he could not forgive for having as its most famous action the planting of a bomb which killed a French-Canadian woman at a factory where French-Canadian employees were on strike against a French-Canadian industrialist: "Whether Pierre Vallières was actually an envoy of the Canadian Communist Party or whether he was acting from his own motives, his actions could not have been more disastrous to the Quebec cause."

This blurring of a wish to spare French-Canadian capitalists the wrath of separatist revolutionaries into outrage at the death caused by revolutionary action disturbed me: if an English secretary in an English company had died instead of a French-Canadian secretary in a native enterprise, would Roy have found that okay? I didn't want to get into a baroque debate on the morals of violence, though, so I contented myself with posing another possibility: would Roy consider independence was worth it, was the all-important first goal, even if it were to take the shape of a fascist regime?

"Fascism," he said, and the tone suggested an answer always at the ready for Anglo-Saxon quibblers, "is a phenomenon of developed, independent countries in some circumstances—Italy, Germany. Fascism—the term means binding all classes together, like rods, halting any class struggle that is in process—is not a prospect in a people coming into its own from colonial status." Which makes me think of the Fanonist term "two-bit fascism"—for dictatorship in colonized but officially independent countries—from that literature that Raoul Roy did so much to make known in Quebec. But at the time I demurred, feeling once again faced with a baroque debate over terms. I simply concluded that Raoul Roy, Lenin lining his bookshelves or no, did indeed prefer independence on the right to no independence at all, and so tried to reach back to the political beginnings of this man who had helped the Shouting Signpainters combine socialism and separatism and who now found himself isolated from them and from everyone else who fought for causes related to his.

I asked him about a part of his experience I'd heard about from an English-speaking friend: his time as a translator into French for the Marxist Canadian Seamen's Union that fought many a bitter strike for the inland sailors on the Great Lakes cargo vessels until a nice, conventional, and, it turned out, high-handed United States union backed by a Canadian Liberal government hounded it off the Lakes. Had that helped form him politically?

He smiled. "Yes, but in Canadian trade unionism I ran into the same situation as a French-Canadian as everywhere else. I formed a left nationalist group which saw some hope in the New Democratic Party, in trans-Canadian social democracy. In 1960 we formed a club, went to the convention, fought for recognition of Quebec's particularity and right to self-determination. No luck. No way of getting through to the supposed left of the colonizing nation. Our group became clearly independentist—I made up this word, in fact, and popularized it by using it exclusively in all our press releases and urging our militants to impose it on the press's mind as being better than the federalists' term 'separatist.' We were called L'Action Socialiste pour l'Indépendance du Québec. We published *La Revue socialiste* and began the first full-scale discussion of the interrelation of the struggle for socialism and the struggle for our cultural, national liberation. This was not easy, for the concept of decolonization was only in its formative stages even in France at the time. But we followed the literature of the field, reprinted Albert Memmi's *Portrait du colonisé* "—in a mimeographed brochure like the magazine, but under the impression "Editions du Bas-Canada" and with a drawing on the green-paper jacket of a muscular, and white, *colonisé* sundering his chains—"and recommended Fanon's *Damnés de la terre* to our militants as soon as it reached Quebec in the early sixties—you know the importance it later took on."

Indeed, if it was not directly at his meetings that the FLQ terrorists became acquainted with this, their bible, it was certainly a result of Raoul Roy's influence in the young left-separatist world at that time. The one young militant of those days he mentioned in particular, however, was not an FLQer but one of my literary dynamiters. This came when I asked him what he thought of joual.

"I can't get as excited about it as some. It will pass. Young André Major was among the lads who attended many of our meetings and I published some of his writings in the magazine. It seemed to me then that he held some sort of literary promise, and I don't think events have contradicted me.

"We had other activities. We opened a restaurant just near here, in one of the shops on Amherst. I wanted a gathering place for militants; we christened it 'Au Mouton Pendu,' because we intended to string up once and for all the St-Jean Baptiste Day parade characterization of the French-Canadian as an unresisting sheep. But it didn't work out. I had three clienteles: first of all the militants for whom it was intended. Fine. But then a series of beatniks who came from other districts, who saw it as an offbeat hangout. And finally, young toughs from the neighborhood: these were uncontrollably wild, smashing the furniture, staging stunts, finally making it impossible to break even."

I thought I could see why this man would have influenced, but lost to other, more easygoing milieux, a group of youths hungry for an understanding of their society's plight. Sympathetic to youth, but seeing no relationship between beatniks and militants, poets and politicals; a Leninist, but sufficiently cold about the social suffering of French-Canadians to set it aside as an immediate concern when he reached the conclusion that national liberation must come first, he was far from the blend of passions which drove his young pupils.

He left me with a souvenir of a final contradictory element from his life. The Mouton Pendu was his second business misfortune in the slums of the east: earlier, just after the busting of the Seamen's Union at the end of the forties, he had gone into the haberdashery business on Amherst but had found that the shopping centers were killing the neighborhood commercial districts and gave up. The souvenir was a paper bag, such as he might have used to wrap me up a pair of underwear or socks in those days. It read:

RAOUL ROY
Articles and clothing for men
1853 Amherst St.   4223 St. Catherine W.
LA 5-3951   CL 9-1230

Now, as he had told me when I first called, he would have to leave for work. He worked evenings, in the newsroom of the federal television network, and took some comfort from the presence there of the odd sympathizer. Say, I'd worked for the Canadian Press, did I know, and here he named a young socialist-separatist who had also found that while waiting for the sun to rise on the new Quebec the most livable life offered him had been in the occupants' news agency, and now in the federal television network. Did I know him? I did, I'd run into him just a few months before, and thinking about him reminded me of a whole series of ironies of the colonial life.

When I had worked for the Montreal bureau of Canadian Press, I had had two colleagues who could be described as Marxists. One English, an immediate colleague on the main, English, desk; the other the French-Canadian socialist who was now working with Roy at the CBC. He was over in the French section, a translator of the vision of the world of our affiliate, Associated Press, for the consumption of the French-Canadian newspaper reader. Apart from adhering to the same, ostensibly universal, understanding of things human, the two men had much in common: both about thirty, both loners, marked by the acerbity of the radical-in-the-establishment, given to skepticism, irony, depreciation of the élans of more buoyant revolutionaries. The Québécois, lean, elegant, would put down *parti pris* for its calls to the working class: "The working class! The working class! The Quebec working class is not ready for revolution, anyone ought to be able to see that with a bit of looking. What does it know of organization, strategy, struggle? Give it ten, twenty years; give it some experience of defeat. Then maybe we'll be able to start speaking of a proletariat here." Or for its theories about joual: "What they don't know is that French here in Quebec has been steadily *improving* since the nineteenth century. Read the newspapers of that period if you don't believe it. Read the court reporting: all references will be to *la cour;* now our journalists overwhelmingly write *le tribunal.*"

The Anglo, round-faced and crew-cut, would also put down the *partipristes:* "With them it's 'If you don't agree, the hell with you.' No dialogue, nothing. I can't go for something where there's no discussion, no listening to critics." Or the general French-Canadian view of the *partipristes:* "So Claude Ryan and his *Devoir* think the boy revolutionaries aren't all that terrible, that they've enriched French-Canadian thought, are the first Marxists to see the light of day in Quebec? It gives you some idea of his level of knowledge. What about the Université Ouvrière?" (This was a small Marxist study group of the Raoul Roy days of left searchings.) And even the longer-standing, less-nationalist leftism of an earlier generation of Quebec socialists didn't satisfy my Anglo friend when it showed up in a rival magazine to *parti pris, Socialisme 64.* I thought an article in its first number on socialism in the United States—Quakers, Wobblies, Debs—would please him with its nonchauvinism, but no, "There they are, off in the clouds with various American movements from the past." Nothing French-Canadian intellectuals could do pleased him, the entire Quebec educated class seemed to him insufferably pretentious, comfortable, inauthentic: "The brilliant-intellectual type of reporter who doesn't bother with facts is *that* thick, of course, around *La Presse.*" Still, he liked ordinary French-Canadians, even wished well to the Pepsi Revolution (*Pepsi* being the Anglo-Montreal racist tag for the French, I have never known why), and ill to the WASPdom from which he sprang. ("What it seems to need is a Lenin to get the thing together.") And my Québécois Marxist was everything he didn't have any use for.

It was mutual. The Anglo was a halfhearted frequenter of the local Communist Party, the only left milieu which seemed to him bearably nonintellectual. The Québécois would sneer at a pacifist group of Anglo-Montrealers, "A Communist front!" reproaching it not with being red, but with being colonial, out of the Quebec picture, radicalism for the rich—like the Communists of Quebec. He would come to work loaded down with papers from Paris and store-bought novels. My Anglo stated that he never owned more than one book at a time—when he finished a paperback, he threw it away. It was very, very mutual, this unlove between anti-bourgeois workers in the bourgeois news factories. *Réciproque.*

A writer in whom everything was present, who told all the basic truths about the colonized Québécois even back in pre-separatist, pre-Marxist, pre-laïcist Duplessis days, was the playwright Marcel Dubé. He has never been associated with the *partipristes* in a precise way, by publishing with their house or writing in their magazine, or even, as far as I know, by socializing with them, but he should be mentioned here. Closer in generation to Gabrielle Roy than to the *partipristes* but a product of proletarian Montreal, his vision surpasses Roy's humane regret of situations and joins the younger writers in fighting them. In one important matter he surpasses them: I know him as a man of the theater, but most of what he has placed in the French-Canadian theater repertory began for him with television, and his statement on Quebec life is part of the era of the TV screen in the French-Canadian living room.

It is the young who fight in Dubé, and most often it is the young women. Listen to his 1953 heroine, in *Zone*. She stands in front of a backyard fence in the slums and tells why she joined a gang of teen-agers smuggling American tobacco into Canada, a gang sprung from this slum soil. Why she loved Tarzan, who has died by the time the French-Canadian cops close in. And when the cops turn lights, moralizings, and brute force on these adolescent French-Canadians who refuse to understand what the regime wants of them, they prefigure the French-Canadian cops who made the adolescent political criminals of the 1960's recite their acts of contrition, as the smugglers prefigure the terrorists. But listen, I quote from memory from an amateur production I saw in Sherbrooke:

> I was nothing before, life was just accepting misery, accepting things the way they'd always been; we were all of us nothing. With Tarzan it was different, we were doing something, we had something of our own. I became somebody then, I was a *smuggler!*

And in 1958 it was *Un simple soldat*, the story of a neighborhood tough who never could make a success of anything, except of being a private in the Canadian army. Here too it is the young girl, the soldier's factory-worker sister, who represents the will to fight; Joseph merely participates in battles. But what to do when the war ends, when there are no more battles? How to fit back in, hold down a job, avoid shooting off your mouth and getting into trouble? Joseph Latour never learns, and when the country is again at war it is like a solution, and Joseph, who never wanted to take off his battledress, goes to Korea and is killed. But first we hear from his lips as plainly as ever in all of Quebec literature just *how* terrible is that "Oedipus complex something terrible" that my friend spoke of as haunting the French-Canadian sub-man:

> JOSEPH (*pounding with his fists on the door to the bedroom of his father and stepmother*): That's right! That's right! Go sleep with fat Bertha. Twenty years now you've been sleeping with her and you don't

love her. But you had to marry her because you didn't have the guts to live alone. (*Falls to his knees on the floor.*) I didn't need Bertha, me. Nor you, dad, nor you neither. We could have stuck it out together, the two of us, all by ourself. But no! You hadta bring her in with us, into our house, all the way into my mother's bed. I've been wanting to tell you that for a long time, dad. But watch yourself, because I'm still here, still around to make you regret it for the rest of your life. The rest of your life, you hear me?

And in *Florence*, where once again it is the young girl who revolts, her old man understands but cannot make her mother, the conservative element to the last, do so:

In school, Toinette, and at church on Sundays, during election campaigns, in the plants and in the offices, everywhere, they've taught us to be scared. They said the best way to protect ourselves was to close ourselves in our houses, in our parishes, out of the way of trouble. When it wasn't the devil's picture they painted us, it was the English, or else some Communist. Outside of ourselves, nobody else was anything but evil and bad. No pleasures allowed, evil everywhere you looked. They taught us to be scared of ghosts and they took away our own things that belonged to us. That's the way they always educated us, that's the way they still are. And that's why we're all a bunch of wet hens! I understand Florence not wanting to share her life with a wet hen.

That was in 1960, the coming to power of the Liberals, the coming to power in Quebec of a progressive petty bourgeoisie, the adoption, in principle, of a will to change. Since 1960, Marcel Dubé's plays have moved out of the slums into the suburbs, up the high-rises, and Jean Duceppe, the actor who first delivered the above speech, now plays plump businessmen whose tensions, nevertheless, are not over. In *Les Beaux Dimanches* he asks his twenty-year-old daughter:

Why can't we talk any more? I don't know what you've become. Separatist, you say; socialist . . .

And in *Un matin comme les autres* he is an amoral ex-nationalist who hates the English he does business with on St. James Street, but most of all hates himself because he does not have it in him to respond to the challenge of a younger woman who, remembering an affair in Paris with an Algerian nationalist who died for his cause, would have *him* become a nationalist militant.

There is irony in Dubé's posing the commitment to separatism as the test of the Québécois's emergence from the old universe of fear. There is something sad in this man, whose entire writing career has been a painful, truthful, noble revelation of the humanity that fights for life in the slums of Montreal, accepting unquestioningly, now that the time of political involvements has come for Quebec artists, the Quebec petty bourgeoisie's petty-bourgeois ideal of liberation. But playwrights, in Marcel Dubé's day, were not ideologists, and whatever his development in the future, the Shouting Signpainters will always owe Marcel Dubé that pain, that truth, and that nobility. And it had all gone into the homes of east Montreal and districts like it all over Quebec; Dubé, ten years before the *partipristes,* had written true popular drama, taken by amateur troupes across the province; had found the way, for which the *partipristes* were still probing, to say revolutionary things to large numbers of ordinary Québécois, whether they go to the theaters, browse in the bookstores, or not. (He had even encountered censorship, when he proposed to have an office-worker character in one of his CBC serials become a separatist. The federal network required that it be changed to trade unionist, that—in days when proletarian playwrights felt called upon to be nationalist revolutionaries—being considered less radical.)

The year I finished my research on the Shouting Signpainters Paris became very interested in Quebec writing, but to someone whose enthusiasm centered around words as combat there seemed to be an obstinacy about missing the point. Robert Laffont brought out his Great Novel At Last, Aquin's *Prochain épisode*; Marie-Claire Blais, who already had an advocate in the English-speaking world in Edmund Wilson, won one of the half-dozen elite literary prizes for one of her novels, also a Paris republication of a Montreal original; and an unknown novelist, Réjean Ducharme, achieved first publication, and hence automatic fame, with France's reigning publishing house, Gallimard.

Marie-Claire Blais I delayed reading for fear that she would turn out to belong to a tradition of French-Canadian fantasts of which I was very weary when the Shouting Signpainters came along, and Réjean Ducharme seems to be the most dazzling fantast of all. His story of a Jewish (yes) French-Canadian girl who lives out bizarre adventures as a nonconformist Israeli infantrywoman (this was 1966) on an unidentified island, at sea, in ports around the world, and in the Palestinian desert is called *L'Avalée des avalés—The Swallowed* (feminine singular) *of the Swallowed* (masculine plural)—and springs from Quebec life in only the most oblique way. I cannot help but feel that the author, a comic acrobat of the language where Aquin is an anguished one, tells his greatest truth in his first chapter when he has his child-narrator say: "I am not interested in what goes on on the surface of the earth." The vaguely timed, vaguely situated character allegorically going through the Quebec *mal de vivre* is well established in Quebec literature, with the lost Catherine of Anne Hébert's *Chambres de bois* the classic case. Miss Hébert long lived in France, Miss Blais in the United States: both, in their declarations, insist they are striving for universality, are wary of the local, the regional, the too precisely political or québécois. Anne Hébert, at any rate, seems to me to be doomed in her search for the human above and beyond the Québécois, to have missed the most human path given to a Québécois in the twentieth century, that of contesting the *mal de vivre* on its home ground. To be, by her very striving for universality, less likely to interest other humans of the universe, by her very unease with her region, regional. Ducharme has outdone her in audacity, in any case, by working into his novel quotes from the Quebec poet Emile Nelligan and some borderline joual, and *still* selling his manuscript to the *métropole*. And Ducharme lives in Montreal, refusing even to go to Paris for the publication of his books, in an anonymity so severe there was a long controversy after *L'Avalée* came out as to whether he existed.

On reading, Marie-Claire Blais' Prix Medicis, *Une saison dans la vie d'Emmanuel,* half supported my prejudice, half contradicted it. Its chapters, all but one, are nitty-gritty enough, but are set in rural Quebec in a world of cruel field labor and theocracy which takes us back to Maria Chapdelaine, the classic French-Canadian peasant girl of French fiction (there is, for example, no word of a TV set in the parlor). The only resistance offered are the delirious writings of a tubercular adolescent. Miss Blais' heart is with him, this dying Emmanuel, and her tale is in no closer touch with the French Canada of

Visitation Street than his jottings are. Until the last chapter, when, suddenly, the saintly daughter glides unprotesting into prostitution and two brothers are grabbed up by mutilating factories and brushed by priestly pederasty. The real world declares itself and real theocracy triumphs.

Parti pris was interested in letters and liberation; the two were about equally present in the founders but each still-segregated interest was bound to attract later adherents for whom what counted was literary liberation, or for whom literature was all right, but you had to get serious at some point. One of the literary-liberation followers was Raoul Duguay, the be-bopping poet I spoke of earlier, who had become *parti pris*'s literary chronicler in 1966. Duguay's politics were summary: separatism, a bit of populism, but nothing to protect him from letting out such remarks as this in a *parti pris* review: "But I nevertheless found the scene where tin cans, fruits, vegetables, everything in a super-refrigerated Steinberg's store comes crashing down in a heap to be (I'm serious) 'the revolutionary act' par excellence against Judeo-American imperialism." In short, a petty-bourgeois left-wing intellectual in whom the leftism is the weaker of the terms, and the petty bourgeois the more pronounced. For whom, if literature and liberation were both Good Things, literature was best of all.

With *L'Avalée des avalés,* he said when the novel came out, Quebec literature begins. It had a father. To this I protest that it had already begun, had in fact found more characteristic paths before Gallimard consecrated it, that indeed even the poetry of Raoul Duguay himself would be enough to make that true. In fairness to Duguay it should be said that he did not stress the Gallimard imprint, the acceptance in Paris, in his appreciation; but there is no doubt that such marks and such acceptances will count in the decolonization of Quebec, and this will be true even with a post-Gaullist France situated several degrees to the left. The population figures simply exclude for the moment the kind of cool autonomy English and Spanish America enjoy with reference to their European founding lands, and this creates certain problems of authenticity for the Quebec artist. But the question arises: How well was France able to grasp what is most authentic in the emerging Quebec culture?

Europe has always had trouble comprehending America, of course, its reactions vacillating between disdaining what seemed, where it was not an actual wilderness, a cultural wilderness, a land without refinement, a culture of ignoble savagery; and overcompensating, enjoying those very rudenesses, that very savagery: jazz, skyscrapers, cowboys and Indians. Or the two were integrated into a more coherent view of the continent: America was cruel and mercantile, but from the *victims* of its cruelty came cries that were all the more human because of that.

Two meetings in Paris gave me the feeling France is at the moment in the disdainful stage of the oscillation. The first was with the popular publisher Robert Laffont. I flip open the novel in whose blank opening pages I took notes from our conversation. The novel is in the Laffont series, now defunct, "The Young Novelists of Canada": maple leaf, distinguished names of the meagre literary opposition of the Duplessis period, and this publicity blurb: "Our aim is to open to the French public the most significant of what is being published in French in Canada; there will, we hope, emerge an image of present-day Canada more complex and richer than the one that has long been imposed on French readers. A new discovery of America . . ." Good will, then, a record of pioneering in French awareness of Quebec. And an openness to the new world: Laffont has built his house, since the war, on translating American successes, adopting American jacket-design techniques, selling via American book-club procedures. As I entered his office, he was saying "Okay" into a phone, and I see in my notes many a remark of willingness to see French literature taken in new directions by such interventions as Quebec writing: "Their language differences aren't errors, it's a new language. And it's accentuating itself; if we don't make our languages converge we'll all be the poorer. Paris is very closed, you know, we have four or five languages of French origin around us that are unreadable to us—3,000 people still speak Provençal—and we are so busy with ourselves; if you don't freshen our views from without I don't know what will become of us."

And yet . . . Was I wrong to hear a bit of paternalism when Laffont said, for example, "I'd be very glad if there were only one language around the world, French." Or: "Regionalism I find very pretty—calling an automobile *un char* . . . Or the argot of the Beatles, of the beatniks." Was I wrong to find all this somehow perfunctory, the leaven in a basic confidence that Paris would go on, would have to go on, judging, consecrating, sometimes finding wanting, sometimes praising what overseas French-speakers had to offer? We spoke of a more recent Laffont French-Canadian novel, this one first published in Paris, not a reprint of a Montreal issue: Marcel Godin's *Ce maudit soleil*. The book, the story of a city-bred clerk in a logging camp, has its rough, tough, "Canadian" aspects, to please the positive, taste-for-the-primitive side of European liking for America. On the other hand, words like *cook* are italicized and translated from the joual in footnotes. My Quebec Marxist wire-service friend defended this: "Do you know the German for 'cook'? And yet, it's just as close to English as English is to French." Yes, but I think that if I were reading a whole novel about people who used the German word for cook, I could figure it out.

"Godin is my author," Laffont told me. "We brought him to Paris, had him work on his manuscript. Not to kill local color—when his loggers speak they have to speak like loggers—just to clarify certain points that were *grammatically* difficult. This is needed if you want to reach an international public; I'm not against taking the opposite course, but if you become regional you must content yourself with reaching the public you have sought. I'm an internationalist. There is, yes, this terrible mistrust of Paris, this complex, sensitivity—it is even stronger in Canadian authors than in other non-French speakers of French. But I think Godin understood. Canadian authors are, after all, lucky, as small national groups go. A first Canadian book has as much chance of selling here in France as any other, and it also has a larger market assured in Canada than a new French novelist can hope for. And their manuscripts are much more readily read here than, say, Czech novelists' books in translation, or Flemish novels. I have one reader reading Czech literature and making recommendations to me about translation possibilities, but a whole staff of French readers."

And then he told me he had in hand what everyone, his contacts in Montreal, the people at the Cercle du Livre de France, his readers in Paris, told him was something big at last, something major, a breakthrough in French writing in America.

"Jacques Renaud?" I asked. *"Le Cassé?"*
No, he said, and turned to consult a secretary about the name, which escaped him. Then:
"Hubert Aquin. *Prochain épisode."*
The second conversation nicely fills out the picture of this problem, because it was with a man who had all the reasons to sympathize with the kind of thing the *partipristes* were doing which were absent in Laffont, the businessman-publisher, for whom political commitment was acceptable, but merely a biographical note on a dust jacket, and who was not likely to be devoured with enthusiasm for literary experiments which carried a heavy revolutionary meaning. The second conversation was in the offices of François Maspero, the most rigorously Marxist publisher in Paris, the man who brought Frantz Fanon to the FLQ, who publishes nothing but revolutionary nonfiction, whose offices are more like a political headquarters than a business office. Publications from left movements in the United States on the desk, young people in sports clothes around. One was Emile Copferman, author of a book on French youth, another on proletarian theater, listed on the masthead of Maspero's magazine *Partisans.* Aware of *parti pris,* reader of even such less ambitious separatist publications as the propaganda tabloid *Québec libre,* a sympathizer:

"There is the presidential campaign now, but as you can see from our latest issue, we don't see any point in campaigning for a discredited pseudo-leftist like Mitterrand. Some on the left even think we should favor the return of General de Gaulle. Well, the one positive element I can see in a victory or in gains by Mitterrand's federation of lefts is that it will be a blow to Gaullist power, it will create an instability out of which a real left program might emerge. But we don't see much point in trying to revivify the old left structures which have fitted in with capitalist structures here, the Communist Party and the rest. Our hope is that there will emerge a new left"—and the same latest *Partisans* he referred me to carried a long reprint from the *National Guardian* of New York on the emergence of this expression and movement in the United States—"which can only take form around the main theme of all of the publishing Maspero has done, the challenge to the developed countries from revolution in the Third World."

It was not, then, pedantic Marxism which would be the basis for Copferman's misgivings about *parti pris;* he too sought a new left, he too centered it around Fanon and the anti-colonial struggle. But when I asked him about *parti pris:*

"What we get from reading *parti pris* here is something very vague, hard to pin down, muddled. No clear revolutionary strategy seems to have emerged, there is merely a series of themes that keep coming back, of irritations the magazine keeps expressing. And their literary ideas are hard to follow. Do they really think revolutionary and popular-language literature can move a population to political action?"

I protested as gently as I could that perhaps some of these problems were not finally solved in Europe either; that, for example, Maspero itself had seemed to suggest a certain interest in the literary, artistic, poetic side of revolutionary politics in publishing *Songs of the New Spanish Resistance*, a French-Spanish anthology of anti-Franco lyrics said to be heard in the Spanish countryside of late. The girl who had done the translation of that book was in the office and she intervened to stress that nothing much should be read into the publication of the songs: "Even their authenticity has since been questioned. We don't know for sure their origin and their diffusion. The purpose of publishing the book was elsewhere."

So I was not to conclude that Maspero's hard-cores imagined modern Spaniards were being whipped to revolt by minstrelsy: the purpose of publishing a *book* of Spanish rebel songs was elsewhere—I could only conclude somewhere in France, in the petty-bourgeois French intellectual left which liked to *think* the cultural objects it lined its rooms with had something to do with the social struggles of peoples out there somewhere. I purchased a copy of *Les Damnés de la terre* at Maspero's book counter and left his student-quarter offices feeling that the clicking into place of the comprehensions on which to base a new, new-left International was still far away, that what the Shouting Signpainters had to say had somehow not passed the translation from joual to French.

I spoke at the beginning of my account of éditions parti pris of Claude Jasmin, author of its second volume, the TV play *Blues pour un homme averti*. Jasmin was for a time one of the *parti pris* stable of writers—he has in fact published more books with the house than any other writer, three at last count—without really being a Shouting Signpainter. This is because there is something of afterthought in his association with the younger writers. He existed as a writer, even as a fairly popular one, before *parti pris*. The novel in which I took my notes during my conversation with Robert Laffont was his *La Corde au cou*, published originally by Montreal's Cercle du Livre de France. He has never contributed to the magazine *parti pris*, nor taken very clear political positions. He has, rather, been art critic, CBC set designer, novelist, playwright, polemicist, a little bit of everything, and of course associated with the general tendency toward loosening the Quebec social system and having sympathy for common folk. Yet Jasmin's second publication with *parti pris* deserves mention, for it blended in with the new literature created in Quebec by the Shouting Signpainters, and hence was testimony to the existence of that literature.

The book was a novel called *Pleure pas, Germaine*. It was written in a joual as relentless as that of *Le Cassé*, although in Jasmin's case the full revolutionary intent of using this deteriorating new-world French cannot have been present. Why, then, imitate the revolutionaries? In an article in *Le Devoir* in the midst of the joual controversy, Jasmin offered this answer, perhaps the most beautiful quick manifesto of joual literature: *"Pour faire vrai."* To be true, to tell it like it is.

But, as André Major noted, Jasmin seems to proceed in the belief that the truth of joual is of limited application in French Canada, is purely proletarian. His manifesto seems to cut deeper than even he intended, for both before and after *Germaine* he has written in standard French: before in *Blues pour un homme averti*, in *La Corde au cou*, a novel whose narrator seems to be of working-class origin, even in another novel with a separatist hero, *Ethel et le terroriste*.

Jasmin's one joual excursion was dedicated to fourteen FLQ members and was a first person account of an automobile trip north from Montreal along the southern coast of the St. Lawrence River to the tip of the Gaspé Peninsula by a Montreal worker who believes he will find there the explanation of the violent death of his teenaged daughter, unclarified by the police. Germaine is his redheaded wife, a native of the Gaspé region he is heading for, and the title is a joual comforting in the midst of tragedy: "Don't cry, Germaine honey." Several themes which Jasmin had found reinforced, singled out in himself by reading *parti pris*, are involved here: the battered, baffled underdog condition of the Quebec worker, with his too-large family, his inflated pride and deflated means, his linguistic inferiority in the Anglo-Saxon economy; the exploration of the land, its vastness, the farmed and wooded backdrop to its squalid cities, its place names, some saintly, some strange and Indian, some English or Scottish, accepted here as piquant, not menacing like the English presence in the cities. And finally, when ti-Gilles Bédard learns, at Percé on the tip of the Gaspé where a mighty square rock stands with a hole in its center out in the sea, that his daughter was not killed, that there is no culprit to be found at the end of the line, and that the young man with the beard whom he thought he would have to kill is a friend, an ally against the exploiters, and is in fact organizing the Gaspesians to fight those exploiters, Jasmin has given his fourteen FLQers in fiction the dream of a liaison between the revolutionary intellectual and the common people they were not able to bring about in fact.

There is a cooked-up quality to all this, however, which makes it at one and the same time the most conscious work of joual literature to come out of the movement and the least passionate; precisely, the most *self-conscious*. But some of the talk is good, some moments have gotten down Quebec speech forms which are real, which needed getting down. Such as this bit, which the publishers extracted to use as a jacket blurb:

> I was eighteen. Signed up in the army. When the war finished up, I checked outa camp. All by my lonesome. And I meet this big redhead, this nice waitress chick at the Roxi Snack Bar, just across from the Empire. And it was during a picture in technicolor with Judy Garland and Fred Astair [sic], with color spilling all over the theater, that I popped the question to my big Gaspé redhead from Bonaventure.

In his next book for *parti pris*, Jasmin was already back to a more traditional way of writing. It was a book of short stories about women, proletarian and petty bourgeois, and was called *Les Coeurs empaillés—Stuffed Hearts*. The intent was to chuckle O. Henry-like at several often-observed sentimental situations rather than to solidarize with the downtrodden, so the language was once again standard. Jasmin has mentioned that these stories were rejected by *Châtelaine*, the women's magazine published in French and English by *Ma-*

clean's. He had no choice but to make a book of them, because *Châtelaine*—and this may have something to do with the development of the short story in Quebec—was the sole professional fiction market in French Canada, the only magazine, apart from a few infrequent literary journals, to publish Quebec fiction.

Parti pris itself, after tapering off into the odd poem, gave up publishing imaginative literature altogether, even by its own founders. Thus extracts from *L'Afficheur hurle* appeared in an early *parti pris* before book publication, among the political texts and factual articles, but previewing *L'Inavouable* before the book came out was something Chamberland was willing to leave to the University of Montreal literary magazine *La Barre du jour.* And the pre-publication extract from Renaud's new novel *En d'autres paysages* was scarcely more than an advertisement in *parti pris.* "Quebec literature needs the éditions parti pris," said the ads for the house, but the *partipristes* seemed to feel Quebec literature could do without space in their magazine—except for criticism, which as often as not dealt with writing from outside their tradition. This may be part of a general trend to the informational, but it is acute in a small collectivity like Quebec. And though Laurent Girouard, André Major, Jacques Renaud, Jacques Ferron have sold a few of their more candied tales to *Châtelaine,* it is understandable that the apparently robust Quebec novel market attracts them and other Quebec writers more.

Jacques Ferron. Another older writer who had come to *parti pris* from a writing career elsewhere and had soon published more there than most of the originals of the house. Two novels: *La Nuit* in 1965, and *Papa Boss* in 1966. These two added to a long list of other volumes—novels, plays, and above all stories, plus articles, letters-to-the-editor . . .

Jacques Ferron had had a political history elsewhere, too, like Gaston Miron. A nonseparatist socialist in the fifties, he went through meeting, election, and convention after meeting, election, and convention. It taught him, bleak though such a life was in the minuscule left of Duplessis's Quebec, some things about the interrelationship of his socialism and his Frenchness. I remember him standing up in Plateau Hall, just back of the Jacques Cartier Normal School in Lafontaine Park, where just about everyone in the now larger-than-minuscule left of Quebec had gathered in the summer of 1962 to attempt to found a Quebec New Democratic Party, a task left undone after the federal party was founded and most provinces had set up their own sections. The meeting was split—and the split was, of course, the reason for the delay—between nationalists and pan-Canadians. At its founding convention the NDP had gone to great lengths to embrace the leftish nationalism Lesage's coming to power had revealed to English Canada, and the result had been a word: *nation*. Long unwilling to call Quebec, or French Canada, a nation (while accepting, oddly, calling its nationalism a nationalism), progressive English Canada at last said okay, you guys are a nation, and we're another, and Canada is not a nation but a country made up of two nations. But it wasn't enough, and the nationalists in the New Party clubs and other formative groups which had sprung up in Quebec in anticipation of the new Canadian social-democratic party's launching wanted a party of their own, not a provincial branch of the NDP. Detailed, oh so detailed, debates on the class-race juxtaposition in Quebec were the stuff of this meeting in Plateau Hall, and Ferron, by now somewhat weary of this debate which had been his life, tried to get at it this way: "The story is told that someone asked George Bernard Shaw if it were possible for an Englishman to be a socialist in India. Shaw said it might be, if the Englishman first *gave up his privileges*."

But would the English socialists of Quebec comprehend? Would they be able to make the leap from their familiar thought patterns on French-English relations, ethnic groups, majorities, minorities, language rights, to the world of colonizers and colonized into which Ferron's comparison led them? Would they be able to grasp the irony of his quoting them an *Englishman's* anti-colonialism? Of course, they would half-understand. My memories from that meeting are of flashes of half-understanding. A French-Canadian official of the United Steelworkers of America: "In the mining industry we have English owners, but we also have the Beauchemins—and they're French-Canadian, Catholic, Knights of Columbus!" An angry English-speaking old leftist from west Montreal: "When we canvassed in the last elections, the people we found in our riding were not all financial potentates." A French-Canadian sociologist:

"There is the notion of 'French' and the notion of 'poor'; somehow they are related, but we cannot quite make them coincide." Another old leftist, this one a Pepsi-lover: "All through our history it has been this way. In the forties, the Bloc Populaire was close in outlook to the CCF, but they couldn't get together." An English-speaking *new* leftist: "What we have got to understand is the similarity of the French-Canadian movement to the American Negro one. For the Negroes, their militancy is closely related to their religion." One of the French-Canadian experts of the federal party: "There are, it seems to me, two kinds of nationalism. One is very healthy; the other I would call a *visceral* nationalism . . ." And a young Quebec socialist intellectual schooled at Oxford, to an older French-Canadian who was angry about some development: " 'I'll pull out my boys,' you say. That's anti-democratic, that whole attitude!"

But we are far removed from Ferron. Except that, while awaiting the acts that would explain to the English in Quebec better than words their relations with the French, Jacques Ferron came closer, perhaps, than any to making comprehensible the scandal of the master telling the slave which forms of revolt are healthy, which visceral. But this is only a glimpse, a fragment. Everything one can recount about Ferron, his long neck projecting out of his baggy blue suit, his hawk nose, his shaven-but-still-black cheeks, his soft, humorous voice, the anger that is nevertheless his overwhelming characteristic, seems a fragment, and the more so when it is a matter of Ferron the writer. For he is the writer in Quebec most difficult to capture, Jacques Ferron. Let us move from the political man to the writer with another glimpse, a letter to the editor—he is a master of the letter to the editor, the world's greatest writer of letters to the editor—which I tore from *Le Devoir* during the Lesage regime, during the Wagner days. It goes:

Wagner au Congo!

Dear Mr. Ryan,

You inform us that Wagner, minister of all the police, tiny head and hairy arm, representative of the English minority in the pau-pau cabinet, may be on his way to Ottawa. Excellent news! But I would like him even more distant. And a man of his qualities does not fit in just anywhere. Ottawa, I'm sorry to have to say it, exists only in tulip time.

218 *Malcolm Reid*

> A gendarme behind each blossom, Wagner minister of the bouquet—it would be cinematic, the man's vitality could not bend itself to it. The country which suits his genius, it's the Congo.
> I remind you that Quebec has its international existence. Lumumba had already begun to rot, but the news of his murder was not yet known. Tshombe wanted to bathe himself in the glow of Washington, to wash himself of it in the company of white souls which never shrink from blood. He was officially invited by Jean-Jean. If he did not come, it was because he was one assassination ahead of time; LBJ had not yet replaced Kennedy and the United States didn't care to sully itself by contact with the recipient of Lesage's invitation. And I remind you of the International Institute of African Affairs, en-Cabined at the University of Sherbrooke. Tshombe, dear Tshombe again! The pious institute was run by his representative in America.
> All these services merit recompense. And the occasion is too good to miss: off to the Congo with Wagner, let him impose his notion of justice via the *affreux*. And he may take with him Frank Scott, who taught him law at McGill.
>
> *Jacques Ferron*

Much of Ferron is here. First of all, the letter is erudite: ten oblique references might call for explanation. Instead I will try to find ten marks of Ferron. The erudition, the facts, the knowledge Ferron had to have to write the letter: information about a possible change of scene for a politician, of Tshombe's movements, of Lumumba's fate, of a pro-colonial African institute about to be set up at a French-Canadian provincial university. "En-Cabined," *cabané*, because the archbishop of Sherbrooke, a pillar of the Quebec right, goes (went) by the name of Joseph Cabana; his brother was long a missionary in Africa and presumably in close touch with the white Catholic right in the French parts of the continent. The anti-clericalism, then. And the irony. The irony! All of Ferron's work is ironic, he has never written a line that was not ironic, did not adjust its nuance into a new irony, look ironically upon its own irony.

It is this irony, together with the erudition, which makes Ferron so hard to grasp. Reading him on Quebec one is overwhelmed by his knowledge of its history, its politics, its relations with English Canada, English Canada's politics, the geography of both. But he never expounds a body of information and then comments on it; the exposition is always the same process as the commenting, and the commenting is—ironic. So what to take literally? All? Nothing? All and nothing. When he says in a reminiscence that he once learned that to be a playwright in Quebec you need a license from the Society of Jesus, and that he applied for one, and received it, from a Jesuit who told him how many plays, including how many successes and how many failures, it permitted him to produce, must one take him seriously? Has he turned up a fact dating from French colonial times which no one else ever remarked upon? Or is he merely being ironic about his favorite subjects, clericalism in Quebec and the métier of writer? Or is he *using* a fact from Quebec history to be ironic about clericalism? Reading Ferron—such sketches have appeared in almost every publication put out in Quebec, left, right, center, since 1950—is like smoking pot, you don't quite know if you know what he is talking about, but everything fits together, makes sense, obvious sense, *yes*.

And yet . . . When he writes, in a column in *parti pris* called *Ce bordel de pays* (*bordel:* whorehouse, but also disturbance, rowdiness, brawl; so that he is calling the country a muck-up of a country, but suggesting that the mucking-around has something to do with somebody prostituting somebody else), that Champlain, surrendering Quebec to the English in the brief British takeover which preceded the actual conquest of the colony, set as a condition the preservation of Faith, Hope, and Charity—and that Faith, Hope, and Charity were the three Indian mistresses of the explorer-governor—is that true? *Ce bordel de pays* ran for about a dozen issues of the magazine, and was a succession of such puzzles, such revelations, such cutting through colonialism to its nerve. Autonomous republics and rebel communes in the history of Quebec. Memories from life in the Canadian army. And angry insights into the American Indian's grinding-under by white society—Faith, Hope, and Charity.

Would I be wrong to recognize in his reference to Lumumba in that letter something akin to his love for the Indian? A shame of his own skin, a hatred for the killers of a black chief? That anger is the reverse side of his irony: the irony is the modulation which keeps the anger under control. Hence the remark about Frank Scott. This man is a poet who shares many of Ferron's concerns, a jurist at McGill

University, a leading English-Canadian socialist intellectual of the thirties, and, Ferron suggests, an elegant sort of colonialist for all that, an all-the-harder-to-shake-off kind of oppressor because of his paternal encouragement of his own kind of humanism among the members of the race his race exploits, his tut-tutting when that race's drives for liberation take paths he finds mistaken. The whole thing is captured in an image—Frank Scott thinks of himself as a friend of French-Canadian liberation, while in fact he teaches in a law faculty which produces the repressors of French Canada (though Ferron is a bit off in calling Wagner English: in spite of his German origins he is mainly, and exceptionally, assimilated to French). In another letter he calls Scott—an oddly frequent Ferron victim, perhaps because he represents colonialism *at its best*—the "chaplain" of Quebec socialism. The priest who stands by in the lay organization seeing that it doesn't forget the sacred values of the British social-democratic high church. (Scott's father was an Anglican archdeacon.) "The next fascism to raise its head in Quebec," Ferron says, recalling Scott's brave legal war on Duplessis, "will not be combatted by these gentlemen; for the next fascism will be English." These were Ferron's allies, it must be remembered, in the days when he tried to be a plain, nonracial socialist.

And the brevity. His letters are brief, his plays are one act, his novels end between the hundredth and the two-hundredth page, and his greatest form is the short story. This is true of his two publications with *parti pris*. Until the appearance of éditions parti pris, Jacques Ferron had published with a house which seems to have been mainly his own and a few friends', the Editions d'Orphée, which had to its credit the most beautifully printed and bound books in the history of Quebec literature, purer even than the fine work done by Roland Giguère for Miron's Hexagone. Immediately the young separatist-socialist house appeared, Ferron identified himself with the youngsters and gave them the manuscript of *La Nuit*. The novel is a mad account of a suburban clerk's night in the city. He is summoned to the morgue, on St. Vincent Street, by a call from a certain "Frank." Frank is both a corpse in the morgue and the guide on a tour from the morgue to the other parts of Montreal which function at night: a strip club called the Alcazar—Aldo's was the name of an orientalized club near Windsor Station—and a brothel on—is it Stanley

Street? The narrator tells of his past: poor, works for an English bank, votes *créditiste* to needle its management, was once a Communist, became one while recovering from tuberculosis in the Royal Edward Laurentian Hospital. Frank introduces himself more fully as Frank Archibald Campbell and fills in his background, largely with quotations from Anglo-Canadian literary lore: Samuel Butler's famous doggerel about the inculture of nineteenth-century Montreal ("O God! O Montreal!"), and several quotations from the turn-of-the-century Canadian poet Duncan Campbell Scott: "What a night! Something was almost ritual about it." He may also be the author of the quotation attributed by Ferron to Frank Archibald Campbell—but it must be remembered that another Anglo-Canadian poet of the same epoch was named Archibald Lampman, and that Frank Scott's archdeacon father was still another: "The Canadians—and by Canadians he meant Québécois—are accomplices more than they are compatriots. They are a strange people, born beneath a foreign domination, a patient and unbowed people who await their hour, who will never completely obey anyone but themselves." Frank falls asleep over a table at the Alcazar and the narrator makes his sally to the bordellos of Stanley Street alone before he returns to his wife's bed in their suburb. Has anything happened? It is hard to say—nothing is changed, yet *La Nuit* is the dream of a man awaiting his hour.

That suburban wife, waiting too, is the subject of *Papa Boss*. One day in her kitchen, she is visited by a seducing angel sent by Papa Boss, who seems to be big money, Household Finance and Niagara Loan, the creditor at the other end of the French-Canadian not-quite-misery. There is, somewhere in the background, the ambiguous neighbor Gérard Pelletier—if Pelletier the friend-of-labor has been commemorated by one elder *partipriste* in Jean-Jules Richard's *Le Feu dans l'amiante,* here we have Pelletier-the-sellout similarly novelized by another senior *partipriste*. And the cold, cruel, hilarious anti-clericalism: a mad, sad nun in her convent garden, composing an endless fetishistic poem, setting the atmosphere in which visions appear to thirty-year-old housewives. In joual, as in English, the consumer taken by the consumer society *se fait fourrer*. Gets screwed.

Ferron's brevity is no doubt easily enough explained. He belongs to that tradition, from Chekhov to Carlos Williams, of doctor writers for whom writing is something for after a day, sometimes a night, of patching up the sick and fearful-of-being-sick. In *La Nuit* we have his usual doctor depreciation: "The doctor didn't have the time to pronounce a diagnosis. Frank died too quickly. He's not happy about it at all, the doctor." But a more complete portrait of Ferron the slum doctor was later painted by a son of the slums who grew up to rebellion and who was helped in this by the family physician around the corner:

> Ferron's office was near my home, and I often went to him for treatment. It was always for the terrible boils that worry and nervousness brought out on my neck. I never went home without a few newspapers the doctor had given me: *France-Observateur* or *L'Express*, which in the fifties were militant weeklies. But we never talked politics. It was just that Ferron had realized that while I waited my turn in the hall, I would devour these papers, which were placed among others on a little table. He had understood that I was hungry for *that*.
>
> I was very withdrawn at the time, and I never dared tell the doctor what was on my mind. Later, when I was cured of my timidity, I saw him only rarely—usually at some literary event where neither Ferron nor I felt really free to talk about "the people across the bridge." There are things which cannot be said just anywhere.
>
> I hope to see this great man again some day—he is still practicing in Ville Jacques-Cartier, without growing rich, simply for the love of men. Meantime, in these pages written hurriedly in prison, I wanted to tell Jacques Ferron that he is not unrelated—far from it—to my present political engagement.

The writer is Pierre Vallières, in his autobiography published by *parti pris* in 1968.

Jacques Ferron is no stranger to the engagements of most of the *partipristes*. Pierre Maheu dedicated his first long examination of clericalism in a 1965 issue of *parti pris*, "to JACQUES FERRON, doctor of incredulity and great unbeliever before the Eternal." This great unbeliever is a man who is capable of accepting the Governor-General's Award in Ottawa one year (it was for his short story collection *Contes du pays incertain*, centering around a favorite Ferron theme, that Quebec natalism and agriculturism plus North American voracity for human fuel have always driven young Québécois who might have fought the country's battles to other fields, other pastures, to keeping a tavern with a *touristeroume* upstairs in Calgary, to burning a pagoda in Korea as the British burned the defenders of St. Eustache Church in 1837), and of piling up one of the biggest separatist votes in the province as an RIN candidate in his home riding a few years later. A man capable of that separatist engagement, a man willing to be expelled from the Parti Socialiste, where most of his best friends were active, because he thought separatism overrode the rest, yet a man also capable of saying, in a play about young terrorists which he published with the University of Montreal students' association *before* the appearance of what he calls, perhaps for *québécois,* or perhaps for *iroquois,* the *effelquois:* "The language is only a pretext. What is finally involved is the dignity of man."

I want to say something about two other not-quite-*partipristes.* First, a middle-aged classical college French professor in Ste-Thérèse who before *parti pris* had written love lyrics for the chansonnier Claude Léveillée:

In the sun of your arms . . .

but, as early as 1959, love lyrics which went like this:

The day that you, my wife, will stretch out on a beach in Bermuda
The day you will no longer darn and patch
The day my dogs will no longer whine with hunger
The day the poet Pior Reimylarsky in Kiev writes his poem of liberty
The day Pal Maleter's widow is consoled
The day when the Lithuanians become again Lithuanians
The day TV commercials smile forth intelligence
The day Ford Motors is nationalized
The day my daughters are owners of the iron of Ungava
And in *La Presse* Saint-Denys Garneau eclipses Maurice Richard

These were not set to music. By early 1964, Jean-Robert Rémillard was offering from his rural base this warning in the eighth issue of *parti pris,* an issue on the strange-to-the-*partipristes* agrarian revolution to be made in Quebec:

For it is important that revolutionary parties act as early as possible to bring the rural masses into the fight for the free republic. They cannot, except at great cost, do without the participation of the countryside. History teaches certain facts. When a revolution which has been born, as is normal, among certain urban milieux does not call upon the peasantry to join it, it sooner or later faces a harsh rural resistance to its measures. France, China, Russia in the twenties—when the peasant no longer goes along, from wisdom or blindness, with the revolutionary chiefs, he either rises openly, or sabotages the agricultural machine in silence. . . .

The farmer knows the necessity of his work, his primary place in production, in life, yet when the time comes to divide up the proceeds he finds the smallest slice of the cake in his hands. Sweat, backache, storms, bills, these gifts are for him. Profits, comfort, ease, and the right to set prices both for what he sells and what he must buy, these belong to a handful of men who can't be touched by his lone and ignorant means.

So he whines, submits briefs, then laughs and goes back to the daily task, until the day when, beaten, he sells out and becomes, according to his age, federal pensioner in the village or laborer in the town.

The revolution which announced only patriotic conquests would leave this man indifferent. But one which, in addition to a redressing of the race, proposed radical objectives of economic reconquest, would not cry in the desert. . . .

For the North American countryman is a new serf, traveling in a GM car, cooking on a GE stove, working with an MHF tractor fueled by BA oil; having, however, the illusion of property, because he is allowed to pay the taxes on it all. He is not so clear about the tribute he must pay to the anonymous sovereigns of the economy and the political order. For the French-Canadian rural man, all this applies, but his masters are of another nation and language than his. Quebec has more unemployed than Ontario, the Quebec farmer realizes a smaller revenue than the Ontario one does. *Et voilà pourquoi votre fille est muette.*

In this context, a nationalist revolution would ease the pain. But only a socialist one could cure it.

And by 1966 the house had in hand the manuscript of the oddest book éditions parti pris has published. With a hoarier taste for the arcane than Chamberland quoting Mallarmé *and* a yeastier yen for the pop than Renaud describing Mr. Fifty, Rémillard offered his *Sonnets archaïques pour ceux qui verront l'indépendance*:

> I have read antiquity and all that I there learn
> On its pink intercom of mad quotations
> Spoke to me of the land where we now crouch

So astride antiquity and actuality, he invokes Anse-au-Griffon with a *"Thalassa! Thalassa!"* and draws Abraham cursing his fate *"en maudit lumberjack,"* says he can no longer quite tell Virgil from Miron and feels that the time is upon Quebec for the wolf to use his teeth and the ram to use his brow. The wolf, could he by any chance be the colonialist? At any rate, the anti-colonialist ram, the RIN symbol, was soon getting help from Jean-Robert Rémillard, RIN candidate in his riding in the same Quebec election in which Jacques Ferron ran in his. But what could an RIN candidate who had so wished the taming of Ford have to say about General Motors, newly arrived in his district? Could the poet from Ste-Thérèse Seminary stick to the independence-now, economics-later line of dead-center separatism when asking for his vote? "The revolution which announced only patriotic conquests . . ." It is hard to believe. Other conquests seemed finally open to discussion in Quebec in 1966. Where the glories of the 1959 wish-poem were so unlikely that the poet made them into occasions when he would *no longer* love his love, a new series of mad hopes seemed almost within reach:

> When Nikita Khrushchev wears my wig
> And Jayne Mansfield my impregnable corset
> When Danny-boy Johnson sings *Turcaret*
> And our misery has a honey breast
>
> When Jean-Baptiste Alair trades in his toque
> On Nobel Pearson's Bomarc toy
> When Pierre-Elliott Trudeau is waxer of our floors
> And we are all a little less eunuchs
>
> When Willie Lamothe twangs out Honegger
> And Rita Beaufouet reads Crèvecoeur
> And debutantes are all our scrubbing-maids
>
> When brokers starve as breakers of our earth
> And you have bust the ten fine toy balloons
> *Then* sing to me your moon o'er St-Clin-Clin!

His latest-dated sonnet in the book—"Algerian Sonnet," January 1965—told what was new in its last line: *"Tu nommes depuis cette fleur Révolution!"*

226 *Malcolm Reid*

The other *pas tout-à-fait partipriste* is Michel van Schendel.

Van Schendel may serve as an example of the slowly emerging type known as the *néo-Québécois*. It was not possible to be such before. If the odd converted Catholic or conservative spirit chose to become a Québécois, he did so at risk of a cold reception from his chosen neighbors. Colonial xenophobia. Even now it is not easy: I have in my head an image of a Haitian standing on a streetcorner in Sherbrooke trying to persuade a Sherbrooke man he did not speak English: that a black man might not be English speaking was inconceivable to his interlocutor. Van Schendel might be more believable for that Québécois-in-the-street—he is a brown-haired, white-skinned, bespectacled Belgian—but he would hardly be any more congenial. He writes articles on the securities market for the newspapers and Lukácsian analyses of nineteenth-century French-Canadian literature for academic anthologies ("Love, with openly declared desire, does not really enter French-Canadian literature until the moment when it is recognized for what it is: a part of the whole Quebec depossession, a historic impossibility," or, "French-Canadian thinkers might have avoided the worst of their rigidity had their rulers praised cultural differences—the praise would have appeared suspect—but the English-speaking colonial bourgeoisie carped just enough at such differences to make the Quebec elites cling passionately to cultural combat and renounce all attempts to master concrete reality"). He is a Marxist and a poet. In *parti pris* he has displayed both those selves, the Marxist in his *"Maladie infantile du Québec,"* which I speak about in the next chapter, and the poet in poems—"Wind, great totem wind . . ."—with the same stranger's feeling for Quebec seen in the title to the collection Gaston Miron published for him back in 1958: *Poèmes de l'Amerique étrangère*.

This is not a *partipriste,* but a man who is able to make himself at home in the company of the *partipristes*. Very largely because of them, he is able to be a Québécois of sorts in a Quebec where if a man is not a Roman Catholic with one of a couple of hundred names, he is not one of us, and we wonder why he doesn't speak English. The political group the *partipristes* went on to form contained, to my knowledge, a French-speaking Portuguese, a Belgian Jew, a Vietnamese, and several varied Anglo-Canadians. It was, I am sure, the first time a French-speaking Quebec political organization which was not the Montreal branch of something pan-Canadian and which had even minimal links with the French-Canadian working class had ever been able to say that. And I know a few American draft-dodgers who are coming along.

Michel van Schendel. *Néo-Québécois.*

When Claude Jasmin called his short story collection *Les Coeurs empaillés,* he was once again outdoing the *partipristes* in assiduous *partiprisme,* for it was the first *parti pris* book with a title which was a literary allusion to another *parti pris* work. The writer he was quoting was Gérald Godin, who had written in his *Cantouques,* "poems in ripe, popular, and occasionally French language" which got their name half from *cantos* or *canticles,* and half from the *cant-hooks* that loggers use to break up logjams:

> At sixteen he went easily
> from poison ivy to lice
> one passion didn't wait on the next
> he stuffed several hearts
> and most of all his own
>
> he carried his soul
> like a useless hard pillow
> like a sawdust doll
> he had no falcons on his arm
> just four or five warts
> the only fortune willed to him
> by some swamp toad
> (or his old man)
>
> his youth his life were nohow royal
> they called him squirt or goddam brat
> according to the days and hates
>
> the only woman he could long love
> was named is named today Beer
> the others betrayed him
> sick or false unwise unwell
> but there's the Precious Blood of Jesus bell

Godin has proclaimed himself a joual writer, even published several essays on the reasoning behind joual writing, something Renaud has never bothered to do, and has done some funny, gentle things with his kind of semi-joual in verse. But it was principally in another capacity that he interested me. He is (at the time of my interview unofficially) the chief editor of the éditions parti pris, and I wanted to ask him how he saw politically committed publishing.

All the individuals to whom I spoke about their work with *parti pris*, except for André Major, for whom it belonged to the past, accepted my attributing what I had seen and gathered from the magazine and the éditions to them; never, or almost never, did they protest "the group decided, it wasn't me." Always "we did" this; "we decided" that. A remarkable melting-of-the-ego-into-the-group, then, within the fairly small circle which actually wrote and edited the magazine. But beyond this? *Parti pris* proposed a socialized life for Quebec, a participation of all Québécois in the ruling of the country; it regularly invited readers to contribute, collaborate, share. Did it have any structures to assure its continued availability to something collective, something popular?

Printed words have always been a very individualistic business. It may be simply "the mob" which demolished the Bastille; it may be "the bourgeoisie," an undifferentiated class, which thereafter came to power. But those who incited these collective acts by written words are remembered by name—Voltaire, Rousseau—and it does not occur to us to include the printer who set their type in their accomplishment. Indeed, it is individualism, capitalism, which has fared best in the matter of freeing words; socialism has criticized capitalist freedom of the word, pointed out its limits, noted that the rich have more presses than the poor, but has never been able to propose a model of freedom to say, to write, to print which was more real than the liberal one. Enmeshed in the realities of freeing men, it has generally felt constrained to enchain words, to make them the servants of deeper freedoms. Paul Krassner, denouncer of the totalitarianism-in-fact of liberal America, nevertheless said, when in Montreal to defend the student editors who reprinted one of the blasts of his *Realist*: "You know, I can't help thinking that America is the only country in which I could publish it." My first questions to Godin were around these problems.

"A book is an event," he said. "Even if it does not sell, does not sweep the country, does not get into the hands of the masses, influence political choices at the moment of appearance, the important thing is that its statement has been written into history. The book will be reported on in the press, provoke reactions, just like a speech or a demonstration—and no literary movement in Quebec has caused so much talk, been so much commented on as *parti pris* and the joual novels. I call it a literary sit-in. We appeared on the scene and said, 'The language is in a mess, and we're going to sit here and write in it, make you listen to it, until the reasons for this mess have been recognized.' We published in our own publishing house, it's true, we didn't walk into somebody else's in the strict sit-in sense, but we were occupying the sacred ground of literature, desecrating the private property of the academicians, the purveyors of pure French.

"When did I first think about the problem? In Three Rivers. A friend told me a story. He was sitting in a park one day reading a book. Beside him two workers were talking. The mere fact of his holding a book made them uneasy, ashamed; one of them turned, seeing he could hear their conversation, and said: *'On parle mal, hein?'* I understood that it was possible to despise oneself for something for which one was not to blame, and it troubled me. At that time I was working as a reporter for *Le Nouvelliste*; every weekend I got to put together a literary page, and one week I did a piece on French-Canadian speech—we didn't say joual then. I advocated its use in literature, quoted juicy examples to prove the vitality of popular but nonapproved speech. So for me it dated back before my political stand, this pro-joual position in writing. At the time I didn't see the whole political picture, although in an industrial town like Three Rivers a few realities were clear enough. I knew there were two Three Rivers, a great proletarian city that was French, and a tiny upper-town that sat on top of it and spoke English."

International Paper, "*la C.I.P.*," is the name of colonialism in Three Rivers.

"My own position was petty bourgeois, in the Marxist sense. My father was a doctor, a poor doctor, but I of course was sent to a classical college—I had to get a respectable education after all. My father's position led to my understanding another reality. When I was at *Le Nouvelliste* I heard of an opening at *Le Devoir* in Montreal. I was interested and mentioned it to my family. Now, Three Rivers was

Duplessis's town, and this was in Duplessis's time. My family urged me not to apply to *Le Devoir*; if I were to work there my father would lose work that depended on the health department. That was it: a father could be made to suffer because his son worked for an opposition newspaper.

"When I did go to Montreal it was to work for *Le Nouveau Journal*. Duplessis was dead and I was like every provincial who comes to his country's capital: I wished to distinguish myself from the big-city fashions. I had already published some poetry, which was why I was in touch with Gaston Miron, but I resisted his political counsel."

From Godin's earlier work I have a populist, joualistic volume called *Poèmes et cantos*, published by a Three Rivers house; and one of the two others I have seen attributed to him, *Chansons très naïves*, seems to have won a European prize, the silver medal for poetry given by Les Editions Regain in Monte Carlo in 1960. This would date from the time when Godin, sojourning in Paris, still thought the salvation for the French-Canadian writer might be in universality, acceptance by Europe, publication by Les Editions Albin Michel. But, he recounts in a *parti pris* defense of joual, he learned better and came home to his real authenticity, his real problem: "Goodbye, Albin Michel."

"There was also Gilles Constantineau," he continued, "a senior colleague at *Le Nouveau Journal* whose ideas were at work on me. One day—Duplessis was gone, separatism was in the air, yet the old clerical order was still very much in place in rural areas—I asked him why the Quebec political situation was so confused. It was not the political situation that was confused, he told me"—here Godin paused, coolly giving this remembered thrust at himself full effect, with pointed finger and wink—"it's you who's confused. At that time I was trying to maintain a position of what I called *le gros bon sens*, good common sense. Not separatist, not revolutionary. For modernizing education, developing competence, technology, preparing the French-Canadian people before contemplating grandiose projects— the very arguments that *Cité libre* later used against us, in short. When *Cité libre*, through Gérard Pelletier, invited the young to speak out, I put it this way: we of my generation do not yet know what ideas deserve our support, offer real promise of accomplishing something, but when we find our ideas, we shall be ready to take up arms for them. And yet when *parti pris* appeared, and André Major telephoned to ask my reaction, it was bad.

"That first number was a catalogue of everything I didn't believe and couldn't accept. I told him so, and he asked if I would like to contribute anyway—even express my dissent in a piece. Now at the core of the early *parti pris* was the idea that a young man could make his stand as exploited French-Canadian in Quebec in 1963 in no more admirable way than by planting a bomb; in short, a glorification of the FLQ, of the terrorist. This I found laughable, and I attempted to laugh at it in a sketch I called "Alberts, or Revenge," which I turned in and which they printed. Why? I suppose it was acceptable to *parti pris* to the extent that I had failed to say what I intended to say and had in spite of myself come out in solidarity with the terrorist's refusal of his world. (I had Alberts the bomber explain his assassination of William O'Neil, the army nightwatchman, by a confusion with Louis O'Neill, the reformist priest.) And so it was that in writing for *parti pris* I became a *partipriste*. I tried to read *Les Damnés de la terre* and could not finish it: the definitive book for me was Jacques Berque's *Dépossession du monde*, which said the same things in more intellectual terms."

We were talking over minestrone in the Italian restaurant below the offices where the CBC's daily public affairs show, *Aujourd'hui*, was "lined up"—with Gérald Godin the lineup man. He spoke placidly, politely, ate with gusto, looked at me humbly from under his kinky peppered hair, with candid eyes and a small candid smile. He retreated slightly when I characterized the *partipristes* as able to voice their political ideas directly only when their audience was small (*parti pris*), being forced to be circumspect as soon as the audience was important (*Aujourd'hui*), caught in the absurdity of infiltration, influence on large groups by minority ones. His political influence was in any case small, he said, he wrote criticism, notes on passing events, "ironic" commentaries, not big articles, deep analyses. This meekness was odd, I thought, for Godin is the only *partipriste* whose writings I had found, not to mince words, a wee bit racist; how could he produce them without hating the English more than this? As to the larger question, well, I'd seen on the schedule for his next show, upstairs in his office, a reference to a "sequence on treatment of Canadian Indians," I'd heard him line up an interview with soon-to-become-separatist René Lévesque, I'd seen scattered around volumes of new prose and verse from Cuba, and I was prepared for his answer: on TV he could nonetheless bring up issues, prod people into thinking about things. Indeed, he feared less the axe of the state network than an English-speaking producer would, because Quebec is "touchy" (the English word in the midst of a French sentence threw me, as such insertions, joualistic or not, are often apt to throw the English speaker who is not expecting such familiar outcroppings in unfamiliar territory) and a French-Canadian employee cannot be disciplined as an English-Canadian one can, without a mighty protest following. Yes, he conceded, perhaps the left should rethink its views on communications in the twentieth century.

Meanwhile, I noted that under Godin's administration éditions parti pris was becoming less precisely the voice of secularist, socialist independentists: their biggest seller was a collection of blackly humorous sketches and love letters by the cabaret monologuist Clémence Desrochers. But beyond the fact that they were anti-nun, Godin could only say that they were a rare example in French-Canadian literature of "realist" writing. (Miss Desrochers's letters, heart-rending in their apparent authenticity and recentness, were addressed to a lost lover whom she playfully called "Cher Anglais" and to whom she confided repulsion in the presence of politically zealous youngsters at the separatist club Le Cochon Borgne. It was known to followers of Montreal showbiz gossip that the singer had in fact broken with an English-speaking fiancé the year before, and the 7,000 sales figure for the book must include more people attuned to popular artists' lives than people likely to be hurt by slights to political zeal. The same melancholy the letters conveyed was also in a song which has the same title as the letter section of the book, "*La Ville depuis*," "The City Since Then," and here Miss Desrochers seems to me to have hit a tone that is new in Quebec popular art, a taking-for-granted that the local lore of the nation can be woven into the fabric without explanation. "I try to forget myself at the counters of Eaton's," she sings, as Cole Porter might evoke Macy's or Léo Ferré the Galeries Lafayette.) It was the kind of ambiguous book with which publishers subsidize less popular and more cutting ones, and would not be an occasion for frowns if it were alone. But it is one of several marginally *partipriste* works brought out by *parti pris* in

1967. One was a volume of widower's dirges by—the Desrochers family was not through sharing its heartaches with *parti pris*—Clémence's father, Alfred Desrochers, a rustic classicist with a Santa Claus beard whose nature verse makes him one of the grand old men of French-Canadian letters. Others were Claude Jasmin's worthy, humane but bland short stories; a book about Vietnam by a Vietnamese settled in Quebec who was almost as cool to the National Liberation Front as to the French and American occupants of *Mon pays le Vietnam*; a collection of pseudonymous anti-Duplessis essays from *Le Devoir* by the liberal (though not Liberal) political scientist Gérard Bergeron, a man clearly of the *Cité libre* generation, politics, and temperament; and a collection of cartoons by Berthio, very funny and very unflattering for federalist fatuity, but previously published in the mainstream press. Each one, like *Le Monde sont drôles*, Clémence's droll title, justifiable enough perhaps, but together a softening of the *parti pris* diet.

I asked Godin if there was anything precise that served to prevent éditions parti pris from becoming just another publishing house. Emile Copferman had told me this had been the fate of René Juilliard in Paris, after leftist beginnings. Again Godin was deferential, unprovoked, cool: yes, there was a reading committee which kept in mind the *raison d'être* of the house; indeed, since the CBC required he withdraw from officially titled participation in *parti pris*, the official boss was Maheu. But the sharpest example of this structure's serviceability Godin mentioned was a negative one: the house had received a witty manuscript pillorying the Church, had liked it, but someone remembered the author's name from somewhere. A check produced a dossier of anti-Semitism in his past writing: he'd published some nasty stuff in the *Quartier Latin*, the University of Montreal paper (which, ironically, has been a platform for *parti pris*-type leftism in recent years). So the odor of fascism torpedoed the sympathetic anti-clericalism. And on the question of the house's mission as a source of popular literature, of books that might just reach the *colonisés* themselves, of books which spoke their language and moved in their circles, Godin said no, he'd lost his illusions about that. Now he wants the jackets of the *parti pris* books sober, slick, bookstore rather than newsstand style; newsstand selling for an outfit with as little capital as *parti pris* is not economical.

For Gérald Godin and for the whole group called *parti pris*, perhaps things are just no longer as clear, the rupture with the old no longer as clean, the choice no longer as blazingly compelling, as when he wrote in the January 1965 *parti pris* of the lesson of his month in Paris four years earlier (he is the only *partipriste* to have done the European bit before joining the magazine): "I will write joual or I won't write at all." Godin's burlesque tales, *Alberts the enfant terroriste*, *Télesse* the horseplayer, are nitty-gritty enough, his poems all display greater or lesser joualization, yet there is his *Cantouque menteur*:

> Sunday Louis Riels
> and living-room martyrs
> weekend suicide-commandos
> and snackbar guerrillas
> tavernutionaries
> all tough and bottle-scarred
> brothers all, my braggart equals
> One day—
> one day we'll have had our fill
> of pissing in our pants
> and it'll be from the barricades
> that we'll rain tomatoes on the English
> and rotten eggs and Leninisms
> before they've unloaded onto us
> the lead of Sgt. Dubois
> of the Royal Vanndouzieme
> stationed at Peel and St. Catherine
>
> But no, my militancy fizzles to avowal
> is false and lying like a dame
> and tearful too but with a truth in there somewhere
> I confess to godalmighty
> and to my land to my Quebec
> my song is false, my song's not truthful
> but the anger is, the anger is
> by the land and by the earth
> and by the breasts of Pélagie

Godin had used, in my conversation with him, the term *sit-in* as a metaphor for joual literature. In one of his (pre-*parti pris*) *Poèmes et cantos*, he writes:

> I'm lonely for french speak to me in french maria
> down there in central park is there an old man with white hair
> dreaming like me maria like I'll dream of you . . .

That dates from a time when he was seeking an American authenticity in New York, in Maria from Spanish Harlem. And though he answered that loneliness for French, returned to the only authenticity which was one, this reference point in black America has stayed with him and he frequently compares joual to what a friend of mine from the Detroit ghetto calls "bootese." This seeking an affinity with the other identifiable oppressed nation of North Americans is what André Major was doing, too, when he reviewed Robert Gover's *One Hundred Dollar Misunderstanding* in *parti pris*:

> If we go to the causes we'll see this misunderstanding is a symbol behind which are to be found all the social and racial injustices which forge the American soul. But just for fun, let's import the theme and see what we get: a student at McGill, living in *Ouessemonte;* a *canayenne* from Ontario Street, speaking joual. . . .

(It is doubtful that Major's French edition of the Gover book allowed him to appreciate it as a sample of a beginning of a bootese literature in the United States, significantly undertaken by white, not black writers.) Finally, Pierre Vallières is reaching for the same thing when he titles his autobiography *Nègres blancs d'Amérique*.

How sound are these affinities, Negroes-White Negroes; bootese-joual? First of all it must be said that there are of course some parallels between the two oppressions, and that the two struggles have recognized this, Vallières in his title, Stokely Carmichael in his telegram of support to Vallières when he went on trial for terrorism. Godin's and Major's instincts are right, and I have relied on the same instinct from time to time in this book, comparing Renaud's *Cassé* to Richard Wright's *Native Son*, using the odd originally black expression when trying to describe the Quebec situation's nuances. Other expressions which were tempting I have eschewed—ghetto for slums, for instance—because it seemed to me they would evoke a false parallel, encourage a leap to entangling conclusions. The essential difference is that where the oppression of black people in white America is a matter of fencing in ghettoes while the police repel any attempt to break out, French Canada has always had an institutional superstructure—police, premier, mayors, school systems—which allowed much of the oppression to be taken into the body of the colonized society in the form of a self-repressive culture.

It is hard to resist, especially when you are a small human group like the Québécois, appropriating other people's searchings and solutions when in search of yourself. Hence the enormous success of two plays in the Montreal theater during the season ending as I write. Both, interestingly, borrowings from the English theater. The Théâtre du Nouveau Monde, the social conscience of the Quebec theater but an institution of the nascent Quebec bourgeoisie nevertheless, adapted Shaw's *Pygmalion* to Montreal in the 1960's: Liza Doolittle was Elise Lacroix, slum girl; Professor Higgins was a bearded intellectual living in a restored house in touristy Old Montreal. She speaks joual, he is resolved to clean it up, pass her at a reception given by Mayor Drapeau. Joual is compared to cockney, and French-Canadian society to capitalist London. That the second comparison falls apart is, I think, plain: professors in Quebec speak a language scarcely different from that of shopgirls, and Mayor Drapeau's court represents the newfound glories of the politically risen notable class, again scarcely distinguished culturally from the workers, rather than some ancient and entrenched class order. The play is rather a wish of the Quebec notables projected onto the stage: they see themselves as a future ruling class of a future total society; they would like to be in a position to satirize themselves in the way Shaw satirized the British bourgeoisie. But they're not there yet.

To the extent that it sees itself as an oppressed group, not yet in power, still needing to satirize and haul down its oppressors, the Quebec neo-bourgeoisie recognized itself in the other hit of the season, *Hamlet, Prince du Québec*. Here everything was simple, simple the way the neo-bourgeois would like to persuade all Québécois things are. Hamlet was young Quebec; his mother, the Church, had lost her first husband, France, and married England. Hamlet, aided by trusty Horatio Lévesque, hindered by the royal serving-man Trudeau, had to find his way back to his true, French, identity. And the tide is turned by the return of his father's ghost, a shadowy figure in a general's cap, arms raised in victory. Of the complexities of the search for identity, nothing; of the class divisions within the identity-seeking nation, nothing (the proletariat is represented by two gravediggers, one assimilated, submissive, anglicized; the other what is called in Quebec *nationaleux*—dumbly patriotic, flag-waving, racist, Groulxist—*he,* of course, is the *good* prole); of American imperialism, of the economic aspects of colonialism, nothing. All there is to it is that Quebec used to be French, was taken over by England, and has to become French again.

Quebec, then, isn't yet the fully developed bourgeois society Eloi de Grandmont would make it in his Quebecization of Shaw, but nor is it the simple, uncomplex, undivided French society Robert Gurik has drawn in his Quebecization of Shakespeare. Its slums aren't ghettoes in the New York, Detroit, or older European Jewish sense, yet its understanding of itself has something to take from Fanon, who's now being read in the black ghettoes, and from Memmi, the Tunisian Jew who came to understand colonialism among the Arabs. Joual isn't bootese, despite the comparisons of the *partipristes*, and it isn't cockney despite the box office boom of a play that suggests it is. What is it? What to take and what to leave in other people's experiences when seeking the sense of one's own?

Joual, it seems to me, is French, but it is veering away from French. The *partipristes* are wrong to yield to the temptation to consider it a new language: it is a sub-language only. It is not, however, a sub-language in the same way that cockney and bootese are; it is not the sub-language of a class, an ethnic group, even a depressed class or a ghetto ethnic group, within a society in which the top levels speak the real thing, the way upper-class Americans and Englishmen speak the English that bootese and cockney are not quite. For the upper classes in Quebec do not speak pure, correct, standard French, but English.

Joual is associated with a proletariat because it is all innocent and naked among the manual working class of Quebec. The workers have no defense against it. The petty bourgeois have a few defenses; they are trying to fight it off, but it swallows them just the same. It is the sub-French of the whole French-Canadian nation, top to bottom, it is the language of a proletarianized society, a society whose very bourgeois or would-be bourgeois are proletarian in relation to the capital-owning ruling class, which is not part of French Canada but which is on top of it. In a sense the petty-bourgeois Québécois who believe they speak good French and the workers joual because the workers say *il fait frette* and they say *une température atroce* are even more to be pitied than the workers: the workers are unconscious, the petty bourgeois are daydreaming.

So joual isn't the language of a class, it is the language of a whole nation, of every class within it. But it is not—and this is the other caution that is necessary—merely a regionalism, a new language, a branching-off from the mother tongue, like American from British, or like Catalan from Spanish. For the differentiation owes too much to the inferiority of the nation in question, too little to geographical separation. Of course joual contains old French expressions lost now in France—the friends of Canadian French are eternally treasuring them—but for every one of those it contains fifty anglicisms. So joual, like cockney and bootese, is what happened to a language under oppression, but not oppression from people who speak the same language as the oppressed—from people who speak another. The people who speak (and determine) the real language, of which joual is a bastardization, are out of sight for the joual speakers. The French are privileged, like Shaw's Higgins, but not on the backs of the Québécois. Their Lizas are among the Arabs and Spaniards in their own *bidonvilles* and their own argot-speaking working class.

And joual is almost barren of the defensive, resilient, and enviable characteristics of those two sub-Englishes, bootese and cockney. Neither the English in Canada nor the French in France envy the vitality of joual the way white Americans do soul talk, the way the English do cockney, because almost every distinguishing feature of joual is a mark of its poverty. When the black American says "y'dig?" after an explanation, the white man can envy him, copy him, emulate him until *dig* is a part of every North American teenager's vocabulary. This is because the black has enriched the word *dig*, has given it a new meaning, has seen more in it than the white man, who first gave the word to the black, ever saw in it. The black man is also defending himself against white intrusion, against being limpid before his oppressor, he is hiding by using *dig* to mean *understand*. He can't hide for long, but when the white man finds out what *dig* means, then the black will discard that feint, that cache, for another, he'll use some other English word in a way that the whites never used it. Similarly for cockney.

But not for joual. The English-speaker has no desire to pick up from his French-Canadian inferior the expression *toffer, to tough*—tough as a verb; he feels he has more mastery of *tough* and of everything else in the English language than the joual-speaker will ever have. For him, to discover that the French-Canadians use *tough* as a verb (it means to endure, to toughen oneself against) is merely to discover that they don't know their English very well, that they've been ill- and half-assimilated. And anyway he doesn't discover that they use this word, for he speaks with them in English.

Nor does the Frenchman want anything to do with *toffer*. First of all, he is unlikely to have any contact with French-Canadians, any occasion to take stock of their language. Then when he learns English, he'll learn the real thing, not the fragments that the French spoken in English America has half-digested in ignorance of what it was really doing. He wants to know what *tough* means to the English-speaker, whereas the French-Canadian just woke up one morning with the word more or less jammed in his consciousness and in his vocabulary; he never made the decision to adopt it.

Similarly, the joualization that *toffer* represents, that any anglicism in French represents, has no defensive or camouflage value for the Québécois. On the contrary, the more English he uses, the easier it is for the English to know what he is thinking, and the more transparent he becomes. It was back when he spoke only French that the colonizer couldn't make him out, for the colonizer speaks no French. (Even joualized French, it should be noted, is fairly opaque for the average Anglo-Québécois.) The oppressed man was most perfectly hidden from his oppressor and could conceal his thought processes most efficiently when he was least worked-on by colonialism. Now he is half-naked, now he has opened up a series of windows to the eyes above.

Where the white American has to chase the Negro behind *dig*, and when he has unearthed him there will find he has moved on, the English colonizer sees the French-Canadian coming steadily over to his side, steadily into the light. Steadily confessing what the English colonizer has always wanted him to confess: that English is clear, French cloudy, that you can tell it in English, that French just doesn't deliver the message. Once assimilated, the French-Canadian could then begin hiding in the dark places of English as the Negro does, of course. This is the process that was fully carried out on the

African languages the slaves in America must once have spoken. Those languages were killed; the Negro came into the English world. Then he began dodging in that world. The French-Canadian has been left enough roughhewn institutional structures—schools, priests—to avoid going through that process in its entirety, and his principal dodge is still to stay out of the oppressor's world. But he can't. Bit by bit the oppressor is sucking him in. The petty-bourgeois anti-assimilationist publishes one anti-joual dictionary; the worker assimilates fifty more English words. One bourgeois proletarian vacations in Switzerland; a thousand proletarian proletarians sign on with General Motors. Everybody, finally, is a proletarian in this scene, because nobody is a capitalist; the English have that. So that's it: joual is the language of all classes in French Canada, but French Canada doesn't have all the classes you need to operate in the capitalist world.

(And hasn't gotten a socialist revolution together yet, either. For a socialist in these circumstances—for a *partipriste*, for example—the only question seems to be, against whom can this revolution best be directed? Do the would-be capitalists within French Canada not have to make their stab at becoming *real* capitalists, a *real* bourgeoisie, at *really* speaking the language better than their workers, before the workers can pass to the attack? It would seem so. It can be said of political issues, as Sartre said of philosophies, that there is scarcely ever more than one alive at a time. The issue now in Quebec is power for the French against the English; everything centers around this, the talk, the press, the politicians. The English in Canada couldn't care less that Trudeau, in *Cité libre* days, used to make socialist noises—he's for putting down the French, that's what counts. He's against separatism, and he's one of them, speaks their language, can maybe calm them down better than one of ours. Same on the French side. Lévesque fights Lesage on social issues for three years, then quits the Liberals on the national issue. French-Canadian workers mostly do not see their class as having anything to do with politics, but they all have their opinions on separatism. Politics is things like that: it is federal or provincial, it is Lévesque versus Trudeau; or it is simply each of them versus his adversaries in his own electoral domain—Lévesque versus the Union Nationale, Trudeau versus the Conservatives. That's politics, and they don't, most of them, think about it often, it doesn't have much to do with their lives. Their nationalism is all they have in the way of class consciousness, and the national question is being settled by others. A politics that would have to do with their daily lives, that they would think about often, that they and not the politicians would settle, would seem to have to await the bankruptcy of that other kind of politics, the up-in-the-air, election-day kind. To wait until parties can no longer pretend to address themselves to the concerns of workers simply by feigning their nationalist accents. Until parties can no longer make "Ottawa," "the English minority," "English Canada," and "North America" stand for *Them,* the rich, in their speeches. Until parties can no longer use "the French-Canadian nation," "our people," "the collectivity," *"les Québécois,"* to cover over, conceal, contain *Us,* the poor. Until, in a word, independence. The groundwork for such a politics of everyday life must, of course, be laid before it can come to flowering. Otherwise, in an independent Quebec, where the new native ruling class is shaky but the workers are unprepared to exploit this shakiness, there intervenes that old Banana Republic solution, that Congolese compromise that was never either necessary or possible even in the less-than-Banana Republic, sub-Congolese days of Quebec: the military takeover. All of which takes us far from joual, unless we read *military takeover,* correctly, as the joual for *independence.*)

I pleaded the positive aspects of joual to Chamberland, and I still believe in them. Joual is, in spite of everything, the meeting of French grammar and American landscape, and the landscape would have shaped the grammar with or without the colonial interference. But the situation in which the Québécois will be able to take joual and love it, develop it, push it beyond itself in spite of its origins, will have to be the same situation I have defined as necessary for taking the old French-Canadian tradition of authority and submission and squeezing from it a new Quebec tradition of insubordination and creation. A situation of combat; a situation of liberty.

When I decided to write about the Shouting Signpainters they were the youngest Quebec writers, the latest generation in Quebec literature, sitting in to win a place on the bookstands. By the time I began my research they had pretty well won their place, and before I was finished new generations were creeping into view. I could not, any more than I could read everything that had gone before, keep up with everything that was coming along, but I was curious. Curious to know to what extent the young writers who were following the *partipristes* were also their followers, to what extent the Shouting Signpainters had begotten children. Some wanderings in the gathering places of young French-speaking and French-reading people one weekend gave some hints.

I dropped into an espresso joint on Clark Street in time for a strange enactment of three—maybe *the* three—ways open to French-Canadian poetry, French-Canadian writing. The joint was La Paloma, *"ce restaurant de barbus-là"* where Ti-Jean went to track down Bouboule. It is a restaurant of young *barbus*, very young, too young yet to get into taverns, the Hut, the Asociación.

The poet who interested me the most was eighteen. He was the first on the program. He read hesitantly:

> Il y a des choses que tu ne comprendras jamais,
> que je ne comprendrai jamais . . .

Then followed, in not-quite-singing rhythms, a rich mixture of lyricism and joual. Obviously a Shouting Signpainter *en puissance*. Abusive colloquialisms. And finally: "Always, we have this air of being about to leave."

The second set of poems was pure French versification, singing, hard to extract a line of thought, a crux, easy to doze to. A real poet, but a citizen of the same Clark Street as me? Hardly: "Aristotle was right . . ." A beautiful girl read these poems, love lyrics all, and I later discovered they were written by a waiter and floor-sweeper at the La Paloma itself.

The third set was pure beatnikery; the reader-writer was the MC who had introduced the evening and he read with the same assurance with which he had announced the hat-passing. One, the characteristic one, was a rather effective imitation of jazz ("Thelon'yus Monk—bop"). This was west coast stuff. Another was about a Negro poet arrested in San Francisco for an infraction of the beatnik-repressing apparatus, an apocalyptic translation from the American, as the French say, about the entire world going beat—not becoming humane, so that withdrawal was unnecessary, but all crowding down the stairs to the La Paloma. I realized I knew this poet, and recalled that he was indeed more a Vancouverite than a Montrealer. What he was doing could better be done in English: for one thing, that's the language Thelonious Monk speaks. And the writer's own travels were proof that no young French-Canadian need content himself with the adapted version if that's the direction he's going in; the real article is just across the border. The guy was the hit of the evening. In Quebec, as elsewhere, the tug to Americanize by direct imitation is strong.

It was the two others, however, I wanted to place side by side for contrast, to referee a debate between. But their personalities and the sweeper's chores made that impossible, and I gave a head start to the *joualisateur,* betraying, no doubt, my *parti pris* in this way.

Serge Gagnon was his name. He reminded me physically of Major, a shaggy blond Major. The same literary black-leather-jacketry to the movements. He was not, he explained, a political poet: "There is no such thing as a primarily political poet; poetry pre-empts politics, and even Mao Tse-tung, insofar as he is a poet, is not primarily political. He, and Vigneault, and Aragon, are poets, comma, whose work may have a political aspect." He is, however, *politisé,* and he again invoked Aragon when I asked about his politics: "I think of the title of Aragon's poem when I'm looking for a way of expressing how I feel: *En étrange pays dans mon pays lui-même.* That's how it is with us, as it was for Aragon during the German occupation of France. Without the Gestapo, but the same. We are colonized, colonized in our daily lives and colonized in our souls."

Later he told me the title of the novel he wants to get ready for *parti pris* soon: *Le Chien dans un jeu de quilles,* dog in a bowling alley, French-Canadian dog in a bowling alley he never built.

But now we were briefly joined by Beathoven, the thin, excruciatingly shy waiter, from a Three Rivers orphanage, author, behind that misspelled nickname, of the second set of poems. His real name, Pierre-André Desbiens (no relation to Frère Untel, he said).

About politics: "I don't understand politics very well; I'm trying to learn. I know that my poems are off in another world; I'm trying to bring them closer to people. What poets do I like? I have read very little poetry. Paul Chamberland says something to me, though."

Gagnon begged to differ. *Parti pris* yes, Major and Renaud were his friends and encouragers; but Chamberland, he said, was "false from top to bottom." (His choice of this expression granted Chamberland one true note—the line from *L'Afficheur*, "Life must be seized again from the top to the bottom.") He was a man, said Gagnon, who walked down from his little house on Bloomfield Avenue in Outremont to the corner of St-Viateur and Park Avenue and contemplated the Greek stores: "Now I feel proletarian, ahaa!" So he was a déclassé, a man who tried to write about proletarian misery without having lived it. But was he, I asked, a bad poet on top of it? And was his political *parti pris* for the proletariat to be rejected too? "Politically? No, you've got to be honest, not politically." As an arranger of words, however, his incurable trouble was that "his vocabulary is false—pedantic, pretentious, unrelated to speech."

Gagnon's own proletarian credentials were sound. He was still living, when I spoke to him, with his family. The personal notes he gave turned him into the Major of five years before, reinforcing the physical resemblance and tempting me to utter the epithet *cabochon*. The father was unemployed (a Major obsession if not a real Major experience), the family made it hard to concentrate on writing, even on the translation piece-work he did, and he planned to move out into a rented room when he could afford it.

He told of an experience that had brought him, his verse, for a moment close to the *colonisés* of his family. At a gathering, Christmas maybe, where others were doing turns, step-dances, singing, he decided to read a poem: "I didn't expect a good reaction, I did it to see how they'd take it. But I got something out of them, something on their faces. My father, uncles, cousins told me it was something new, weren't quite sure what to make of it, but—and this is a typical working-class family—it did say something to them. That encouraged me."

I had found a marked trace of *partiprisme*, then, but no out-and-out disciples. I turned up further traces in coffeehouse surroundings that weekend, in a *chansonnier*. This might be a good place to define this term and talk about the greatest Quebec *chansonnier*, Gilles Vigneault.

A chansonnier is a song-maker, a singer-composer. That is, he renders the whole of his creation: words, music, performance. There are few, of course, who are equally good at each of the three tasks, and

Vigneault consecrates this rule by being the greatest of them all without having a voice. Not, however, without skill as a performer; I wonder if it is not perhaps as a performer that he is greatest of all. André Major says joual literature has no place on paper, just may have one on recordings; Vigneault has put it there with his St. Lawrence North Shore coastal sailor who plans his first trip to Quebec: "Maybe I'll come back speaking English. (*Laughter from the audience.*) Ah, you laugh, but if you've got English you can get any job you want on the North . . . on the South Shore too, for that matter. Any job you want—foreman, timekeeper—if you know enough you can even end up *boss*."

This patter is the centerpiece of a song which is rousing in tune and chorus, but one cannot think of anyone but Vigneault performing it. His more sublime songs have been sublimely performed by other, female singers, Pauline Julien, Monique Leyrac. Even the Parisian Catherine Sauvage attempts one of his reels—on an all-Vigneault record she has made called *French Songs of Canada*—making it a French imitation of a Tin Pan Alley imitation of a cowboy song, which is not, oddly, all that far off.

But this is marginal. I am persuaded that it will be Vigneault as total phenomenon who will sooner or later take Quebec to the world. For Vigneault is in a sense too good to be true, premature, and this enables the onlooker to say, as Miron feared they would say of him if he published, "Look, they have talent, they produce artists, we're not keeping them down, they're recognized internationally." He is a great international popular artist and an accomplished poet who has come out of a people still not counted as a nation by other nations, still an unaccomplished identity. His songs express Quebec with a certainty that, according to the rules, ought to be denied to the uncertain human being who is the colonized person.

Like the best popular artists in the United States, and, I would guess, in the rest of the Americas, he is at once the old Quebec, the folkloric Quebec, the rural and conserving Quebec, and the new Quebec, the contesting Quebec, the open-to-the-world and constructing Quebec. He does not spurn the world and cling to his archaic barn dance; nor does he spurn the barn dance and copy the manners of peoples he considers up-to-date. He makes the barn dance tell his new story (like, yes, Bob Dylan singing the preoccupa-

tions of an urban and automated generation of Americans with the guitar and harmonica of Woody Guthrie's rural and folkloric U.S.; or like Woody himself, already blending Old West and New Deal).
Thus:

>Iron, titanium
>Underneath the ground
>Nickel, copper
>And what the copper brings
>Capi*tal* and me*tal*
>Billions and bond-coupons
>We've got the youth
>Got the arms
>We've got—gotta hurry—
>Gotta get the job done
>Want to see that promised future
>Shining oh so bright.
>
>. . . Where there used to be a village
>Now a town, a city, suburbs
>Ten religions, twenty tongues
>And old men in their silence
>So look me in the eye, will you,
>And tell me what they'll use for happiness.

And when at the end, after that last verse, he sings the chorus again, and returns to that future shining bright, he pauses, and there is a lowering of the voice into the throat, a sigh of irony before he says it, *"Du plus brillant . . . avenir."*

For that's U.S. Steel's, Noranda Mines', cutting open of the land, still locked in human winter. There is a building of the land that could take place, that will take place, that would plant summer in winter, and this Vigneault prophesies to a fiddler's reel:

>I've got cement, got glass, got steel
>To build my village sixty stories up—
>And not wreck the grass in my back yard—
>
>And I've got roads that know my foot
>I've floors that know my jig . . .
>
>I've got a land to lead, to guide
>Somewhere between money, and fuel oil, and love

It's too big to sing, so I shout
It's too far to walk, so I run.

It is a country boy, of authentic popular origin, who speaks here, but not a proletarian. His father is a fisherman who spent most of his life as a federal inspector of fisheries. Thus Vigneault is ambassador from the rural working class to the middle-class youth of the cities who listen to long-playing records, read verse, frequent coffeehouses. They are separatist, the characteristic members of this youth, cultured, left wing. They need assurance that their cause is, or can be, a popular one. Vigneault gives that assurance; he distills rustic discontent and frustration to the point where it almost goes over into conscious revolutionism: "If you know enough, you can even end up *boss.*"

Gilles Vigneault is not a *partipriste,* but connections are there. The group to which Vigneault belongs is that of the Jacques Ferrons and the Pierre Vadeboncoeurs, the Longueuil left. If there is an old left in Quebec to which the *partipristes* can play new, this is it. Ferron is a family doctor in Ville Jacques-Cartier; not far away, in Longueuil, Michel Chartrand, union organizer, veteran of Asbestos, Ferron's fellow-veteran of meeting and convention after meeting and convention, is a printer. Ferron's sister, a novelist too, is married to Robert Cliche, who for a time took on the task of Quebecizing the NDP; they live in the Beauce, the *rural* South Shore of the St. Lawrence, across from Quebec. Ferron's brother Robert is also a South Shore doctor, also a socialist. Chartrand, at a meeting of the political formation that was the expression of this left, the Parti Socialiste du Québec, would joke from the chair: "If Dr. Ferron and Mr. Vadeboncoeur can interrupt their philosophical conversation for a moment, they might help us count the vote." All have been more or less nationalist: Cliche will say he's giving the NDP a last chance, Chartrand will walk out of the NDP—after leading it in the days when it was the CCF in Canada and the Parti Social-Démocrate in Quebec —to found the PSQ. Ferron will be hoofed out of even the PSQ when he runs for the legislature with the RIN, but sometimes it will seem that only the Rhinoceros Party, founded by himself, his brother, Chartrand's daughters, others, as counter-absurdity to the 1965 federal elections, is lunatic enough a fringe for him. Vadeboncoeur, the Christian, will rebuff the *citélibristes* in whose magazine he wrote, will say that Quebec nationalism implies socialism, that nationalism is the one constant of Quebec life, that socialists must find the way to make it give forth its socialist secret. He, like the unbelieving Ferron, will salute the *partipristes* as his continuers, will contribute occasional pieces to the magazine, but unlike Ferron will not give them the manuscript of his next book. "Perhaps he feared we would refuse it," Gérald Godin wrote in an affectionate review in *parti pris* in which he characterized Vadeboncoeur as a *curé de gauche*, a renegade preacher. He *will* publish with Les Editions de l'Arc, a tiny house whose main output is the texts of the songs of Gilles Vigneault. And the printing for the house is done by Michel Chartrand—one volume of Vigneault lyrics even contains a hand-written typographic instruction from Gilles to Michel, and in Vigneault's father's home in Natashquan there is a Quebec woodcarving of a flight of gulls, a gift from that same politician-printer, who also prints Vigneault's concert posters (though on records, where the money is, it is Columbia that has him).

The accumulation of details is perhaps arbitrary, but nevertheless it is clear that Vigneault, in his forties, is of the generation that saluted *parti pris* rather than belonged to it. His salute was concrete: in the second issue of the magazine the blurbs included "stories—gilles vigneault, nina bruneau." Inside, Vigneault's contribution was two sketches, one a memory from the inevitable North Shore—the six-year-old boy who watched the fur merchants fleece his trapper father—and the other a couple of allegorettes on imprisonment and freedom: a mason-jailbird repairs his own wall the better to escape; a just-released prisoner is rearrested by a cop to whom he has unwisely identified himself as "a free man."

These token adhesions to *partiprisme* are not Vigneault's only such gestures; he gave a poem on the workingmen of Quebec to a PSQ paper Chartrand put out, and his name was on the PSQ membership list, even if he did not show up for all the separatist-socialist functions he promised to. But he does not go beyond tokenism. Like most of the greatest of the great, he prefers being analyzed to analyzing, he would have his work speak for itself, and there has been little trace of him elsewhere in *parti pris*. Maheu told this story about him in a more recent issue:

We earn our bread as we can, and I happen to work for a big advertising agency. I tell myself no trade is unworthy, it consoles me. But the other day I was asked to telephone Gilles Vigneault ("You know him, maybe you could convince him"): a big firm, American naturally, wanted to use a quotation from him in its advertising. I do so, against my better self; on the other end, the answer is prompt: "You'll tell them they'll never have enough money to buy one word," said Vigneault. Rarely has a no made me as happy. The following night I was at his concert at the Comédie Canadienne; I'll only say he was equal to that reply. No one knows as he does how to say a people seeking birth, how to blend past and folklore in a future which transforms them. Vigneault gives us all a taste for not being for sale.

Others have mentioned him in passing. But when *parti pris* wanted an article on Quebec song for its issue on the literature seeking birth, it was Stéphane Venne, a chansonnier of much more modest proportions, who did the piece. "It began with almost all the elements already present in one man," he wrote, meaning Félix Leclerc, the great lone chansonnier from just before the present flowering, whose rustic traditionalism Venne, like many another Quebec artist, has not been able to exorcise except by the adoption of a conventional and alien Paris–New York urbanism. How Vigneault managed to surpass the traditionalism of Leclerc without rejecting his origins Venne is trying to get at when he says, "Make no mistake: for a public 90 percent city dwelling, Natashquan is exotic, elsewhere, distant. One doesn't even feel the urge to go there. No peasant poet Vigneault." As one who has felt the urge and slaked it, even more as one who has heard, from a table near where Vigneault was singing, one young Québécois boast to others, "You know, when he does his recital in Natashquan, it's not quite the same . . ." I have to contradict this. But Venne's basic meaning is sound: Vigneault is one thing around which a new Quebec, not any longer the country-priest Quebec, the return-to-the-soil, the Félix-the-*Canadien*-leaning-on-his-fence Quebec, but a Quebec which will enclose that old Quebec, can build.

All the chansonniers are that, and I have to resist a cataloguing that would turn into a roaming essay on the Singing Signpainters. Let me just tell about Claude Dubois.

Dubois is the chansonnier I came upon the same weekend I heard the poets recite at the La Paloma, the occasion for this definition-via-Vigneault. Thin, pale, with his muddy locks brushed forward over his brow, dressed in the tight-panted style of the fancy duds of the working class of the industrial world until Carnaby Street hit, he climbed on stage with assurance and launched into a sweet ballad of life at the corner of Sanguinet and Vitré: "A well-heated shack, where we all froze quite well . . ."

Then a cynical, yet still beautiful, song, rendered in a voice with some of the quality but none of the roughness of Vigneault's: when he was younger (this at eighteen), he asked a girl down the street to go out with him. She said no. Why, he asked. *"C'est pas de tes affaires, p'is c't'une affaire de famille."* After this introduction, the song: "You've gotta love your mother, you've only got one mother, and so you've gotta love 'er, ya-ya-ya-ya-ya-ya . . ." The whole family, father, sisters, brothers, gets this treatment, the whole of family love is reduced to slum small talk, a cheat, a diminution of the person. Like everything else about slum life, but maybe worse, because this is something the prevailing ideology designates as noble, something which, because it is forced on you, you call a sacred fulfillment. The song rejects but does not replace.

Dubois, when questioned, is unaware of, or unwilling to avow, the revolutionary character of his songs. He even seems drawn in other directions than this spontaneous rage against the slums, to have taken to heart the reproach that all his songs sound alike, a reproach of friends, he says. He works his act up to one of his more elaborate and less beautiful songs, called "Century of Speed" and as conventional as the title suggests. And he tells about his big song, in the works, a rambling piece which has, to judge by his description, something of the style of an artist he speaks enthusiastically about, though he didn't come to him by casual paths: Dylan. For Dubois has been hired by the same company that produces the American chansonnier's work, Columbia. His boss, Dubois says, told him: "Take these home, listen to them, and try to exploit that style, because it sells." " 'Go to hell, you're making me sick,' that was my first reaction," he says. "But I went home and listened, and this guy is really something. He's even anti-American, he tells the United States off in so many words in many of his songs. But I don't understand English at all, you know, I had to have a friend translate for me."

He goes on to speculate about his own chances in the American market, in American showbiz, and to anticipate a promised meeting with Dylan when he comes to the Place des Arts. Rawly expressed by a youthful artist, this is a tug I was astounded to find in the most hard-core Shouters (as with Renaud's desire to write in American). Dubois is very ingenuous about it. He doesn't speak English, but isn't he appealing, he seems to be saying, isn't he gutsy and original like Dylan, won't the Americans forgive him this little language thing? They won't, of course. America does not forgive the unmelted in the melting pot, at very most according foreign-fad currency to Aznavour-in-translation or Montand-in-guest-appearance.

I asked Dubois if he were an *indépendantiste*. This is a precise word in French, and I used it to make a yes or no easy, but I didn't get one. "That depends on what kind of *indépendantiste* you mean." For a young Québécois this is a way of saying no. And yet there is a certain sympathy, there has to be. Was he a socialist? "Very," he said, again somehow throwing the question cockeyed. He mentioned Léo Ferré, the leftish French poet who was singing in town at the time, and called him a great socialist, which indicated that he saw socialism, too, less as a precise option than as an aura of brotherly love salted with satire of the high and mighty.

Were his joual songs addressed to joual speakers?

"They are addressed to everybody. My father finds them nice, a little hard, but okay. He is a carpenter at Angus Shops—you know, the CPR shops? I was born at the corner of Sanguinet and Vitré—I talk about it in my song—but when I was about ten we moved out to the South Shore. I went to school at the regional high school in Chambly. Why move? To have a better life, to be happier. No, no teacher particularly encouraged me. Nor my family. Singing came of itself. Not even the atmosphere, chansonniers everywhere, no, not even the climate. I think I'd have been a chansonnier ten years ago, too, yes. My songs don't resemble anyone else's, wouldn't you agree?"

I mentioned Vigneault and Raymond Lévesque, that other singer of east Montreal: "Hm. Of course, Vigneault is everywhere, Lévesque is everywhere. But I don't think I got my ideas from them. I've been making my living singing for about a year now—I quit school, moved out."

He had come from another club, sung another date just before the performance I'd seen in a coffeehouse not far from the district he sings of. And I recalled having seen him earlier, further west, in the Asociación Española, singing what struck me as lively—though at first hearing not beautiful—joual. When, later, Dubois's records began coming out, they seemed to me to be a happy failure of record company to efface the artist. They'd dressed Dubois in folk-rock denim cap on the jacket, but inside the voice was still pure, the melodies French. The attempt to take him in hand had done some damage: a trite band accompaniment cancelled out Dubois's nice guitar plucking without bringing him anywhere near the hard-rock sound of Dylan's band-backed albums. His first record mostly contained the repertoire he was singing when I dropped in on him; his pre-Columbia repertoire, including some of the sweetest airs since Vigneault. His second must be the fruit of Columbia's hothouse work: the jacket dada, the lyrics surreal, the orchestration pale rock. This was sadder, but not yet disheartening; here and there an image, a note or two, a saving beauty. And some of it was not Columbia's fault, but simply Dubois's immaturity, inability, for example, to go beyond the romantic cliché in describing the city, the whole city, the smog and madness. But Dubois was still going forward.

Others have gone further than he toward singing the way the models from the environing culture impose, others have more slavishly imitated rhythm and blues, beatlemania, folk rock. I have heard a thin, pale, classical-collegian youth belt out the "baybe, baybe, baybes" of the Otis Redding songbook in a provincial nightclub, a "grill," perhaps finding a part of himself in them, as many a Québécois finds a part of himself in Willie Lamothe's arrowhead pockets and joualizations of Hank Williams. And then there is the slide into tedium that always threatens the traditionalists, the chanteuses and *chanteurs* who choose not to nourish themselves from the Afro-American, or Afro-Americanized-French, environment and find themselves with nothing more recent than Piaf and Paul Whiteman as sources. It is not every artist who has the sure step of a Vigneault, and even Vigneault perhaps did not have it at twenty. Authenticity is a search, and in that search the young voices of Quebec can draw from a brief, uneven, yet distinct pulling-together of a Quebec way of living the twentieth century and the North American continent. They can draw from, or they can simply breathe in: I learned some months after my conversation with Claude Dubois that though he does not care to attribute to any of his teachers his coming to song when a high school student in Longueuil, though the naming of influences is painful to him, he in fact maintains a warm friendship with a young teacher from those days, and that teacher is one of the founding circle of *parti pris,* a man given to replacing a Chateaubriand passage with an André Major story in literature classes.

In a 1950's poem, Gaston Miron seemed almost to be calling across to the young writers who would come after in a passage addressed, on the surface, to his own wished-for poem, to the very thing to be created:

> Poem, I tried to bring you into being

The Quebec in which Serge Gagnon and Claude Dubois will be men is different from the one in which Jacques Renaud and André Major grew out of adolescence. Much is still as when Miron wrote; colonialism has not been toppled. What is different is that the project of toppling has been enunciated. The poem has been brought into existence. The revolution not yet, but the poem has children.

6
The revolution not yet

Who has heard the Shouting Signpainters?
  Writers who proclaim a political intent, who want to change their surroundings, who are not content to comment on them, cannot escape this question. It is the question of efficiency: Have the words the *partipristes* hurled out touched the speakers of joual? Has colonialism anything to fear from these books?
  The reaction from colonialism seems to indicate that it fears the authors, but not because of their books. To harass the authors will perhaps discourage their producing more books, but no censorship has fallen on *Le Cassé*, *L'Afficheur hurle*, *La Chair de poule*, as long as they have not ventured out of the bookshops. (Jacques Renaud's mother did tell me that a scandalized browser managed to get *Le Cassé* removed from the shelves of the French-Canadian department store Dupuis Frères.) There has been one seizure of a *parti pris* work for obscenity, that riot of the unconscious which bourgeois society represses for good measure: it was a very Gérald Godinesque book published as the breakout of a savage talent hiding in a Montreal warehouseman named L'Oiselet. The one plainly political suppression struck a book whose author was already wanted by the police for his acts. *Nègres blancs d'Amérique*, by Pierre Vallières, accused of sedition. I have mentioned his book; in this chapter I will speak of his acts.
  That restriction to the bookstores does, of course, put a sharp limitation on the number of Québécois beneath whose eyes the *parti pris* output ever falls. The manual working and rural class of Quebec

never go into bookstores; if they purchase reading material it is on a snackbar counter or at a newsstand, or is by peddled subscription. So how about newsstand distribution?

When I was in Sherbrooke, a city of some 70,000 which receives every Montreal daily newspaper within the day and whose stands generally stock the same range of French, American, and Canadian magazines as appear on Montreal newsstands, I couldn't find *parti pris* on sale. There was some possibility, I recall, that the University of Sherbrooke (French, Catholic) bookstore stocked it, but I had to buy it on trips into Montreal. There it was on every fairly well-stocked stand, and I saw the same was true in Quebec City on various visits after my return to Montreal. I also used to see the *parti pris* books, that first wave of Renaud, Chamberland, Major, on the odd drugstore newsstand. But no longer.

The retreat to the purely literary marketplace after an at least scattered attempt to break into the mass-readership one seems to be partly due to *parti pris*'s losing faith in the mass-marketability of its offerings and partly forced by the unwillingness of newsstand owners to display them. The newsstand owners' refusal I have heard explained as both distaste for the content of *parti pris* and a simple inability to sell it, in there among the *photo-romans* and the tabloids. In either case, the pessimistic leftist book importer who distributes the éditions parti pris doesn't much try to push them beyond the bookshops, and the big magazine distributor who handled the magazine did not manage to put it in any but the most intellectual news shops.

Bookstores are amazingly frequent in downtown Montreal streets, even in outlying districts, even in the east end: French bookstores, English bookstores, bilingual bookstores. And the class that has always been the public of *parti pris*—petty-bourgeois, bohemian-intellectual, establishment-intellectual-wanting-to-keep-up-with-everything, some white-collar, some student—frequents them. Hence the magazine's circulation *in Montreal* is probably about what it would be under any system of distribution. Elsewhere in Quebec bookstores are scarcely to be found. If *parti pris* had the same potential audience in Sherbrooke, Quebec City, Valleyfield as in Montreal, that potential was largely lost for lack of newsstand distribution.

The limitations were plain from the start, even in the blush of the magazine's early circulation climb. "We never intended *parti pris* to be a mass-audience news or propaganda paper," Chamberland told me. "Everyone I know would like to start a weekly," said Maheu, clearly suggesting that such a project was something else again from *parti pris*. And Jean-Marc Piotte wrote for a mass propaganda sheet in 1965, when he was publishing more ponderous articles in *parti pris*. These three *partipristes*—Chamberland, Maheu, Piotte—were victims of the panic *parti pris* nevertheless inspired in at least the submissive levels of colonialism. I have spoken of Chamberland's short-lived teaching career and the gag employment ad *parti pris* ran for him and his comrades. Similarly, Maheu taught literature, at the Collège Saint-Laurent, the year *parti pris* appeared and his contract was not renewed. For a long time Piotte could not find work after the end of his stint with the Bureau d'Aménagement de l'Est du Québec, a federal-provincial rural uplift project in the rugged Gaspé peninsula for which he was a community organizer.

All were re-absorbed into respectability with time, in each case because they accepted intellectualizing within the establishment's structures: Chamberland (after a stretch as a writer of employee-training material for the state electric utility) and Piotte as higher-learners in Paris; Maheu as copywriter in an Anglo-Saxon advertising agency. Politics as a hobby, okay; fooling around with the minds of our young, our poor, no.

André Major was also unemployed during this time, and his re-absorption was most thorough of all, engaging his whole self and not just his office hours. He had been sacked by the Catholic Action weekly for secondary-level students, *Vie étudiante*, for which he was writing *Le Cabochon* as a serial. This was the noisiest establishment whack at the *parti pris* menace, and it was probably the Catholics who ended up with the worst of it since *parti pris* defenders were the bulk of their papers' staffs and resignations forced them to close down their whole string of youth publications. But cooler heads praised *Le Cabochon* when *parti pris* published it, and the beginning of the killing of André Major with solicitude was on. It was cruel, three years later, to read Jean Ethier-Blais reviewing the novel in the literary section of *Le Devoir*: one could not of course take Mr. Major's improvised ideology seriously, but what sensitivity, what talent, he purred, in precisely the tone Major later adopted in *his* murmurings as junior reviewer for that same serene *Devoir* lit. sup.

Good boys, but keeping bad company. That had been the line on the FLQ, and that was the line on *parti pris*. When, in this same period, the right pulled out of the Rassemblement pour l'Indépendance Nationale, which had sought to be an ideologically neutral umbrella for all forces within Quebec society working in the drive for separation from English Canada, one of the sins with which the rural and ruralist physician-leader of the dissidents, Dr. René Jutras, reproached Pierre Bourgault was frequenting "the Marxist journal *parti pris*." Bourgault had published his campaign statement for the presidency of the RIN, which he went on to win, in the third issue of the magazine. (So little founded was Dr. Jutras's fear that Bourgault would Marxize the party that a couple of years later *parti pris* was printing the position papers of one of its *real* children, Andrée Bertrand-Ferretti, who was trying to oust Bourgault as a straw separatist who would make independence painless for big money. Bourgault's chief claim on the early sympathy of *parti pris* seems simply to have been his youth.)

Behind this kind of panic was the fear, the intimation, that *parti pris* spoke for youth. If not all youth, then at least the "future elite" to whom the French-Canadian watchdogs' own ideology had always given a golden importance; if not immediately, then soon, very soon if there was not massive retaliation. And indeed the virus kept cropping up. The University of Montreal student bi-weekly, long rebellious, declared itself flatly socialist the second year of *parti pris*'s presence on the scene (interestingly, not separatist, socialist). The next year, 1965, it was separatist too, and announced it was no longer playing the game of objective reflector of student life, but was a *journal de combat*. The student council panicked and squeezed out the editors, but meanwhile the Laval University, University of Ottawa, and University of Sherbrooke papers were leaping in with similar *prises de conscience* (in these cases, usually in the more familiar order of *indépendantiste* first, then maybe socialist). And the *next* year the *Quartier Latin*'s personnel were more *partipriste* than ever.

Behind the cooling of the retaliation, the acceptance of the *parti pris* presence, was perhaps an establishment realization that this crystallization of youth around the *parti pris* themes was not, after all, shaping up instantly, that insofar as it recruited youth to separatism it could serve the establishment's own uses of nationalism. Socialism?

That was a big word. Panic had perhaps been premature, the reaction of the least sophisticated elements of the status quo.

The *partipristes* themselves knew that it was not an analytical monthly and a virulent literary school that were going to bring North American capitalism down in Quebec, and their magazine spoke of ways of fleshing out the assault. *Parti pris* had editorialized against the ousted socialist editors at the University of Montreal: to the phrase from Lenin—"When the university moves, everything moves"—on the masthead of the paper the students brought out to compete with *Quartier Latin, parti pris* replied with Lenin's strictures against infantile leftism. A newspaper was not a thing to be thrown away; it could help bring an unawakened public to revolutionary positions. How then to proceed with the wider public, on *la Catherine*, in the *ruelle Saint-Christophe*, or *pas loin du pont*?

Already others had made *parti pris* more than a publication, a new presence on the newsstands. Revolutionary *publications* had been seen before in Quebec, even in the fifties. I have in my files a luxuriously printed *cahier* of left-nationalist reflections called *Québec libre*, in which a bit of Kerouac and de Beauvoir in with the Québécois indicates that this is not the old closed nationalism (1959); the mimeographed Fanonism of Raoul Roy's *Revue Socialiste* (1960 and forward); and a printed but collegian left-nationalist magazine called *Jeune-Québec* which a friend who later went into one of the post-FLQ terrorist movements showed me around 1962. I also have an older magazine, *Place publique* (1952), in which free-thinking intellectuals of the Duplessis period who found *Cité libre*'s left-wing Catholicism too mild for them denounced election-peddling in darkest Quebec and U.S. napalm-bombing in the Korean War. But these magazines had the weakness of sharing too much with *Cité libre* (their age) and too little with the French-Canadian landscape (they felt the tug of Canadian Communism as an anti-obscurantist force, but they also felt its anglicizing, protestantizing, denaturalizing effects on the mundane life of the French-speaker who fled to its milieu). They could not be the successors to *Cité libre*; they could only be a marginal hard-left group of castoffs from Quebec life.

That was what was new with *parti pris*: the claim to be the next step after *Cité libre* had been seized and possessed. The claim was made overtly, in *parti pris*'s ridicule of the *citélibristes* ("It is a tradition that nations erect monuments to the great men of the past: hence we suggest that the city of Asbestos put up one to Gérard Pelletier."). This sort of thing rang true in *parti pris* in a way it could not with those who were still torn between their admiration for Pelletier, the pro-labor reporter on the Asbestos strike scene, and their inability to pardon his Catholicism and political timidity.

It was claimed, this successorship, and the claim stuck. Neither *parti pris* nor *Cité libre* were full-fledged professional journalism like, say, the French *Maclean's*, set up in the early days of Liberalism in Quebec with the collaboration of some combative journalist-writers but above all with the backing of the big Toronto firm's slick advertising apparatus. *Parti pris* had no nonpolitical ads, unless you count one for "Pétro-Montréal, Inc., fuel oils, Marcel Chaput, président." But like *Cité libre* it was printed and distributed professionally, not artisanally, and like *Cité libre* it went beyond the meeting halls and salons into the marketplace. Its circulation grew fast: a thousand subscribers, perhaps four times that in total sales. *Cité libre* had reached Frère Untel in Saguenay; *parti pris*, I know, reached the Camus-reading progressives at the University of Sherbrooke, who were shocked by it in 1963. I have heard a bus ticket collector, a socialist formed in the unionization of the province's private bus line, tell movingly in a speech how the discovery of *Cité libre* years before had put the first spark of contestation in him. No doubt the future will bring forth similar testimonies from the working-class militants *parti pris* reached in the sixties.

Cité libre became a name for a tendency in Quebec, but it was a tendency without an organization. The *citélibristes* saw their anti-Duplessis combat as being carried on by the trade-union movement. Toward the end of Duplessis's days, Trudeau called for an electoral front of all democratic elements, but no such merger took place and the Liberals alone profited from the debacle. But the Liberal rise became a sort of *Cité libre* coming-to-power, as the magazine's circle placed men in many a position of power, and not merely in government. In the same way *parti pris* also became an appellation for a tendency, a gang, a milieu. There began to appear in the magazine more and more precisely stated invitations to those who felt they belonged to that milieu. The more-than-magazine nature of *parti pris* began to seek organizational shape. In the first issue it had been:

"We'll do our part by organizing discussions, meetings, etc. We welcome readers' comments, and articles in any field—literature, politics, social research—for total liberation demands total thought. And even to subscribe to *parti pris* is an act: it helps prove the real emergence to self-consciousness of the revolutionary group . . ."

The second issue contained an editorial on the imprisonment of the FLQ which said the young activists' intransigence freed their sympathizers from *their* prison, "turned us resolutely to the future"; it was followed by these two "Notes: —The staff of the student paper *Le Garnier*, of Quebec, comes out officially in the latest issue for the independence of Quebec. One article was entitled: 'For a proletarian revolution.' Youth knows where it's going. —We said in our first number that the public's reaction would indicate whether we had a right to speak for youth. We had to reprint the issue; it was sold out in a few days."

In the third, Piotte editorialized: "Revolutionary youth (including *parti pris*) would be willing to be active in a party clearly socialist, independentist, and secularist. No existing party, the RIN and the PSQ any more than the others, meets this definition." (This was the Bourgault issue.) "If we can make of neither of these a true party of the revolution, then we will have to create this party . . ."

The editorial in the fourth was a "letter to the reader" which returned to the theme of reader-as-member-of-the-group, of magazine-as-expression-of-the-new-consciousness: "Since we wish ourselves revolutionaries, we cannot consider our readers an amorphous, female mass awaiting our ideas. *Parti pris*'s function is to help the revolutionary class become conscious of itself, of its strength: by definition we are a sort of magazine-seminar."

We were now into 1964, and the next four issues, in the early months of that year, continued in this vein: "For the moment we have only our refusal of compromise, but that is a first breach in the wall that separates us from the exploited. . . . We mean to force that breach . . . for *parti pris* will make sense only if it prepares what is to come," said Chamberland in the February issue, and Maheu opened a "What Is to Be Done" column with: "The party that will make the revolution is still unborn, and *parti pris* is worth what hope is worth. Our job is to keep calling for the revolution until it finally comes forth, to say things that aren't yet quite true so that they become true. . . . In France, they've learned that if you throw marbles under the feet of police horses, they stumble, that if you throw oil, they slip. The police have dogs in reserve, which will panic us when they're first unleashed. But the Negroes have learned that the dogs go for the throat, and with an arm to the throat plus a punch to the dog's snout . . ."

In March, Piotte warned that "it's not at our desks that we can study techniques for action"; Maheu urged "massive and organized demonstrations, propaganda by tracts, slogans, paint, coups d'état" (which he corrected next issue to *coups d'éclat,* or surprise moves, attributing the error to super-militancy on the part of the printer); Michel van Schendel wondered whether "the starting point for revolutionary action should be the backwoods, where anger is strongest"; Piotte and Chamberland urged *partipristes* to be in on the upcoming formative meeting of the Parti Socialiste, "a turning-point for Quebec socialism" because it would decide whether to reject all ties to pan-Canadian socialist movements; André Major saw more hope in underground groups which had recognized "the impossibility of any separatist party's being effective inside the legality the system accords"; and the back cover told of the beginnings of the extension of *parti pris* beyond a magazine: "the éditions parti pris announce the publication of: *la ville inhumaine,* a novel by laurent girouard."

In April, at last something specific: "*Parti pris* has, for some time now, been participating in panels, meetings, discussions. We stress our interest in this type of involvement. —To all groups that have written or telephoned us to arrange meetings or even to join us, we stress that such collaboration indeed interests us. But it is tied to setting up an office for the magazine, which should take place this summer." But while there was a sharpening there was at the same time a looseness of the politics of liberation in Quebec: in a column on a new clandestine-but-moderate separatist group, Robert Maheu noted that "it is said that in Algeria in 1953 there were no fewer than forty-five movements or organizations for independence; only fools refuse to see vitality in the similar Quebec situation." This was also one of the least *partipriste* issues *parti pris* ever put out: the theme was Quebec cinema, and there were articles by only vaguely politicized filmmakers. And for the one and only time in the magazine's history, there was a not-responsible-for-opinions-expressed disclaimer after the editorial. The May issue was silent on the problem except to mention one of those "panels, meetings, discussions" at the Jacques Cartier Normal School.

The next issue was one of the most *partipriste* ever: thick like a book, it announced from its burnt-brown cover nothing less than a "portrait of the colonized Québécois—his alienation—his sexuality—his psychology—his liberation." In the editorial Camille Limoges told the practical men of Quebec liberalism that the socialist-separatist extremists were the real realists now. In his column Pierre Maheu called for the realization of this realism in "a movement of popular liberation" which would make independence a proletarian cause, the cause of the fans who cheered at a Montreal Golden Gloves tourney when Reggie Chartrand's protégés appeared with *"Québec libre"* on their dressing gowns. The back cover announced four things: the next issue would be *parti pris*'s manifesto for '64–'65, the magazine invited advertisements, it was moving to 2135 Bellechasse Street, where a club parti pris, to which one could belong for a dollar a month, would hold meetings.

The Champagneur Avenue meeting place had been Maheu's apartment, not palatial, in a block of run-together old houses like in the slums, but Outremont-old, oaken, kept up, tranquil. The Bellechasse address was over in Rosemount, a basement in a new apartment building, shabby-new in this district down the mountain from Outremont but up from the slums to the skilled workers who inhabited it. "We're in every night of the week," said a further notice in the next issue. "Our initial investment was $1,000," said a letter to the reader following the promised manifesto, "but we must move on from this artisanal stage. It's go forward or retreat, and so we've rented a new office for the magazine, with meeting hall and secretariat. But all this costs money. We've done the carpentry, painting, curtain-sewing, etc., ourselves, but we can't buy chairs, typewriters, files, and a mimeograph for less than $1,500, and rent, phone, and stamps cost us $150 a month. . . . So you'll forgive our insistence; you will find in this issue a membership form for the CLUB PARTI PRIS." The emphasis ran through the issue: "For months we've been insisting on the need for a true revolutionary party, ending a good half of our articles on that note. But we haven't gone further than pious hopes. What structures would this party have? Hard to say in advance, something to be created in the crucible of action. The very idea of a democratic revolutionary party is new in Quebec; the club parti pris will try to develop it. But the subject is immense, and no country in the world has yet invented a satisfactory democracy." How would the club go at it? "It won't be a platform from which savants will discourse," read the back-jacket notice, "for the simple reason that we have no savants in our land. But it won't be 'social' either, a conversational rendezvous; it will be a place for precise discussions, with each participant invited to draw on his particular background to enrich the group. Directing things will be an animator, who will be firm on method but loose on content. And if you don't like him, you'll change him. . . . See you soon."

The manifesto sketched in the climate of Quebec in 1964: the first FLQ in jail, but a new one robbing garrisons and publishing *La Cognée*. This sheet was mixing some socialism with its separatism, *parti pris* was joined by *Socialisme 64*, a little magazine of older, more academic, more trade-union-tied socialists. A "new left" was born. And on the other side, "police repression of revolutionary groups, raids on their offices, arrests of newsboys selling *Québec libre*, 'preventive' arrests, exclusion from jobs for some militants, exclusion from the media for some opinions, and above all a bourgeoisie on the attack even against very moderate unions: Fashion Craft, *La Presse*, Dupuis Frères . . ." André Major drew the background of this last lockout from time spent in the grand old French-Canadian department store's stockroom a bit earlier, capturing everything, as usual, in one brutal, physical image: "After an hour of work, sweat, dust in the nose and throat, neons burning our eyes." Major managed to find one fellow-worker who'd known one of the FLQ, but the others were so varied and split that only a very harsh (and French-Canadian) management could have made union solidarity replace backbiting. In the same issue, Raymond Villeneuve of the FLQ wrote to the magazine from jail: "They won't let us read Lenin, but they don't object to Adolf Hitler." This from a terrorist who was the prisoner of old conservative French-Canadian nationalism until very shortly before his going underground, as is indicated by his biographical sketch in the pro-FLQ pamphlet *Les Résistants du FLQ* by Bernard Smith, which quotes his adolescent texts appealing to "the mystique of the fatherland." In the same September 1964 issue Chamberland, who had editorialized in the May issue that the Quebec liberation movement would be socialist or nothing, conceded that the workers might have to support the bourgeois independence drive for the moment. And Piotte tackled, half-earnestly, a self-criticism of the *partipristes* and their integration-on-paper of socialism and separatism:

> Pierre Maheu asked me to rewrite my opening paragraph. You don't start a self-criticism by talking about *Cité libre*. But to criticize *parti pris* I must review what we have been, and we have often defined ourselves in relation to *Cité libre*, criticizing in it a part of ourselves. So I must again speak of it, but let us hope it will be the last time. So! . . . Formed in either the school of Sartre or in Marxism-Leninism . . . we habitually posed a dilemma, an intellectual problem, and then went on to solve it with deftness and brilliance. Our method was deductive, schematic, filtering Quebec reality (which we knew mostly from texts anyway) through the concepts of Memmi, Fanon, Berque, Marx, and Lenin. We were something new in Quebec thought, but not, let us simply say, in the universe. . . . Some reproach us our philosophical language. But can you blame a man for having a good vocabulary? I'd be happy to handle the language like Paul Chamberland. A rich vocabulary helps ferret out the richness of reality. In a colonized country the odd character who possesses more than four thousand words is rare; let us not throw stones at him. But it is true we must clarify our lexicon, without, however, neglecting complexities. One word of explanation: our magazine is not aimed at the workers of town and country. It is a magazine, and to reach them we would need a newspaper. It's simply that you do not destroy a tank with a rifle. But we do have to define more sharply the words we use. How many times did our professors of philosophy tell us, Paul? "Define your terms; think of Socrates!" Forgive me, masters, for forgetting your wise teachings. We have gargled words: revolution, violence . . . Let's make them fit our reality. Many, too, have criticized our dogmatism. But when we asked them to define it, answers varied. Some said we deformed reality; them we pass over in silence. Others didn't like our vulgarities, whether labelled as such or mingled with our serious writing. They amused us in the writing, we didn't take them seriously, and it's a bit hard to understand a mind that does. Disrespect for human beings? But a human being is not an essence, he is what he does, thinks, wants, says—not ten years ago, but now. Our tone was dogmatic? Aggressive, yes, impolite, yes. We were popularizers, we were pamphleteers. But it is true one need not always be bad-tempered. . . . It seems to me we oscillate constantly between the revo-

lutionary desperately in quest of the better world and Emile Drolet [Laurent Girouard's hero in *La Ville inhumaine*], the disabused, the man who hopes no more. . . . And there was our romanticism, as in my "notes on the rural milieu," in which I describe at length a situation where people are exploited, then conclude that we must create a revolutionary party. Must, in a word, make the revolution. When and how? I do not say. For I am incapable of making the leap from the situation I describe to the revolution I prescribe; a romantic incompetent. . . . But the era of romanticism is past: the reading of Fanon and the theft of dynamite do not suffice to light a revolution. More realism is needed . . . (and you're invited, comrade).

"There is one thing you must understand," Jean Racine told me when I went to him for the story of the movement *parti pris* founded. "That is this: that we intended, when we started out, to make the revolution. To make it, to cause it to happen, by our own will. We learned better, but our intention was no less than that."

The club parti pris, or the Mouvement de Libération Populaire, as it later called itself, collected two hundred people, most but not all young, many but not all from already political petty-bourgeois backgrounds. Racine was secretary when I spoke with him. He had come from the RIN, from the family of a commercial artist in a drab suburb. Others were slum kids just recently initiated into petty-bourgeois intellectualism.

Shortly after the founding of the club in Montreal, the idea of a club in Quebec City was announced. The Mouvement was to sigh later that it had never, despite this contact, despite an envoy sent to the Lake St. John region north of Quebec, really managed to exist outside Montreal. And I am aware of no one who was able to put into literal practice Fanon's calm advice: "The nationalist militant who decides, instead of playing hide and seek with the police in the cities, to put his fate in the hands of the peasant masses never loses." The *parti pris* issue about Quebec, *Québec, capitale de roi-nègre*, which came out in May 1965, was a contemplation from a distance: citations of sociological documents were frequent, the list of contributors was not the most familiar, there was a transcribed tavern conversation with an unemployed man from bleak St-Roch which contained some joual jazz. The brightest bit was a *boutade* at the end, a photo of an African carving resembling Jean Lesage—"The plate shows a statuette of the Teke people of the western Congo. We understand it to represent a black king, traitor to his nation, who once lived there. It becomes a fetish to protect oneself against his tendency to return to haunt and vex humans. Note the rich symbolism of the dagger (a type of gouging tooth) held in the right hand, and the cock's crest, indicating fatuity and irascibility. And, like Oedipus, his feet are broken since he lies with his mother who is in Ottawa. Known to the people as 'Ti-Jean la Taxe.'" The same from-afar qualities were to be found in the occasional *chroniques régionales,* such as Laurent Girouard's account of a trip through the Abitibi country on the northern Ontario border.

The Mouvement's activities at this time included meetings, discussions, and political education forums aimed at training those who were already in the socialist-independentist orbit, and support of strikes in Montreal enterprises large and small, foreign and native, private and state.

Such labor revolt, particularly in the public services, was a marked characteristic of the last year of the Lesage regime (Lesage was in power from 1960 to 1966). *Parti pris* commented with satisfaction on the strikes at Hydro-Québec, the provincial electrical utility, and at the Quebec Liquor Commission; they had brought out the class conflict in the wage system even when the national state becomes an entrepreneur, and they had expressed a certain national consciousness in that they were organized by the all-Quebec labor organization, the Confederation of *National* Trade Unions (CNTU), which began as the Catholic Church's stopgap to secular trade unionism and with time and secularization became the native rival to U.S.-based unionism. I remember a night in the main park of the textile town of Valleyfield, where Mouvement militants had been called to support a strike by employees of a metal processing plant. Here the national, not to say the racial, character of the conflict was clear, since the company was a subsidiary of Noranda Mines, the big Toronto complex which extracts precious metals from far-flung areas of Quebec's northern soil, and the particular conflict was a spontaneous one based on the workers' irritation at an English-speaking supervisor—such walkouts happen often in Quebec. The chief political intervention was by the RIN, whose leader, Pierre Bourgault, had spent several days with the strikers. There was tension in Valleyfield —the town's conservative mayor had ordered his police to prevent the public rally in the park from linking the strike with politics, and Bourgault had agreed to speak only of independence, letting the issue at the zinc plant go for the moment. But the left was there too, and Pierre Vallières took the soapbox after Bourgault to defy the cops with an outburst tying the grievance of the zinc men to the general exploitation of the province, and was quickly hustled away by the police.

The strike with which the Mouvement most closely associated itself, however, was neither against the provincial state nor against Anglo-Saxon capital. It was against one of the small French-Canadian enterprises which, along with Jewish and other ethnic-minority businesses, occupy that marginal ground in Quebec capitalism not held by Anglo-American interests. The company was called LaGrenade Shoe (yes, in English), and was owned by a family of brothers of that name. The CNTU had unionized the small shop staff, and the strike dragged on as LaGrenade operated with scabs. MLP militants made placards in their headquarters, now downtown on St. Denis Street, and joined strikers on their picket lines in the north end of the eastern slums. They attempted to explain their politics to the strikers and they helped them resist the entry of scabs, a process which resulted in tangles with city police accompanying the scabs through the lines and a famous photo of Pierre Vallières, then secretary of the MLP, kicking spectacularly as constables removed him from the picket line. The photo and the press coverage made the little shoe factory's labor dispute known all over Canada, but although it became a touchstone for Quebec revolutionaries, it did not in reality strengthen the workers. The company dismissed them, the strike "rotted," as Quebec union jargon puts it, and the workers went elsewhere: the defeat became the socialist-separatist movement's as much as the union's, and though the MLP pulled out of the picture with as little rancor as possible among its members, resentments remained. Vallières and the Mouvement drifted apart, and Jean Racine replaced him as paid permanent staff.

LaGrenade had been one attempt to make things happen, and further attempts to make things happen were to come. But the MLP decided to try a program of finding bases in the working class before strikes or other extraordinary moments of class war cropped up, and the result was the St-Henri project. Now even it seemed wrapped up, Racine told me, sitting in the rough-planked MLP office on the third floor of a little commercial building on St. Deni Street, the Frenchest and poorest of Montreal's business thoroughfares, amid cubic packs of unsold back copies of *parti pris* and tangles of placards ready for any demonstration: "*Le Québec aux travailleurs,*" "*parti pris,*" "*Appui aux grèves.*" Very thin, pallid, with black-rimmed glasses and an intense brow crowned with stiff, black, swept-back hair, Racine was a cool revolutionary who had begun in the RIN, moved left, and been so feverishly active in the MLP office that when Vallières left it seemed only natural to give him the job. "Now?" he asked. "Now the MLP is in a process of thought and transition." That morning he had had to contemplate a mutilated door, the result of a forced entry the night before. "Some far-right type from Toronto," he said nonchalantly. The Mouvement had been through more upsetting harassments than this, and those mostly from the authorities. As aboveground callers for the fall of the Quebec order, and as incorrigible street demonstrators, MLP members were sharply watched by Montreal police, provincial cops, and the RCMP (the three of which had, after the FLQ bombings of 1963, announced the joint formation of an "anti-terrorist squad"). The Mouvement had a lawyer-member ready to step in at any moment and defend demonstrators who found themselves in city courts. For graver cases it kept up good contacts with criminal lawyers through such legal-trouble-weary members as Yvon Husereau and Michèle Saulnier, the teacher accused (and acquitted) of complicity in a plan to blow up the Statue of Liberty for which a group of American blacks and a Quebec woman were convicted in New York courts. And it set up with members' dues a bail fund to free militants imprisoned and charged after demonstrations and police crackdowns. It even had to deal with stoolpigeons: "We found out one guy who had joined us was a police plant. We went to the guy and told him we were onto him, and he just faded out of the picture: we never heard of him again."

For the story of the St-Henri experiences, Racine told me, Yvon Husereau was my man. But it was Racine who had put the experience on record in the magazine, his only contribution, though as MLP secretary he edited an internal bulletin called *Le Militant*.

("And Gérald Godin," he added, "wants me to write something for the éditions, it doesn't even have to be a tragedy, just anything, so he can say he's dug up an unpublished work by Jean Racine.") This official account of the experience ran in the February 1966 issue under the title *"chronique du m.l.p./*work in the working-class milieu":

> In September the Mouvement de Libération Populaire began an offensive meant to resolve the great contradiction of North American socialist movements: their lack of a base in the working class, the class of which they claim to be the avantgarde. The term "avant-garde" would be justified even if, without controlling the whole working class, a party contained the most conscious workers, but the notion has too often been the excuse of parties without any serious links with the mass of workers. . . .
>
> This is why, last summer, we supported numerous strikes (LaGrenade, International Envelope): to contact workers at a moment when a clash with their class enemies has brought their class consciousness to a high point. But the approach was incomplete; it didn't permit systematic politicizing, attempts were restricted to quick conversations on the picket lines.
>
> So in the fall we worked out a plan for distributing political tracts at factories in Point St. Charles and St-Henri. This district was chosen for several reasons; it is the zone of heaviest industrial concentration (more than 800 heavy industries) in Canada, many workers live in the district, the inhabitants are more and more aware of their situation of inferiority (and aware that this situation is caused by capitalism) because of the generally bad quality of lodgings in St-Henri and Point St. Charles. The plan was weekly distributions of tracts at the gates of four or five factories and at nearby homes, to touch the workers at several levels. But despite the favorable response of workers, we were never able to push the experience to complete success (which would be—the creation of cells of the Mouvement de Libération Populaire in factories). This failure, which is at the same time a success in terms of the education of our people, had been predicted from similar failures by the CP. But the Communist Party (of Canada, at the time) was working on a much more limited scale—distributing their newspaper, *Combat* (which isn't going to politicize anyone), usually to seek votes in some election. . . .
>
> No, our lack of success in creating cells in workers' districts is probably due to addressing workers at the wrong moment, at a moment

when consciousness of exploitation was not as high as in a strike. And then the MLP lacks the organization to carry out such an enterprise through an entire district. Though it's not the subject of this article, we've got to realize that in militancy, leadership, and equipment, the Mouvement de Libération Populaire has serious failings. . . .

In three of the factories we have worked on, however, contracts are now being negotiated. In the three, strikes seem likely. What we will have to do . . .

Fine, but I wanted to know more specifically what had happened in this confrontation between Shouting Signpainter and *colonisé québécois,* and so I grabbed Husereau when I next came upon him (in a bookstore looking for "something good, something solid, not apologia, on the Communist movements in Western Europe").

"It is impossible to total up the results of the experience," he told me. It was an experience of the period after the Victoria and Dominion Day demonstrations of 1965 had revealed a certain popular audience for separatist agitation, and after Vallières and his followers had joined *parti pris,* strengthening its concentration on the working class as the audience for revolutionary propaganda and its promise of working-class power as the theme of that propaganda. Racine's summariness and Husereau's reluctance about drawing up balance sheets made it hard even to obtain facts about the experience. But before that, a few facts about Husereau.

He was the chief mover of the action and the author of the handbills the MLP volunteers handed to the St-Henri factory people. He was not even twenty at the time of the St-Henri project, but he had already gone through several stages of revolutionary development: I have the front page of the conservative tabloid *Montréal-Matin* for September 4, 1964, which headlines "There are twelve!" Around the headline are the courtroom photographs of those arrested in a Montreal firearms-store robbery in which the robbers killed one store clerk and the arresting police another. Yvon Husereau is there, in a chequered bush shirt, incorrectly identified in the caption as Jean-Guy Lefebvre, twenty-six years old. His name, spelled "Hussereault," appears under another face, presumably Lefebvre's, and his age is given as eighteen. The fates of the dozen were unequal: those who, like Husereau, were arrested in the bush, in the terrorist group's camp, were released as unconnected with the shooting (not without having spent several months in jail); two who were on the scene, François Schirm and Edmond Guénette, were convicted of murder and condemned to death (later life imprisonment). In the camp police seized the evidence of the group's political self-education: publications ranging from *parti pris* and the European anti-colonial literature it looked to, to the scholarly English-language Marxist magazine *Monthly Review* from New York. Husereau's politics were already far from simple at the time of his arrest, and after it his development led him to frequent the headquarters of the nuclear disarmament movement in Montreal, a cosmopolitan English-speaking milieu which extended hospitality to left elements among French-Canadian youth in the hope of making contact with the majority population of Quebec. A newspaperman friend of mine around this time thought he saw a story in the conversion of young French-Canadian terrorists to Gandhianism by the patient efforts of Russell-like nuclear pacifists. How much of such a process took place I would hesitate to say—the ex-terrorists quickly formed their own group, lodged in the pacifists' basement—but the sojourn at the Montreal Peace Center on Ste-Famille Street undoubtedly opened Husereau somewhat to North American perspectives on political action in Quebec after an adventure based on its Cuban aspects. The American Negro movement took his attention during this period, as did the American New Left's concern with the problem of spreading initiative and power among participants in revolutionary movements. This problem has never ceased to concern him.

Husereau's group called itself the Groupe d'Action Populaire, "GAP," and it distributed tracts in taverns and published a tabloid newspaper called *La Voix des chômeurs*, intended as a rallying-point for the unemployed. The summer after the Armée Révolutionnaire du Québec's adventure in the bush, the summer of 1965, was the summer of the street demonstrations in Montreal; the Groupe d'Action Populaire was involved, as well as *parti pris*. *Parti pris*'s summer issue headed its editorial on the May 24 events with a post-demonstration quote: "We are no longer dealing with separatists, but with authentic revolutionaries.—Adrien Robert, chief of police of Montreal, *La Presse*, May 25, 1965." The same issue contained Pierre Vallières' plea "for the union of the left": "We join *parti pris* less to write in the magazine than to fight with the Mouvement." And the back pages carried the membership form for the club parti pris, which had been running for a year.

In the fall issue *parti pris* printed a long evaluation of the Quebec political conjuncture. It announced:

> One year ago, *parti pris,* after a year of existence, published a manifesto. It contained a quick analysis of the Quebec situation, a history of the independence movement since 1960, a criticism of existing parties, and the conclusion that the next step was action and the forming of a revolutionary party. The manifesto invited readers to organize themselves to make the revolution of which we had spoken.
>
> Now we publish a new manifesto. But this one is not at all in the same spirit. Not that we've changed our minds, but this time it is not a handful of writers for a magazine who are expressing their ideas, it is a political movement which is defining its positions. For last year's call was heard. The club parti pris has taken shape, *Révolution québécoise,* the Groupe d'Action Populaire, and the Ligue Ouvrière Socialiste [the Trotskyists, who later pointed out they were friendly but had not *joined*] have joined it, and it has become autonomous, a much more important thing than the magazine that gave birth to it.

All of which had been somewhat anticipated in the first issue of 1965, where, along with its articles "for a Quebec literature" (a memoir on *Le Cassé* by Renaud, the announcement of coming publication for *L'Afficheur hurle*), there appeared "advice to demonstrators" in the light of the Queen's Nightstick Saturday in Quebec City ("Since cops have orders not to hit above the shoulders, nylon jackets are particularly good—billies slide on them; and young ladies should not wear high heels"), a report on "private information meetings" and a "political education committee" the magazine proposed to launch, plus, on the back cover, an ad for a public meeting in the (yes) Montreal Policemen's Brotherhood Hall where Maheu would speak of "Quebec Tomorrow: Fidel Castro or Tshombé?"

So Husereau and his GAP comrades decided in 1965 that GAP belonged with *parti pris*, and very soon after the group entered the club, Husereau, despite being a youngster even in the Mouvement's young ranks, had established himself as one of the group's sages. Familiar in detail with French-Canadian labor history, raised in an anti-clerical atmosphere even in his home, he had tried pure Third World Fanonism in the Laurentians, had been exposed to New Leftism with its North American preoccupations among the ban-the-bombers, and now found himself among European-oriented Marxist-Leninist-Sartreans. Since Quebec was (a) colonized, (b) North American, and (c) French-speaking, its search for a revolutionary path was likely to draw on all three of these sources without being identified with any of them, and Husereau was well placed to attempt the synthesis. He told me about how it went when the attempt was made in St-Henri.

"We operated like this: we got up early each morning—our tract had been prepared beforehand—and went out in a group, in cars and on foot, to the gate of a chosen factory. We handed out our tract to the workers coming off shift, and if we could we talked to them, explained what we were doing, answered their questions. This was easier for some of us than for others. Mario Dumais, for example, is a solid militant, knows his stuff, and was always with the volunteers, but he has trouble voicing his ideas in that kind of atmosphere. Others have the knack. One of these was Claire Dupont. Claire pep-talked the workers and would sometimes find herself in the middle of an arguing, questioning group. She always had the answers."

What kind of message was presented to the men and women of those St-Henri plants? Here is a sample. A tract by Husereau, one of the weekly series he wrote, this one dealing with the media, and one of the few pieces of Shouting Signpainter writing known to have been read by serious numbers of Quebec industrial workers:

crush
the profit-makers!!!

The government controls television and radio;
Big business controls the press;
Government and big business are hand-in-hand!
This we know, because . . .

        THEY MAY DO THE TALKING,
        BUT WE DO THE PAYING!

The people have a voice . . . but it's hardly ever heard:
THE PEOPLE HAVEN'T GOT THE MONEY TO MAKE
   THEMSELVES HEARD . . . BY THE ORDINARY MEANS.

But:

> COULDN'T THE WORKERS ORGANIZE
> THEMSELVES
> AND CREATE THEIR OWN MEDIUM OF
> EXPRESSION???
>
> WHEN YOU THINK ABOUT IT . . .
> . . . WHY NOT???
>
> IT'S A MATTER OF GETTING STARTED . . . AND THAT'S
> WHAT WE'RE DOING!!!
>
> WHO WOULD DARE
> OPPOSE THE INTERESTS
> OF THE WORKING CLASS??!
>
> *let's get together!*
> *we will win!*

It was signed with the MLP name, address, and phone number.

"I know for sure that the literature we distributed had its effect." Husereau talking again. "One day we arrived at a factory for a distribution and a girl at a second-floor window waved to us, holding up that week's tract and pointing to a copy posted in the plant. Another time I sat down in a restaurant with a St-Henri man who didn't know I was involved in the political action taking place in the district—I posed as a delivery man with a truck parked outside, a ruse I often used to find out how people were reacting. He told me yes, he'd read our stuff, others had too, and they'd been interested. How much? That, again, you can't say for sure."

Why drop something that was working this way? Had it come to a dead end? Husereau was hard to get an answer out of, but others among the propagandists I spoke to attributed the halting of the effort partly to his own touchy and unpredictable character. "The group was never able to get together on its plans," a Belgian schoolteacher–computer programmer–militant who was involved told me. "Yvon would decide what was next, and one day we simply found out he'd decided the thing couldn't go any further." "Husereau was a difficult guy to work with," said a girl, who was enthusiastic and who would plainly have gone on getting up at dawn for the factory-door propagandizing if it had continued.

And there were the arrests. These were not Yvon Husereau's doing, but that of the Montreal police charged with policing the squalid slum streets of St-Henri, a village-like ghetto off by itself in the west of Montreal, below its railway approaches. Police would pick up loose pairs of distributors and whisk them off to the district station: no charges would be made, the arrestees would be released, but spiriting away activists without their comrades knowing what had happened had its demoralizing effect. "That was another way we could feel the workers' sympathy for us," Husereau said. "After this had happened a couple of times, workers would tip us off by phone when the cops hit some of our members, so we could take action to get them out."

Husereau is sure a better technique, a renewed drive at social animation, could make the *parti pris* message meaningful to French-Canadian ghetto-dwellers:

"You'll notice that all our texts drive home social and class themes; there is no nationalism, no call for Quebec independence. Why? Because we learned in our contacts at LaGrenade, International Envelope, other strike situations, that the national side of the Quebec worker's exploitation is if anything better-developed in his mind, separatism is further along than socialism. French-Canadian workers are nationalist: that's a fact, a basic, no socialist program that ignores it can get anywhere because it's too deep, too real a grievance. But precisely because it is so clearly drawn it's not what you have to hit. It's the class demand you've got to charm up from his unconscious."

Husereau said all this with just a hint of a whine, with the defensiveness that is a basic part of his personality. He has undoubtedly been discouraged, in his already mounting years of revolutionary activity, to find the revolution so hard to charm up to waking life, and in more recent months he has withdrawn from activism into way, way-out Marxist scholarship. Somehow the old revolutionary methods have missed a few of the essential characteristics of North American life, he is convinced, and what is needed is a "post-Marxist" science of revolution which will look deeper into the motives of the common man of late welfare-state capitalism than the old Marxism ever did. The territory he is into is lonely on the newborn left in Quebec, and in my most clinging recent image of him he is hunched over a table at the Asociación Española in his red-and-black hunting shirt, hair in bushy curls, sad smile on his young but slightly puffed face: "I tell you, the essential sentence of the century belongs to Aragon: 'The future of man is woman.'"

Somewhere between the first announcements of the club parti pris and the LaGrenade–St-Henri period, there appeared another magazine with the same preoccupations as *parti pris*, and almost the same size and shape. It was called *Révolution québécoise*, and the papers announced that its founder, Pierre Vallières, had launched it with the declaration that it would be Marxist, and being Marxist it would be hard to avoid being Leninist. The inspiration, then, would be the Russian Revolution and the world socialist movement that followed it. Now *parti pris* had never been ambiguous about its Marxism, and its members also looked to the first socialist revolution of the century for lessons. But they referred less often to Russia than to Algeria: their inspiration was the postwar decolonization of the dark-skinned world, a development in which the performance of white socialists had often been shabby. The outsider's logical question was why *Révolution québécoise* existed apart from *parti pris*, and I remember putting it to a promoter of the magazine manning a booth at the University of Montreal a few weeks later. "We're not hostile to the *parti pris* group," he told me mildly, "but we reproach them with a certain dogmatism." By this I took him to be referring to the violence of the language of *parti pris*, crashing down on the colonialists in Ottawa, the capitalists, and the native clergy collaborating with them. From the start *Révolution québécoise* was nationalist but less clearly separatist, asking if independence was indeed a step to the class liberation of the French-Canadian worker and expressing skepticism about the more purely cultural themes of *parti pris*: this was the Leninist coolness to the life of letters. In general *Révolution québécoise* was a chillier affair, a duller magazine than *parti pris*—even its shape was the usual rectangle—without, it seemed to me, achieving any greater popular appeal.

The approach drew a certain sympathy from me nevertheless. I remember taking the latest issue into a French restaurant while a reporter in Quebec City, flipping through this newsstand find instead of the menu, thinking: This is a less rich brew than *parti pris*, less successful journalism, yet perhaps really closer to the way things are? The relationship of the national emergence of French-Canadians to their liberation from the physical burdens of exploitation is still open to discussion, isn't it, and that physical exploitation is still the major scandal of the world, even the dark world? I opened the magazine over supper and read what was perhaps the most interesting article it published during its short existence: Charles Gagnon, one of its staff, deflating the joual program for French-Canadian literature traced by *parti pris* with the commonsense argument that joual had no future, no academy, no fixed address—"When Joual Puts on Airs" was his title—and to ennoble it was to glory in one's own wounds, a masochist's glory. Every French-Canadian knew his language was French, and if he also realized that he did not speak French correctly he realized something shameful, even by his own standards. Yes, I said to myself, true, though perhaps it misses the point of the joual movement, which is to transform shames into glories, commonly shared absences into rallying-points for fighting back. The article seemed to me to have correctness where *parti pris* had profound, sensed truth.

The truth at the heart of the joual movement was at length demonstrated by Gagnon himself, in circumstances which take some recounting.

Perhaps the names of Pierre Vallières and Charles Gagnon mean something to the non-Quebec reader. I first became aware of Vallières when he was writing news commentary for two unlikely publications, *La Presse* and *Cité libre*. *La Presse* has always displayed a curious helplessness before socialist and separatist leanings among its staff; several cleanings-out of the stables through lockouts, firings, and disciplinary measures left the paper still being composed by seemingly self-reproducing young men of the left who keep it a journal of protest in spite of itself. The cleanings did have Vallières as victim at one point, though, and the same thing eliminated him from *Cité libre*, where he briefly shook things up by debunking the notion that the changes Quebec society had gone through since the death of Duplessis were a revolution. There were other things about Vallières: he had been a seminarian with a religious order for a time, and the usual wry remarks were made about exchanging one mission for another; and his voice was heard at separatist demonstrations and in the conventions of the Confederation of National Trade Unions as a delegate for the journalists' union. That voice was, of course, a socialist one in both the separatist and trade union contexts; true to his Leninism, Vallières had his steady belief in revolutionary mobilization in the trade union, the organized worker, and *Révolution québécoise* turned again and again to this theme. Lost strikes are the revolution set back. The refusal of the unions to see the revolutionary direction of their own action is a betrayal of their members, as when the miners seized the town of Asbestos, then, told to do so by their leaders, set aside the baseball bats which were their only arms and allowed the provincial police, who had more than bats and no such pacific orders, to repossess the town for the owners.

Well, Vallières and Gagnon did join the *partipristes*, along with the others of *Révolution québécoise*, in the spring of 1965; Vallières was soon the MLP's secretary. For this period, I remember a night at the Swiss Hut. This was before Vallières had ruled that there'd be time for another beer after the world had been changed. He was there, we found ourselves at the same table, or did we find ourselves first in the same argument—"Our French is as good as any spoken anywhere!" "Come on, you guys yourselves have glorified joual, made a language of it!" "Not me! Not me!"—and placed ourselves at the same table? We exchanged names, occupations, other introductory topics. Was I any relation to John Reed, you know, *Ten Days That Shook the World*? I said no, but if I ever wrote about the Quebec October I'd ask him to write a preface, like Lenin.

By the time I began work on this book, Vallières and *parti pris* were apart again. Rumors circulated about him: he was in Yugoslavia studying workers' control of industry; he was underground. Then, months after the last had been heard from the picket lines at LaGrenade, a bomb delivered in a cardboard box at lunch hour exploded in the company's offices, killing the owners' elderly woman secretary and injuring one of the LaGrenade brothers. *Le Devoir*, in an excellent in-context report of the explosion, said the company's "social policy" had aroused indignation: the following day it retracted and said it intended no suggestion the bomb had any legitimacy. But everyone knew the bomb had to do with the strike, and soon the screws were on left separatists. One militant was asked to talk to police, did so with his lawyer in a restaurant, then, a minute after his lawyer left him, was seized by the same police and held for a day and a half without his friends knowing where he was. Released, he walked with a friend everywhere—until he went alone to the corner for a paper and was kidnapped again. To hear him tell of the interrogations, the blows, the physical irritations, the cops making him recite childhood-learned prayers, is to be taken back to Maheu's images of activist as insubordinate child, cop as confessor. And what these pious kidnappers wanted to know was where was Pierre Vallières.

In the fall of 1966 arrests began to be made of the new FLQ, the one that had published the mimeographed paper with the shaking fist sketched on the cover, *La Cognée—The Hatchet*—the one that had said that the anti-social behavior of the LaGrenade brothers had called for a bomb, and that had in recent numbers spoken of violence as a "social phenomenon," a fact of life even before revolutionaries turn it against the existing order. (*La Cognée*'s language had swung to the left since earlier days when separatism was the overriding theme of its articles.) At length it was clear to the public that it was Vallières who was being sought. *La Presse* systematically pushed the story into its inside pages, but *Montréal-Matin* knew people were intrigued: it filled its front pages with headlines. Vallières and Gagnon were in the Laurentians ready to give themselves up, said their lawyer; but it was not in the woods that they turned up, it was in front of the United Nations. They carried placards declaring themselves political opponents of the Canadian regime who had been chased from the country as criminals. They were arrested, jailed in New York, photographed by the *Daily News*—interested in such goings-on like its sister tabloid *Montréal-Matin*—and called in the caption "two Quebec separatists." On Canadian state television before their arrest they had defined themselves with nuances; in English they more or less accepted the characterization as separatists. But to the French film crew in New York they said that the FLQ's bombs were aimed equally at Anglo-Saxon and French-Canadian capitalists, because the real liberation of Quebec would be that of its workers from all capital. A New York lawyer fought their deportation back to Canada as they kept up what propaganda they could from their cells. This consisted largely of a demand for the status of political rather than criminal offenders, but more penetrating was a letter which the cooperatively published youth paper *Jeune-Québec* received from Gagnon. Charles Gagnon had berated joual in *Révolution québécoise,* had written the odd *parti pris* chronicle (an unfavorable review of Frère Untel's second, cooled-out book) after the *Révolution québécoise* group joined *parti pris,* and was a teacher of literature at the University of Montreal; but his father was a farmer in the Gaspé and his letter was addressed to him. The elder Gagnon lived in the joual world, and that world seemed very far away and hard to reach for a Marxist lecturer at the University of Montreal, even if his father was a Gaspé farmer.

> Old Jules,
> After reading Georges's letter, which I received today, I thought of writing you because he said you were maybe not saying just what you thought of my affair . . . I was curious to know; I thought of asking you to write, then I said: why not me? I call you *tu* for the first time; perhaps for the first time I really talk with you . . . We've got lots of time now, a pensioner and a prisoner. We have to make use of it.
> I don't know where to begin. I have many things to tell you, and yet I don't want it to be too complicated, because except for a few pages of your missal or in *Vers Demain* [the white-beret social-credit paper], I know you've never read very much. You've told me about working as a cook in your father's lumber camp. A small camp, as I recall.
> Then you got married, bought a farm on credit. I remember the year, 1917, when you got married, and when you sold it in 1952 you were still paying Farm Credit. But you still believed Duplessis was the little man's man. That, I have to say, I don't understand.
> Yet you knew you were being robbed: you swore, yes swore like hell. Against taxes, the bosses, the mayor, the notary, the dentist, the manager of the co-op, and maybe, I'm not sure, sometimes the priest, too. You felt it: those people weren't with you. You worked your land from May to October, you went to the camps from November to April, you still couldn't afford the things you wanted, because you had ambition, you had pride: good horses, good harness, a good four-wheeler, being able to pass in society, not looking like you were asking for charity.
> If we never talked about these things before, it was because you were in the camps all winter. It was funny: I had a father for half the year. A mother all year, and brothers and sisters. And finally it was as if you weren't quite part of the family. We didn't know where to put you, or where to hide ourselves when you came back.
> And there were the catalogues. Dupuis, and most of all Eaton's and

Simpson's, which were full of good things we dreamt about and you couldn't buy us. But that wasn't the worst, because very young I'd accepted—my mother said it, and later the priest—that there were rich people and others who weren't rich. And there weren't many riches in Bic, outside the church, the presbytery (less rich, but big, clean, warm), and two or three houses. So the riches in the catalogues were a little easier to forget.

But it's amazing, eh, the way men who speak, or spoke in those days anyway, of poverty being accepted with a good heart, lived, along with the notary and the doctor, in the nicest houses in the village? Then there's the biggest building of each village, with central heating and empty four-fifths of the time.

I can't forget those winters; after a night shivering on my bunk we headed for Mass, three miles away, in the sleigh, we arrived frozen, feet, nose, everything. Into the church. It wasn't warm, but better than outside: what could make some Québécois anti-clerical and not believe in God? He's got some funny friends, God has, some very funny friends. As long as there are slums in Montreal, and there are; as long as there are shacks in the Gaspé, in Portneuf, Lake St. John, Abitibi, and those exist too—whenever I see priests' houses like I've seen in Montreal and in Ste-Anne-des-Monts in the Gaspé when I was there last summer, as long as the men who live in them talk of accepting poverty and wealth, you will have to count me out of the believers.

Vallières published his own account of the *Nègres blancs d'Amérique,* his own autobiography. He had the right to write it. At thirty he had already been through a revolutionary itinerary which took him from a Franciscan monastery in Quebec to the Manhattan House of Detention for Men, where he began to put together the five-hundred-page testimony his extraditers would not let him deliver in their courts, the story of a Quebec slum boy whose exposure to the possibilities of the intellect gave him nothing but pain until he decided to live for the revolution, the opening of those possibilities for all the slums.

The book is unliterary, unembellished, unsubtle, uncouth—but not illiterate, and it is full of a kind of savage readability, true with the pathetic truthfulness of the man who across the tavern table sobs out the story of his life and rants his what-is-to-be-done. It will, I am sure, be read for many years and it will, I am sure, be a part of the political education of many a *cassé*, many a *barbare*, many a *cabochon*.

For that, despite his letters, is what Vallières is. His book is a politics of chickenflesh. Letters he has: many people who know Vallières, who have been involved in political action with him, will be surprised on reading *Nègres blancs d'Amérique* to learn that this is a man who has wrestled with Husserl, haggled with Heidegger, and "read all the great theologians whom the Church has excommunicated over the last twenty years: Rahner, de Lubac, Congar, Daniélou." But they will find here, too, the reasons a French-Portuguese acquaintance naturalized to Quebec politics had for seeing Vallières as the carrier of a mute, very québécois, very un-European anger, "a guy, finally, not nuanced in the least." There is the early childhood in the heart of the east, in the heart of slum Montreal, the pigtails seen torn bleeding from a little girl's head by a street bully; there is the adolescence in the "suburb" of Longueuil Annex, where the houses were made of beaverboard. There is the awareness of oppression in the quarrels of the parents, the once-rebellious locomotive-repairer father who worked at the CPR Angus Shops, the resigned wife who had tamed him. There is the nonacceptance of oppression in the classroom farts, and the filling of that nonacceptance with the content of the French left-wing magazines on Dr. Ferron's waiting-room table. Then the seeming out: the years in Montreal bohemia, as a white-collar wage-slave, as a contemplator of Cézanne's onions with friends who had also curled their anger back inside. Gaston Miron was there, and *Cité libre* was pleased to accept the young intellectual rebel's essays on the slowly emerging Quebec consciousness, but it didn't bring the revolutionary to birth; the escapee from Longueuil Annex had to make one last attempt to make his escape good, in Paris, before he could force himself to turn again to that mire and ask its dwellers to rebel. In France, Vallières says, unnuanced and unannounced, he discovered what a Marxist working class was. It does not seem to have been a complex educative process; simply an admission that this was what he wanted, this was what would make him a man: teaching the Quebec workers to be hard and brave like those French agricultural laborers. An ideal. Like a *béret blanc* or an artist in a garret. Oh, Marxist, yes; materialist, and realistic, concrete, worldly, all that; but let there be no quibbling about idealism versus dialectics, Pierre Vallières was what they would call, in Longueuil Annex, *"un gars qui suit son idéal,"* and his ideal was egalitarian.

An egalitarianism that would make him scoff at the Soviet Union's stratified socialism, and not be so sure about Fidel Castro or Mao. And true to this unintellectualism, a thousand philosophical problems are debated, hashed out, in *Nègres blancs*, and a thousand readings are reviewed, but it all comes down to one thing: to fink or to act, and once finking has been left behind, the problems that it seems to *me* intellect must resolve are not even discussed. (He had one relapse into religion, that spell in the Franciscan monastery, but embracing that kind of idealism never seems very real in this book where all past attitudes are scoffed at as soon as they are evoked, not given any lived-in quality: they were so many false stops before assenting to the commonsense of revolution.)

The national question? Must socialism pass by independence? Will the workers' nationalism merely enthrone the national bourgeoisie? Is the . . . No, *they're* the cheap labor merchants, *we're* the niggers. Of course one is separatist, of course socialism will be a Québécois thing against confederation. Waiting for the Canadian workers, *ça a pas de bon-sens, voyons.* The national bourgeoisie? *"A incinérer, camarades!"* He'd seen Mme Justine de Gaspé-Beaubien go around in her wheelchair delivering Christmas chocolates to her late husband's office employees; that was all he needed. Get serious. Even socialism is scarcely defended, shown preferable to social credit, reformist trade unionism, pacifism. It is an *idéal.* No more to be said.

Little said, either, on the neo-FLQ. This is partly explained by Vallières' belief, even while writing the book, that his movement was a going thing, would survive his own prosecution. You don't give away the inner life of a functioning underground. But not even a word on how much continuity there was between the first FLQ and his, whether it was organic, whether he knew, had worked or conferred with the originals, before or after their capture, or whether it was just a naming-in-honor, an identifying with others who, too, all Quebec knew, had had the *idéal.*

To reproach such a man with idealism is like reproaching Voltaire with insolence: he is thus or he is not: he has anticipated you—" '*Cré-Vallières, tête de cochon!*' you'll say," he interjects at one point, only to go on in the same *tête-de-cochon* vein. The best thing to ask of this book is what is this Quebec which makes such men? To those who would criticize him without even the comradeliness of a fellow

Marxist who does not see things his way, he is so indifferent as to embarrass them with riches of self-revelation. Hence the bald exposure of his sexual frustrations, from the disappearance one day of the little girl whose breasts he used to nibble underneath the porch, to the empty, arty married woman into whom for a time he was "ejaculating my virility as into a silken doll." There was the friend's wife in Montreal he used to covet as he talked to the friend of transcendance; there was the friend's wife in France who, having allowed him one evening to "stroke her shoulders, her breasts," that maternal breast again, counseled him to go home to his realities. And there was the love of his life, of whom he still daydreams in the Manhattan House of Detention—"It's crazy how imprisonment makes you sentimental." Those who smile at the motives of a revolutionary who has made such confessions are Vallières' least concern.

> Hey, Georges! What are you waiting for to make up your mind? And the rest of you, Arthur, Louis, Jules, Ernest? On your feet, lads, and *all together:* to work! We'll have another glass of beer when we've done something besides talking and always putting the blame on other people. Each of us has his little share of responsibility to assume and to turn into action. The sooner we are united, lads, the sooner we shall win. We have already wasted too much time in vain recriminations. Now we must go on to action.

Those words are from the book's peroration, and from the closing passage, too, of the prosecution's requisitory against him when he stood trial in the Court of Queen's Bench on Notre Dame Street East, a year and a half of prison after his arrest in New York. "Let Vallières go," said the prosecuting attorney after quoting from *Nègres blancs*, produced as Exhibit C-313 by the prosecution the day after it appeared, "and you know what to expect." Enough of the twelve middle-aged French-Canadians in business suits in the jury box got the message. The Crown had not been able to provide a clear link between Vallières and the LaGrenade bomb. The best it had gotten, despite vast tolerance from the testy judge for every piece of relevant or irrelevant paper or speech it chose to present, despite his overruling of objection and request after objection and request put by Vallières as his own attorney, was a mumble from the youth who had actually planted the bomb (and who had been convicted, had served a two-month sentence, and had been freed months before the Vallières trial) that Vallières had at one point sort of suggested he should do something like that. But what had become plain in the course of the trial was that the system had between its paws a revolutionary of a relentless kind, one who had hectored, organized, and written (his past writings were produced by the ton, those of the most varied, but always revolutionary, kind—and a good many of his past readings too) and would not stop hectoring, organizing, and writing until all men were equals, the workingman equal to the property owner, the man who gets nudged by the cop equal to the man who gets called for jury duty. The man was a leader, a persuader—his assumption of his own defense only emphasized this—he was one who *could* make young men plant bombs, never mind whether he had been shown to have done so in this case. The first Quebec political leader, in fact, that justice had gotten its hands on: other terrorists who had been through the courts, those who, if not leaders, were ringleaders, had been unknown before their arrest, unrecognized, could be written off as obscure nuts. But Vallières, who had worked at *La Presse* under Gérard Pelletier, who had edited *Cité libre,* who was known to Pierre-Elliott Trudeau, who published his autobiography in the midst of his trial? This was Top Terrorist, and he had to be hit with Number One Crime.

For some of the jury this was apparently sufficient: Vallières was in charge of the whole thing, what did it matter if the fatal bomb hadn't been tied to him? But one, François Charpentier by name, silver haired and lean, had already set himself apart during the trial by his questions to the witnesses (he wanted to know what the lightly sentenced accomplices had been told and had not been told by police and prosecutors discussing their coming testimony with them; he never clearly learned) and had a question for the judge. Court reassembled to hear it: Did the specification "at the H. B. LaGrenade Shoe Factory" have any special significance in the charge? No, said the judge, not at all, it was simply that you had to have a time and place in an accusation. The jury retired again, and the question, it would seem, became why quibble? Why insist on that bomb in particular? Why not—come to think of it—take the door the judge had left open in his speech to the jury, where he said you could convict for manslaughter? He didn't say, but sentence could be as low as a year or two for that. A compromise. That way everyone can go home, everyone would be happy. And so the jury announced its compromise, and the judge asked Vallières if he had anything to say. The hectorer from Longueuil Annex stood up:

> I wish to say that if I have today been found guilty of involuntary homicide, and no matter what sentence the court places on me, it is precisely because the court allied itself with the Crown, not to expose the facts as they were brought before the court, nor to direct the jury toward a verdict based on the facts, but to no other purpose than to condemn at any cost an accused so treated from the start.
>
> Mr. Chairman, the only thing I have to say is that I am not at all guilty of the crime with which I am reproached and for which I am convicted today. I have to say that the jury here was deliberately led into error. I have to say that today is the conclusion of a political trial, a conclusion which does indeed have its logic. I have to say that perhaps the interests of a particular class were defended, were very well represented before this court through this trial. I have to say that this court, in fact, is a court tailor-made to get the man it wanted to get.

And then the judge, Yves Leduc, about to retire, noted for his clemency in ordinary cases, a magnanimous man, announced *his* compromise: "In view of your clearly belligerent attitudes, I sentence you to imprisonment in perpetuity."

The public was excluded from the court for this denouement, the public whose age and dress marked it clearly as sympathetic with the defendant and likely to break its decorum at the verdict. Vallières' day in court was a rallying point for a socialist-separatist movement sagging in inactivity amid the speed-up of bourgeois separatism's drive to independence. Vallières-Gagnon had become a term in Quebec politics, the names on a poster, a committee, an anger, a comradeship so linked that it was a cause for outrage when the Crown announced it planned to try the two separately. Vallières had prepared one part of the defense, Gagnon the other. Gagnon's style was everything Vallières' wasn't, soft-spoken, witty, elegant: "the representatives of Her Majesty," he always called the prosecution, "my comrade," he always called Pierre. Even his writing style was all classicism and ellipse. But in an essay in the back of the *parti pris* edition of *Nègres blancs* and in a piece for *parti pris* written from jail, he made it clear that if the style was nuanced the commitment was not. *Les Têtes à Papineau*, the hotshots, from *Nègres blancs*: "Objectivity? I fear we must make up our minds to forget about it. I am even more categorical on this point than my comrade Vallières . . . and I am as reluctant to distinguish theory from practice." *Pourquoi la révolution*, from *parti pris*:

> Our left wants to remake the world, render it habitable simply because it finds it uninhabitable. . . . A strategy which hopes for effectiveness must prolong the real consciousness of workers, and not be guided by those petty or big bourgeois who condescend to interest themselves in the workers. . . .
>
> Let us mention a few of the fundamental elements of this consciousness. It is a confused consciousness, particularly in a heavily colonized land like Quebec; it is confused because consciousness is language, and often in such lands the workers have no language except one that speaks of daily realities: this makes political, even trade-union, consciousness impossible. It is this absence of language which causes working-class "consciousness" to be mostly anger and revolt, often without a precise target: pure anger it might be called, sometimes turning on the workers themselves, in guilt, masochism, auto-destruction (read and reread Fanon's beautiful pages on this in *The Wretched of the Earth*, or Memmi's in *Portrait du colonisé*)—sentiments rife in every tavern and grill in the province. Thus a revolutionary strategy does not mean repressing these destructive feelings, but giving a more and more precise, a more and more political, object to them. It is through them, through their many forms, that the now-abstract sense of fraternity that inhabits the heart of every exploited man will find its concrete way. Speeches, pamphlets, tracts—these alone cannot do the job, for they are but the Word, and we have seen that the Word, for the workers, is not yet flesh. The bourgeois, who possesses the world by words, cannot understand that.

Even from jail, even reduced to the doubtful Word, Vallières and Gagnon were serving as prods to getting things together. Between their trials, Pauline Julien and Jacques Larue-Langlois got together some of Quebec's best artists to perform for the money Vallières needed to appeal his conviction. "Songs and Poems of the Resistance," at Gésu Hall, owned by the Jesuits: Georges Dor sang a new song, from an envelope note, his most political ever (*"Coeur de Castro, coeur de Mao, grand coeur/de Guevara"*); I got my first glimpse of Gilbert

Langevin, singing joual protests (*"Abattez-moé, abattez-moé"*); Claude Gauvreau, Borduas' friend, emerged stiffly from reclusion to read nonsense epics for the rebel in Bordeaux Jail; and Gaston Miron broke his silence with a *Text for Pierre Vallières* that strode out toward the day when—did I grasp it?—we would be "each a self/and each as well in each." The Quatuor du Jazz Libre du Québec did a sort of "Set for Pierre Vallières," which saxed into the "Internationale" at the end, and backed Robert Charlebois and Louise Forestier in a new kind of Quebec rock'n'roll which took from Telegraph Avenue without ceasing to be Visitation Street.

Vallières went underground. Husereau had plunged into books, into the theoretical storing-up for revolution. Were there any other choices for *partipristes* faced with the fact that the Mouvement de Libération Populaire had not managed to "make the revolution, to cause it to happen." The MLP as a whole decided there was one.

Racine had told me to be at the MLP's next Thursday night meeting to see what its reassessment process had produced. The third floor of the Edifice Sleepex was packed. I greeted Husereau, sat down beside Chamberland. The new issue of *parti pris* was circulating, an advance copy Maheu seemed to have brought: it contained a piece by him on "parties and elections" and a rigid exposition by Husereau on the correct cell structure for a Marxist party. In the back of the room, leaning against the wall, I spotted Godin; against another wall, Jean-Marc Piotte in black leather; a little later, Miron came up the stairs.

Racine was up front, behind an apple-crate lectern. Beside him, Michel Mill. Moustached, speaking an excellent European-flavored French with a just-under-control stammer, Michel Mill is a Trotskyite known to his Toronto comrades as Mike Miller. The Trotskyites of English-speaking Canada were the one left group in the colonizing nation which had recognized the importance of *parti pris* within the Quebec movement and undertaken to court it. (The Trotskyite tendency in Canada exists alongside the pro-Soviet Communists, whom they revile, now alongside some Maoists, with whom they do not agree on what is wrong with the pro-Soviets, and finally alongside the social democrats of the NDP, who are always purging them from their ranks. The familiar pattern of left dissension in the industrialized countries of Western Europe and the U.S.) They had done so in their usual disciplined way, whose spirit was well expressed by a unilingual Trotskyite I spoke to around this time. She reproached herself briefly for not having found the time to learn French since her arrival, then admitted: "Our French comrades are developing so well we hardly have to do anything at all about them now." As Racine told me: "We had already read Trotsky and were familiar with his positions." Indeed, the works of the outcast prophet, in Paris paperbacks, are more generally available in French than in English Canada. Most MLP members, unaware of the constellation of lefts in English Canada, merely accepted the Torontonians with amused comradeship and puzzlement as to their precise purposes.

Mill was active in the MLP and on the committee that studied where it might go from where it was: short of cash, frustrated in its attempts to form a working-class base, unconvinced the moment was ripe for arms, bombs, or secrecy. And he was now reading that committee's report:

The MLP's best hope for creating a working-class base was to get closer to the unions. This was not easy. Some unions whose strikes the Mouvement had offered to support had rebuffed a separatist-revolutionary group which had often knocked the timidity of North American, including Quebec, trade unionism. But a political party containing both trade unionists and Marxists not antipathetic to *parti pris* already existed in Quebec: the Parti Socialiste du Québec, a nationalist offspring of the nationwide New Democratic Party, (The PSQ served as provincial social-democratic party in Quebec, since the NDP had decided not to open a branch office here as it had in other provinces.) On the issue of independence, the PSQ wasn't out-and-out separatist, but could be described, as it was by its chief advocate within the MLP, Jacques Trudel, as "independence without the name," meaning full powers for Quebec within the confederation or else.

Racine didn't agree with this description, but put it this way: "Getting our way on independence isn't the important thing for us now; the important thing is to find a working-class audience. So rather than debate nationalism with the PSQ, we ask them not to back down on their policy, but simply to sweep it under some carpet, not to talk about it for a while. Later, we'll see."

The leaders of the MLP who were deeply steeped in Marxism like Racine were able to be cool about independence because of their Marxist coolness about the interweaving of things. I recall Racine, challenged in the Swiss Hut one night to justify the PSQ move to a rabid separatist who did, however, consider himself a Marxist: "You want to do dialectics? Okay, we'll do dialectics: independence is a form, not an end." And some MLP leaders—Maheu, Chamberland, Piotte—had been in the PSQ back when it was declaring its independence from the NDP; *parti pris* had even carried a *chronique du psq* in early issues. They weren't afraid of working with men like Jean-Marie Bédard, a Marxist nationalist labor organizer who'd been through every political mill on the left in Quebec in the preceding twenty years and had a strong affection for the *partipriste;* he and others in the party were, as Maheu put it in a *parti pris* editorial a bit later, "no more a part of the generation which gave up without a fight than we are part of the Pepsi Generation."

Rank-and-file MLP members, who had trusted the Mouvement to express their blend of socialism and separatism, with both felt to be essentials, were less sure. There was discussion, questions from the floor, and the establishment of one clear condition for undertaking negotiations with the PSQ: the party would have to give different tendencies the right to organize within its ranks, and the MLP would do just that, keeping up an "organic" existence even after merging. For the rest, Maheu interrupted a quibble to say, "We're authorizing our representatives to negotiate with the PSQ, eh, not conducting those negotiations here and now?" The dissenters, warned of the PSQ discussions in documents that had gone out to members before the meeting, were not even present to protest. They had already taken their option: they'd joined the RIN.

Why did the MLP not do this? Why be the Bolsheviks within a social-democratic party and not the Communists within a national liberation front? I had put the idea to Racine. "The RIN would have been very glad to have us," he said. "Bourgault would have given us the same concessions we're asking from the PSQ—more, even. His attitude toward us has always been urbane: sooner or later, he was sure, we'd see we needed allies and come around to the RIN as the only separatist movement which can do the job."

(This was the position the RIN finally found itself in with relation to René Lévesque's movement when he started it.) Racine continued:

"Instead we choose the little PSQ. Infuriating for quite a few, this decision of ours. But what we need is not to add a bit of noise to the already loud separatist drumbeat in Quebec, it's to get roots in a workers' movement. We know there are trade unionists who are sympathetic to our view of the Quebec working class's position, and these men are in the PSQ. Precisely because the PSQ is nothing now, we can affect what it will be, we can build it. The RIN we couldn't swing more than a few degrees to the left: the petty bourgeois control it, and will continue to do so; it's their baby, not ours."

Within the month Maheu was standing up at the PSQ convention saying the party should get ready for the forthcoming elections:

"I would cite the case of the social credit movement in Quebec. They began to use television seriously to penetrate the population in the early fifties. Their vote in the first elections they ran in was minimal, but from then until their sweep in 1962 there were only *three elections*. If we renounce participating this time because of our own weakness, our uncertain unity, we put off all hope of being on the map for ten years or more. We must go in, and let our unity come in action."

This from a man who spoke for the magazine that had scoffed at electoral politics—the Québécois had always sold his vote, and he was right to sell it, the guilty were those who bought it from him. Maheu's justification of his new sound drew on the latest issue of the same magazine, an issue devoted to social credit, the *rightist* movement of the Quebec poor in the 1962 federal elections which so shocked the Quiet Revolutionaries. In it Godin had outlined the long evangelization by white-beret *créditistes* for whom social credit was a revolutionary para-religion but not a political party. They had been at work before Réal Caouette of the electoral *créditistes* took to the provincial TV screens. *Parti pris* even dug up a Rumanian bookseller from Bleury Street who was an ex-functionary of the Communist government of Rumania *and* a fancier of Major Douglas's doctrine, in order to relate *créditisme* to Marxism. And Maheu's own article had carried the title "The Ambiguity of the People," meaning the people's capacity for fighting its cause in the name of anti-popular ideas.

This ambiguity was perhaps at the heart of *parti pris*'s turning to electoralism. Yes, the Québécois despised electoral politics, sold his vote to the highest bidder. Yet to him that was still politics, the only politics there was. Husereau said it, recapitulating the St-Henri experience, Racine said it at the MLP meeting: "For the Quebec worker, the only political gesture he can make is casting his vote every few years; to help him over the hurdle from the old politics to revolutionary politics we must first give him the chance to make that gesture for his own party, transform the one political act he already knows of before we can show him there are other kinds of political acts."

So the Shouting Signpainters, and the young people who had heard them, learned about committee rooms and leaflet distribution. They worked, uneasily, with other Quebec socialists who had already participated in election campaigns with the NDP. The votes they scraped up—only three socialists ran, all in moderate Montreal ridings where the NDP had done passably in the federal elections, plus a mysterious fourth in the Lake St. John region—were, as Maheu feared, minimal: they did not even attain the objective of bettering the also-neophyte RIN that Racine, who became the PSQ's permanent secretary as he had been the MLP's, had set for himself. This plus the jolt of the Liberals' narrow defeat and the return of Duplessis' party, the Union Nationale, caused real disappointment among MLP militants who had gone into the PSQ, and pretty soon *parti pris* was having second thoughts, wondering if independence wasn't a prerequisite, if the RIN, after all, wasn't the right place for the Bolsheviks.

But there had been the experience of yet another attempt to find the language of the ordinary east end Montrealer, and Maheu, an advertising man, had gone about it the way the pamphlet that follows indicates. It is what a Shouting Signpainter had to say when he knew his words would be thrust into the hands, literally, as in Husereau's tracts, not figuratively as it might be said of *L'Afficheur* or *Le Cassé*, of the *colonisé* he meant to liberate:

THE PARTY OF THE QUEBEC WORKERS

worth 10 . . . a psq vote is worth 10 . . . a psq vote is worth 10 . . . a psq

THE OLD PARTIES   BOURGEOIS PARTIES

THEIR FINANCES

Here is what the former chief organizer of the Liberal Party, Jean-Marie Nadeau, had to say:

> "Their organizers travel to Paris, New York, and Toronto on the eve of elections. They visit the same antechambers of the big firms which have interests in Quebec." (*Political Diary*, p. 11.)

The old parties are controlled by their coffers.
Their coffers are filled by big companies.
The old parties are controlled by the big companies.

THEIR MEN

Bosses, financiers, lawyers, more lawyers. The members and candidates of the old parties are fat bourgeois. They don't know your problems. They've voted themselves $18,000 salaries. And how much do you earn? Can these characters represent you? The two old parties change platforms like shirts, and bring them out only at election time. Was the Liberal program respected?

THEIR PROGRAMS

Their only real program: helping the big companies, helping the Americans exploit our resources, helping the bosses exploit our work. The old parties have no ideas, they have interests. And they've passed an election act which gives them still more money to protect their interests.

VOTE FOR THEM, AND YOU'RE VOTING AGAINST YOURSELF

QUIET REVOLUTION +
POLICY OF GRANDEUR = OFFICIAL PATRONAGE

The government used to help small companies with small contracts for paint or roads. It was a small capitalism, and an under-the-table patronage. Today the government helps the big companies with the General Investment Corp., and with its anti-union policy. It's big, electronic-brain capitalism, and big, official patronage.

The big companies need energy:

The government buys up hydro power, borrowing the money in the United States, and produces energy for them.

The big companies need specialists:
   The government reorganizes education, pays to train men who will later work for the companies.

The big companies need prestige:
   The government pays for Places des Arts and World's Fairs and lets the slums multiply.

It's all very nice.

But it's done with our money.

The government nationalizes losses; takes over the money-losing jobs. Why not nationalize the profits, the paying sectors?

The policy of grandeur is: THE NATIONALIZATION OF LOSSES,
                                      THE PRIVATIZATION OF PROFITS

TO BE DONE WITH OFFICIAL PATRONAGE,
WE   NEED   A   WORKERS'   PARTY

THE PSQ   WORKERS' PARTY

ITS FINANCING
   The PSQ lives by the dues of its members. It is a popular and democratic organization. The program is adopted by the members. The PSQ is run by its members.

ITS MEN
   Workers, office employees, students, union men—these are its members. They have the same problems as you. This is a party that represents you. It is a party of all working men.

ITS PROGRAM
   The PSQ is a party of ideas. A party which knows what it wants and says it clearly. The PSQ favors:
   A REAL SOCIAL POLICY
      —through fiscal reform, full employment, a minimum wage of $1.75, health insurance that is universal, state run, complete, and free, education that is really available to all, comfortable lodgings at low rents.
   REAL PLANNING
      —by the nationalization of financial institutions and natural resources, the creation of a Quebec state bank, and the control of decisions in enterprises by the workers.
   REAL LABOR LEGISLATION
      —which gives all wage-earners the benefits of unionization.
   A FREE STATE OF QUEBEC

—the PSQ wants to make Quebec a free state, with all the powers the growth of the nation demands; it would take a new constitution; and if English Canada is not prepared to let us have these powers, Quebec should declare her independence.

VOTING FOR THE PSQ IS VOTING FOR YOU

Pierre Maheu has personified *parti pris* around the province since its beginnings. Never yet a novelist (he says he plans to write a novel), poet (he says he wrote poems as an adolescent "but I've got them well hidden"), "creative" writer, author of no book, he is the one voice which has been heard in pretty well every issue of the magazine, the voice which speaks for *parti pris* every time there is a conference, a round table, a panel discussion, or a brooding director's first feature movie to speak for it in.

He is a seductive representative. As a writer, cool, clear in the deepest waters, personal and general in a very smooth blend. And all three strands are always there: now the national consciousness will come out, now the socialist, and now the laïcist. As a speaker he is as seductive as his prose; he has abundant black hair, an ever-so-slightly babyish face, a quiet tone marked by a voice which almost cracks from shyness every few sentences.

"I resisted getting involved in any political movement for a long time," he told me over coffee in the booth of a restaurant across the street from the Parti Socialiste. My wife and I had invited him there after a speech on economic planning and computers (Sartre's *Temps modernes* is one of his big sources on such nonliterary subjects) to the socialists. We'd suggested the Asociación Española, but "I can't stand it anymore, can you?" And in the restaurant a grimace in our direction on lifting his coffee cup to his lips, the same pained sensibility before the mundane and grating in this city with only one kind of coffee in nine out of ten of its restaurants and only two or ten rendez-vous for its intellectuals to choose from. Ever since we've called restaurant coffee *café maheu*.

"It was my brother who kept nagging me," he went on. His brother Robert wrote occasionally for *parti pris* in the early days, and I'm not sure it wasn't perhaps Robert Maheu rather than Pierre who sold me my first copy. "He was in the RIN, I was in nothing. I was an intellectual and all that, I read Sartre, Sartre was my guiding light, and of course when my brother said I had to commit myself, it hurt, because commitment, well, I was for it. But somehow it didn't seem to me to apply here in Quebec. To me, people here were stupid and it was no use committing yourself to them. All I wanted to do was get out of this place."

In a late *parti pris,* à propos of the intellectual contortions clericalism forces on the Québécois, Maheu let the reader in on a little of his pre-*parti pris* self, quoting from a diary of those days and placing the stupidity elsewhere:

> "Normally, commit oneself to the group to which one belongs by one's situation. But if one belongs to the wrong group? I am bourgeois, Catholic, French-Canadian (absolutism, etc., and a lost cause). Solution: disengagement, deconditioning. Attain generality." *Merde,* how dumb I managed to be.

"Then came the FLQ. My God, I said to myself, history can happen here as well as anywhere else." His brother's needling took effect. Studies (in letters) at the University of Montreal put him in touch with other intellectuals who had also been waiting for that proof that Quebec was not excluded from the human story and were now in great haste to move in and play their part. There were some at the U of M, some at the Jacques Cartier Normal School, some working, some bumming: they came out of the RIN, the Communist Party, the NDP clubs that didn't satisfy them, they talked FLQ and Fanon, Sartre and Marx, and they brought out *parti pris* in September 1963 while the *effelquois* were still before the courts and the PSQ was emerging from the NDP. That was the beginning. There followed the whole itinerary I have described. It was the outcome of this itinerary I mostly wanted to discuss with Maheu: where *parti pris,* after three years, was at.

First of all, he told me, he was at wanting to relax a bit. That novel, and a few other projects, called. As a result he was giving his last courses at the PSQ, was cooling it in the RIN, where, the last issue of the magazine had just announced, *parti pris* now felt the work of clearing the air had to be done:

> We don't relish the idea of working with the kind of people who now make up the RIN. We have no illusions about them, few have gotten beyond a purely petty-bourgeois aspiration for political independence,

the republican forms. But it seems to us that this stage must be gone through, that a drive for this independence in outward forms must be undertaken, if only to clear the air, to settle that accursed national question and make it possible to hasten a confrontation between the conflicting classes within the nation.

How, then, did he see things now?

"It isn't a crime anymore to be associated with *parti pris*. You remember the first period, when the whole lot of us lost jobs, were excluded from public debates, were anathema. That's over. Now we're called upon to speak at discussions, even by the clergy, and our politics are tolerated by employers. The idea, the independentist-socialist-laïcist idea, has made its mark, is part of the picture in Quebec." And Maheu was to let his job on the executive of the Mouvement Laïque come up for election without contesting it. The secularization work was also falling behind independence in importance.

Yeah, I agreed, but wasn't that an ambiguous victory? *Partipristes* were not only accepted—they often held jobs where they influenced, molded, touched society. Yet there they played by other people's rules. Maheu in his advertising agency helped shore up the consumer society he denounced in his essays; Godin and Renaud at Radio-Canada put together shows which, even if they always stuck in a bit of their disquiet, remained finally (like my dispatches for the Canadian Press) bolsterers of the existing order. And at Cockfield Brown, at the CBC, the audience was huge, was in fact the proletariat they hoped to see revolt: as soon as they wielded some serious instruments of persuasion, they did so according to other people's rules. The order seemed to have stamped *parti pris* "safe." Go ahead and publish in your spare time; eight hours a day you'll help us close people's minds.

Maheu felt attacked, and I was a bit sorry I'd made it sound that way, but this is what he said: "As for me and my ads, my product escapes me just like any other worker's; I too am alienated in my work."

"You could carry that argument to an extreme," intervened Jean-Marie Bédard, the old-Marxist trade unionist who led the PSQ and was one of the friends of the *parti pris* youngsters among its old guard. He'd joined us for his snack before heading home from party headquarters. "You could say the worker who puts in his eight hours is helping the capitalist exploit because he is contributing to production, profit, the success of the enterprise. But . . ."

"The ads I write I don't have final say on, nor have I usually originated them. We do a great deal of translation from English, naturally. And when the time comes to write the ads, there are small decisions I can make, peanuts if you wish, but the difference between retaining my sanity and being completely alienated. First of all, if the message I am required to write is utterly at odds with everything in me—a call to the reader to celebrate with joy the centenary of Confederation, say—I simply write it as badly as I can. In other ads, for consumer products, where I am indifferent to the brand that is being pushed over another brand, well, I can at least strive in my copy to bring people toward new ideas, new forms, modern tastes, everything that is forward looking. I can try to open the reader's mind and sympathies. We've had our little triumphs, too—in all our ads now, because of our deliberately using that form, addresses are given as 'Montréal, Québec,' rather than the old 'P.Q.' "

I didn't rub it in. He went on, on another tack:

"And I do not want to say that I detest advertising. I'm fascinated by it: in a socialist society I would be very happy to explore what role advertising could play. I learned something about this recently at the Montreal Advertising and Sales Club. The speaker was a Czech whose work is precisely that: advertising in a socialist context. He said that on Czech TV, instead of commercials with every program there is a program of nothing but commercials once a week. And here is the interesting thing: it has a higher rating than any other program on the network. Beyond the horizons of a repressive society there remain the questions of taste, of preference, of individualization of human life. Even with the same salary, one man can choose to embellish his body, another to fill his stomach with good things. The ad can be his guide to fulfillment of his individual leanings. It can do the opposite of conditioning the society to conformity, of making the mouth water for the article that will give a man the same status as his neighbor; it can help him be himself."

For his part, Maheu leans toward elegant dressing, and almost always wears a hand-woven Quebec tie, though most recently I noticed him wearing a tie fashioned from the same gray worsted material as his double-breasted suit. He is married and has children, and his main concern at the time was breaking down the religious monolith that weighs upon Quebec family life. "I was married by a priest myself," he shrugged when I asked him what progress the Mouvement Laïque had made on civil marriage. The shrug seemed to say, We're still in the real world, I have to be Catholic like everyone else on the big occasions. He mentioned that the Dominicans would always marry you at their Outremont monastery without a fuss.

His speeches to the Mouvement Laïque, his articles in *parti pris* during this period, all turned around the same theme: the God of French Canada was preventing the man of Quebec from emerging. Man always dies so that God may be born; the rebirth of man depends on the retreat of God. How to bring this about? Not, certainly, by begging the believers in power for a little corner to be atheist in, a ghetto for the abnormal. For there is a unanimity in any society which ghettoes only irritate: the hope for the unbelieving in Quebec was in the creation of a new unanimity, around new, nonmystical values. But what? Maheu rarely answers that question when he is debating religion, but we have to assume it is a socialist unanimity, a common belief in man fraternally building his universe.

Here enters the snag. Socialism is everybody's business, most of all that of the poor. But the Church has the poor securely, and as long as that is so the break from the Church will always be the struggle of those who have the leisure, the countervalues, the *privilege* of not believing in God. The Church will always beat the freethinkers over the head with their masses of believing poor. The liberal priests, the ones who will marry you if you have trouble with the parish priest, are the Dominicans of Outremont, and where does the spokesman for the new, humanist unanimity come from except that same upper-crust-of-the-underdogs municipality? As long as agnosticism radiates out from Outremont and not up from the poor it will be another parvenu snobbery.

Maheu has illustrated this truth better than I can. "Call it Ti-Pop," he wrote in a late *parti pris*:

> And what is *Ti-Pop? Eh bien*, the *Ti* is Quebec, like in *"Chez Ti-Jean Snack Bar," "Ti-Lou Antiques,"* or simply, *"Allo, ti-cul."* And the *Pop* is, if you wish, Pop Art. But this doesn't particularly involve art. It is rather a culture, our old culture, *la Culture Ti-Pop*. Ti-Pop is an attitude; it

gives aesthetic value to the objects of the Ti-Pop culture. Get the idea? A bleeding cardboard Sacred Heart inscribed "Why blaspheme me?" An election poster of the Duplessis period. The heart of Brother André in alcohol—but also the dolls in Godbout's film *Le Monde va nous prendre pour des sauvages*, folk crafts—it's all food for Ti-Pop. Both nostalgia and sarcasm, irony and pleasure, rediscovery and rupture. In the case of strictly religious objects, sacred hearts, holy pictures, Extract of Annals (a miraculous concoction created by an excellent lady who boiled back issues of the *Annales de Sainte-Anne* for rubbing on the sick), Ti-Pop makes aesthetic things of sacred ones, renders them profane, hence an attitude of profanation. Elsewhere—the way I like the songs of Madame Bolduc or Private Lebrun, or the smile on the face of the watcher of the TV show *Les Cailloux*, accustomed to Ferré or Léveillée, when he is presented with singers like Allan Mills or Hélène Baillargeon, that smile of happiness among familiar things and of reluctance to admit one's happiness, or Godbout's tenderness about his dolls—here Ti-Pop is simply reclaiming that part of our past that is reclaimable.

And in this announcement he had launched a fad among the hip French of Montreal. Committees met to plan exhibitions of Ti-Pop objects, rock'n'rollers Ti-Popped to electric guitars ("When Maurice Richard by skill and luck/Reached 500 goals, got a golden puck/Ti-Pop was there!") and the Ti-Pop Catechism went forth to the Ti-Populus:

> He who spits in the air gathers no moss. And since us French-Canadians, born as we are for a crust of bread, well, we well know that there is no greater wealth on earth than knowledge. But on the other hand, you can't always have your way in life, and since books aren't worth the paper they're written on, though if it moves it's obscene, you can't carry things too far because of what are the neighbors going to say? So whichever ways you look at it, the Ti-Pop family that prays together stays together.

I attended a conference in the winter of 1966–1967 in which Maheu participated, a teach-in on the war between religious and secular forces in Quebec. He quoted Sartre: "Man loses himself that God be born." He summarized Quebec culture of the previous century in the folk theology *"L'éssentiel c'est le ciel."* And he concluded that atheism, his own atheism, was impossible even in the Quebec of the day: "God exists; it was he who caused me, for example, to lose a couple of jobs." He developed themes he had been treating in issues of *parti pris* since turning his political activism to the Mouvement Laïque. Atheism was impossible and so, it struck him, was faith, where God was imposed by the surrounding culture; the only thing which would make either possible was the birth of a "new culture" in which no metaphysic would be imposed. The common values of the society would be in other fields. This utopian vision was largely lost in the anti-clericalism of the occasion, God still weighing heavily on both believers and nonbelievers, and a friend, in a conversation afterward, sighed to me: "Maheu's new culture—I don't know . . ." (But as the conversation went on, my friend bowed somewhat to my speculation that the very fact that Maheu drew his inspiration from French Marxism, and the preservers of Catholicism theirs from the French worker priests, suggested that the future Quebec would be one divided between progressive forces *à la française* and traditionalist ones forced to accept the French framework for debate. "It's true we're becoming more and more French, even to the Michelin tires on the *métro*," he agreed, and soon we were imagining international festivals of French song in Natashquan at which Parisian and Sénégalese competitors would vie for patronizing praise from the Quebec critics for their not-bad-at-all stab at the jig and hoedown.) The new culture is not here; what is here is something that Maheu's speeches always refuse and reject, yet know is the reality: the agnostic ghetto.

The ghetto exists and is beginning to equip itself with its own institutions, its own gathering places, its own folklore. It feels superior and is winning the contempt of those outside it: it is in fact no ghetto at all, but an elite, not the old doctor-lawyer-priest elite of *Le Devoir*, but a left elite, a *petite gauche* which chuckles at the people with their Ti-Pop ways. And the people know. A friend, no Outremont boy but a man of modest origins from east Montreal who at normal school found the revolution and helped found *parti pris*, told me of an experience while searching in a religious articles shop for *ne-me-blasphémez-pas* posters and plastic Jesuses for a Ti-Pop exhibition: "At first the shopkeeper and the others didn't know what sort of thing I wanted, so I decided to try to explain the idea to them. They caught on. 'Ah,' one said, 'what it really is, you're laughing at us, eh?'"

And Les Sinners, the rock group which grabbed Ti-Pop, saw it too. In a publicity interview they described one of their aims as proving that *"des tis-gars d'Outremont"* can make it, a Ti-Pop takeoff on the line of the slum demagogue in Quebec, that all he is he owes to himself and his constituents, because he's just a kid from Ste-Marie. The people have their opinion of the populism of Outremont.

Quebec writers had always vaguely known it, and *parti pris* made it explicit: the intellectuals need the people even to make their own atheism livable, for as long as this ghetto is associated with privilege, the inhabitants of other, crueller ghettoes will help the persecutors persecute it. This intellectual's dilemma—bound to the working class by principle, but to the bourgeoisie by life-style—is the traditional one in industrial society and recent *parti pris* thought has been around that side of the Quebec situation—its industrial side. Now the masters most often cited are not Fanon, the black voice of Algerian protest, Memmi, the Jewish analyst of colonial psychology, or Berque, the French academic and administrator whose life has been describing North Africa to the French—but Antonio Gramsci, the Italian Marxist philosopher-militant, André Gorz, the French strategist of European Communism amid postwar prosperity, Lucien Goldmann, the relater of modern European literature to modern European politics. The term most often used is no longer colonialism, but neocapitalism. The perspective was always French, even when the Arabs were the subject under discussion—I know of no French-Canadian revolutionary who speaks Arabic or is aware of the literature of the Third World in the Third World's languages. Raoul Roy told me: "Ben Bella didn't speak Arabic. It's as if Bourgault couldn't speak French. There is also a linguistic problem in Arabic which is comparable to our own and should remind us not to get too excited about it: there are two Arabics, the literary and the popular, sharply differentiated."

Roy seemed to have felt that showing that what is important in the way of North African political thought passes by Paris dealt with the problem. And on a less demanding level, Laurent Girouard said: "I was once interested in doing some scientific work in Honduras, where a friend had already established himself. I started studying Spanish, with the result that I now get along in Spanish a bit better than I do in English. But when I proposed an effort to learn the language of Latin America, of Castro, among my socialist friends, perhaps to open up contacts with other American liberation movements, the response was zero." He smiled.

On the level of consciously situating themselves between colonial and industrial approaches to the revolution, the moment of greatest clarity was perhaps the manifesto of 1965–1966, the magazine's only real turning point, the moment at which it ceased merely stating its view and began trying to act on it. Its view had been original; its action, while audacious, has been drearily familiar in its frustrations. In the last issue of the magazine before this manifesto the final chorus had been sung to the *parti pris* song cycle by a group of intellectuals all a bit older, a bit less exclusively associated with the *parti pris* view, than the originals. One after another university professors Jacques Brault and Marcel Rioux, French-born movie critic Patrick Straram (who extended his contribution into a continuing column of self-study), poet Gaston Miron, physician-storyteller Jacques Ferron, testified to their conversion to the themes of *parti pris*. In the same issue Pierre Vallières announced his group's adhesion to *parti pris*: if he had not converted to its view, he had become convinced of the need for the entire left to pull together. And the issue gave its account of the moment that was the peak of the drama of Montreal as a colonial town with a testy native quarter, the street demonstration of May 24, 1965. Then the manifesto of an anti-colonial magazine become a Quebec political movement appeared, and it captured the conjunction: "Quebec is a land at once colonized and industrialized, in this it is unique, and no pre-existent ideology can be applied to it. In its thought, its methods and traits, the Quebec revolutionary class will have to invent its socialism. Though linked with the world struggle against imperialism, the Quebec revolution will work only if it assumes all our peculiarities, if it is resolutely Québécois."

It is hard, though, to assume one's uniqueness. Quebec has never amounted to anything; other countries have. If it wants to make its mark, must it not, then, do what they did? Come out of its nonexistence the way they came out of theirs? It is hard to avoid thinking this way, hard to take off in flights of spontaneous invention of one's own road, when one is aware of the smallness and limitations of one's land. One always seeks models.

This seeking of models is bound to make Quebec something of a little France. The French model imposes itself on its intellectuals through their reading. The American model imposes itself on its proletariat through the forms of their work, but the European model will not be as easy to keep out of the forms of its struggle as it is in the United States. And its business class will reflect this tension by being half-French, half-American, in the manner—but without the resources to back it—of the modern French capitalist.

One other country comes to mind when imagining the Quebec of the next few decades, another country which has been Latin under United States pressure and which has shown some marks of an industrial and cultural confidence in a basic structure of colonization. Quebec is bound, it seems to me, to be something of a northern Mexico. The left-wing domination of intellectual life, without the resources for revolution, seems to me a particular likelihood for the period before the working class's race-class resentments become a class consciousness which operates against the national bourgeoisie as well as the Anglo-Saxon one.

It is already clear that the bourgeois smoothing-out of those resentments is not working. On the promise of upgrading French across the country, the Confederation-savers ask French-speakers not to pursue their own upgrading by aggrandizing the Quebec government. The dead-ends this leads into include, for example, the new immigration rules, designed by a *Citélibriste* in Ottawa, Jean Marchand, to reply to the separatist accusation that immigration is rigged to help the English. Immigrants will now be favored according to a system of points, and in the Marchand chart knowledge of French earns you the same number of points as knowledge of English. This, then, is fair, bicultural, a gain; it eliminates presenting Canada to apprentice citizens as an all- or almost all-English operation. But at the same time it fails as an accurate test of the apprentice's adaptability to Canadian life, which is in fact greater if he knows English than if he knows French. That the real Canada, and not the paper one drawn up in the *Citélibrist* immigration department, operates in English, is something that immigrants know better than anybody. Take away their right to be anglicized, as the Roman Catholic schoolboard in the largely (not majority) Italian suburb of Montreal called St-Léonard learned when it tried to do so, and they rise in anger. In St-Léonard the election of unilingualist school trustees was a victory in an unproductive cultural institution which left the Italians' reasons for wanting to be English untouched in the factories of Montreal. It was like Mr. Marchand's immigration policy, it was not realistic, it was not enough to turn the tide. The old immigration policy, weighted to the English or the anglicized, reflected reality but offended the bicultural square deal. The new is fair but up in a cloud. The choices before federal legislators addressing themselves to Quebec claims will more and more be such choices between unrealistic fairness and unfair realism. The alloy of justice and realism is difficult, will certainly not be made on the morning of the independence of Quebec, and seems bound for a long while to be over-understood in the pages of intellectuals who cannot act on it, and acted out in the angers of workers who do not understand, but find that for their work there is no justice and for their Frenchness there is no reality.

On a wet winter night in the middle of the Vallières trial, the French east end of town came to knock at the English west. Workers from all the labor movements, socialists, separatists of all tendencies but hard right, marched around the town of Mount Royal, second only to Westmount as an address for the wealthy. But Mount Royal also contains a 7-Up bottling plant, and the plant's truck drivers had been on strike, with scabs replacing them, for six months. Municipal manual workers were also on strike—reason enough for a march on city hall and placards caricaturing Old King Reginald, the chief magistrate of this dormitory for Montreal center. And a bus load of strikers from General Motors came down from St-Thérèse, a rather different kind of suburb north of Montreal.

One placard read: "The lousies don't live in the riding." Pierre-Elliott Trudeau, the *Citélibriste*-in-chief in Ottawa, sat for this district in parliament. He had once given a famous interview to Toronto television in which he listed among Quebec's blemishes its "lousy French." In either French or joual *lousy* has only the literal meaning of creeping with lice and this insult went into the separatist treasure chest. Now the lousies had come west to convey their anger to the scrubbed, and when windows of finance companies got broken along the parade route, and provincial police reinforcing the local cops moved in with their clubwork, driving back the truckers and those who were there sharing their anger from the factory where they hurled sticks and built fires, Pierre Vallières, who had felt that anger back in Longueuil Annex, who was in jail for not forgetting it, for understanding it, could understand again.

I thought I would have to end by saying that *parti pris* was a moment, a past moment, when the whole structure of the domination of Quebec appeared at once. That until *parti pris*, the overall structure had never seemed clear. That its three strands—the material, cultural, and spiritual alienation of the French in America—had been identified before *parti pris* and stretch back to the very beginnings of French-Canadian life. That a debate was constantly going on as to how the various parts fitted together. That each strand had had thoughtful attackers who sensed that their struggles were interwoven, but whose obsessions always led them to consider the other two unimportant: independence first, organize the workers first, get the priests out of the schools first.

For as I ended my inquiry the three strands seemed to have reclaimed the *partipristes*: the Parti Socialiste and the RIN and the Mouvement Laïque divided them up, and they would have to fight anti-nationalist trade unionists here; separatists of the Rockefeller's-not-afraid-to-invest-in-Quebec variety, or of the go-easy-on-the-Church-people-are-still-Catholic one, there; or again, the Protestants and *mange-curés* of pure secularism. The MLP gave its people to these several strands in 1966, and the magazine split apart over whether to support René Lévesque's independence movement in 1968. Lévesque's was one of the partial programs of transformation which was much talked about then, as was the futuristic Montreal world's fair and the beautiful subway that glided you to it. The year 1966 killed the partial social transformation of the Liberal government; the partial national program of the Duplessist return became the talk.

But I reread. 1970. The moment is still here. The Liberals are in again, the Lévesque movement gnawing away at them. And on the left, small groups—one of them calls itself the Front de Libération Populaire—are still reaching out to the rage of Montreal.

Partial programs, you see as you come across the city on Dorchester Boulevard, have attempted to spare your eye the dwellings in the eastern streets which feed into the boulevard. They have erected multi-colored plywood fences across the ends of house rows. But there are young people who know what is behind those fences, who are painting on them the alphabet of revolution. They learned this alphabet in these very streets, or learned it in other schools. A child has fallen off a balcony in east Montreal since Chamberland spoke of the *ruelle Saint-Christophe,* and a judge refused his mother damages because the child was illegitimate. Since *Le Cassé,* an unemployed man has beaten his infant son to death with an ashtray and asked the police who tracked him down, "Is he dead?" And last week or a week like it, not far from the bridge, a funeral procession of motorcyclists, the police patrolling nervously, buried a knifed young cyclist named Fidel.

The young people I am speaking of will not stop shouting until the walls come down.

Selected Bibliography

parti pris writing

parti pris, revue politique et culturelle, 38 issues from October 1963 to Summer 1968. (A selection of articles was published by François Maspero, Paris, 1967, with a preface by Jacques Berque, and republished by éditions parti pris in 1971.)

Laurent Girouard, *La Ville inhumaine,* 1964.

Germain Archambault, *Le Taxi: métier de crève-faim,* 1964.

Jacques Renaud, *Le Cassé,* 1964 (translated into English by Gérald Robitaille as *Flat Broke and Beat,* Bélier, Montreal, 1968); *En d'autres paysages,* 1970. (Also by Renaud: *Electrodes,* poèmes, Les Editions Atys, Montreal, 1962.)

Paul Chamberland, *L'Afficheur hurle,* 1965, republished in 1970 with a few changes and a note on how the author felt about it then; *L'Inavouable,* 1968. (Also by Chamberland: *Génèses,* Cahiers de l'AGEUM, Montreal, 1962; *Terre Québec,* Librairie Déom, Montreal, 1964.)

André Major, *La Chair de poule,* 1965; *Le Cabochon,* 1965. (Also by Major: *Poèmes pour durer,* a selection from before, during, and after *parti pris,* Editions du Songe, Montreal, 1969; *Félix-Antoine Savard,* "écrivains canadiens d'aujourd'hui," Fides, Montreal, 1968; *Le Vent du diable,* novel, Editions du Jour, Montreal, 1968.)

Jacques Ferron, *La Nuit,* 1965; *Papa Boss,* 1966. (Also by Ferron: *Contes du pays incertain,* Editions d'Orphée, Montreal, 1962.)

Claude Jasmin, *Blues pour un homme averti,* 1964; *Pleure pas, Germaine,* 1965; *Les Coeurs empaillés,* 1967. (Also by Jasmin: *La Corde au cou,* Robert Laffont, "Les Jeunes Romanciers canadiens," Paris, 1961, since made into a movie by Pierre Patry; *Ethel et le terroriste,* Librairie Déom, "Nouvelle

Prose," Montreal, 1964, translated into English by David S. Walker as *Ethel and the Terrorist,* Harvest House, Montreal, 1965.)

Jean-Jules Richard, *Journal d'un hobo,* 1965. (Also by Richard: *Le Feu dans l'amiante,* Chezlauteur, Montreal, 1956; *Ville rouge,* Editions Tranquille, Montreal, 1949; *Neuf jours de haine,* Editions de l'Arbre, Montreal, 1948.)

Jean-Robert Rémillard, *Sonnets archaïques pour ceux qui verront l'indépendance,* 1966.

Gérald Godin, *Les Cantouques,* 1966. (Also by Godin: *Chansons très naïves, Poèmes et cantos,* and *Nouveaux poèmes,* Editions du Bien Public, Three Rivers, 1960, 1962, and 1963.)

Clémence Desrochers, *Le Monde sont drôles,* 1966.

Robert-Lionel Séguin, *La Victoire de Saint-Denis,* "collection centrentenaire," 1968.

Pierre Vallières, *Nègres blancs d'Amérique,* 1968. (Translated by Joan Pinkham as *White Niggers of America,* Monthly Review Press, New York, 1971.)

Pierre Vadeboncoeur, *Lettres et colères,* 1970. (Also by Vadeboncoeur: *L'Autorité du peuple,* Editions de l'Arc, Quebec, 1965; *La Ligne du risque,* HMH, Montreal, 1963.)

French-Canadian literature

Albert Laberge, *La Scouine,* édition privée, Imprimerie Modèle, Montreal, 1918. (Réédition-Québec was prevented from republishing the book by Laberge's heirs, but a 1971 pirate edition is available from Anatole Brochu, Shawinigan, and Gérard Bessette includes excerpts in his *Anthologie d'Albert Laberge,* Cercle du Livre de France, Montreal, 1963.)

Lionel Groulx, *Notre maître, le passé,* Bibliothèque de l'Action Française, Montreal, 1924. (Later volumes, Granger Frères, Montreal, 1933, 1937, 1944.)

Ringuet, *Trente arpents,* 1938. (Translated as *Thirty Acres,* McClelland and Stewart, "New Canadian Library," Toronto, 1958.)

Gabrielle Roy, *Bonheur d'occasion,* 1945. (Translated by Hannah Josephson as *The Tin Flute,* McClelland and Stewart, "New Canadian Library," Toronto, 1959.)

Marcel Dubé, *Zone,* Leméac, "Théâtre canadien," Montreal, 1968 (first published in 1955); *Un simple soldat,* with *Le Temps des lilas,* Institut Littéraire, Quebec, 1960; *Les Beaux Dimanches,* Leméac, "Théâtre canadien," Montreal, 1968.

Michel van Schendel, *Poèmes de l'Amérique étrangère,* Hexagone, Montreal, 1958.

Anne Hébert, *Les Chambres de bois,* Editions du Seuil, Paris, 1958.
Gilles Leclerc, *Journal d'un inquisiteur,* Editions de l'Aube, Montreal, 1960.
Les Insolences du frère Untel, 1960. (Translated by Miriam Chapin as *The Impertinences of Brother Anonymous,* Harvest House, Montreal, 1965.)
Gérard Bessette, *Le Libraire,* 1960. (Translated as *Not for Every Eye* by Glen Shortliffe, Macmillan of Canada, Toronto, 1962.)
Marie-Claire Blais, *Une saison dans la vie d'Emmanuel,* 1966. (Translated by Derek Coltman as *A Season in the Life of Emmanuel,* Farrar, Straus and Giroux, New York, 1966.)
Hubert Aquin, *Prochain épisode,* 1965. (Translated under the same title by Penny Williams, McClelland and Stewart, Toronto, 1967.)
Réjean Ducharme, *L'Avalée des avalés,* 1966. (Translated by Barbara Bray as *The Swallower Swallowed,* Hamish Hamilton, London, 1968.)
Gaston Miron, *L'Homme rapaillé,* Les Presses de l'Université de Montréal, "Collection du prix de la revue *études françaises,*" Montreal, 1970. (This is all the work Miron wants in print.)

From elsewhere

Albert Memmi, *Portraite du colonisé,* 1957. (Translated by Howard Greenfeld as *The Colonizer and the Colonized,* Grossman Publishers, New York, 1965.)
Mordecai Richler, *The Apprenticeship of Duddy Kravitz,* Paperback Library, New York, 1968. (First published in 1959.)
Frantz Fanon, *Les Damnés de la terre,* 1961. (Translated by Constance Farrington as *The Wretched of the Earth,* with a preface by Jean-Paul Sartre, Grove Press, New York, 1965.)
Herman Buller, *One Man Alone,* Centennial Press, Toronto, 1963; *Quebec in Revolt,* Swann Publishing, Toronto, 1966.
Poésie/Poetry 64, Ryerson Press/Editions du Jour, Toronto/Montreal, 1964.
Jacques Berque, *Dépossession du monde,* Editions du Seuil, Paris, 1964.
Michel Bernard, *Le Québec change de visage,* Plon, Paris, 1964.
Lucien Goldmann, *Pour une sociologie du roman,* Gallimard, "idées," Paris, 1964.

Records

Gilles Vigneault, Columbia FL-312, Montreal, 1963.
Claude Dubois, "Poésie et chansons," Columbia HFS-9070, Montreal, reissue of a 1966 release.
Robert Charlebois, Louise Forestier, Gamma GS-120, Montreal, 1968.

Index of Names

Aquin, Hubert, 169–73, 179–80, 207
Arango, Gonzalo, 190
Arcand, Denys, 28
Archambault, Germain, 61, 62

Beaudoin, Marie-José, 77
Bédard, Jean-Marie, 290, 297
Bergeron, Gérard, 233
Bernard, Michel, 168–70, 172
Bertrand-Ferretti, Andrée, 257
Berque, Jacques, 37, 183, 231
Berthio, 233
Bessette, Gérard, 57–58
Blais, Marie-Claire, 206, 207–8
Boisvert, Réginald, 53
Bolduc, Madame, 300
Borduas, Paul-Emile, 111–12
Bourgault, Pierre, 25, 173, 198, 257, 266–67, 290
Brault, Jacques, 186, 303
Brochu, André, 27
Buller, Herman, 109, 130

Caouette, Réal, 291
Cathelin, Jean, 84
Céline, Louis-Ferdinand, 160
Césaire, Aimé, 49
Chamberland, Paul, 27, 38, 40, 63, 64, 89, 97–145, 150, 157, 172, 179–80, 185–86, 194, 215, 244, 256, 260–61, 263–64, 288, 290, 307
Chaput, Marcel, 21, 25, 26, 163, 198
Charlebois, Robert, 288
Charpentier, François, 285
Chartrand, Michel, 247, 248
Chartrand, Reggie, 10, 262
Chénier, Jean-Olivier, 106, 124
Cohen, Leonard, 129–31
Copferman, Emile, 211–12, 233

Depocas, Jan, 111
Desbiens, Jean-Paul (Frère Untel), 16–17, 20–22, 25, 34, 280
Desbiens, Pierre-André (Beathoven), 243
des Marchais, Gilles, 144
Desrochers, Alfred, 233
Desrochers, Clémence, 78, 232–33
Dionne, Yvon, 27
Dor, Georges, 287
Dubé, Marcel, 203–6
Dubois, Claude, 249–53
Duceppe, Jean, 205
Ducharme, Réjean, 206–7
Duguay, Raoul, 134–35, 208
Dumais, Mario, 140, 273

Duplessis, Maurice, 17, 23–24, 109, 220
Dupont, Claire, 273
Dylan, Bob, 92, 128, 245, 250–51

Fanon, Frantz, 21, 24, 25, 26, 37, 38, 49, 164, 165, 200, 212, 237, 264, 265, 287, 302
Ferré, Léo, 251
Ferron, Jacques, 106, 215–23, 225, 247–48, 282, 303

Gagnon, Charles, 277–81, 286–87
Gagnon, Serge, 243–44, 253
Garand, André, 81–86, 137, 145, 167–68, 183
Garneau, Saint-Denys, 112, 168
Gauvreau, Claude, 111–12, 288
Ginsberg, Allen, 128
Girouard, Laurent, 52–61, 112, 127, 174, 215, 261, 266, 302
Godin, Gérald, 61, 196, 227–35, 248, 269, 288, 291, 297
Godin, Marcel, 210
Goldmann, Lucien, 167
Gorz, André, 302
Gramsci, Antonio, 143, 302
Groulx, Canon Lionel, 108, 177
Groulx, Gilles, 179–80
Guénette, Edmond, 271
Gurik, Robert, 237

Harvey, Jean-Charles, 34
Hébert, Anne, 33–34, 35, 103, 197, 207
Hébert, Jacques, 17, 22, 61, 62, 152
Hénault, Gilles, 186
Husereau, Yvon, 268, 270–75, 288, 292

Jasmin, Claude, 54, 60–62, 212–15, 227, 233
Julien, Pauline, 132, 245, 287

Laberge, Albert, 56–57
Laffont, Robert, 209–11
Langevin, Gilbert, 163, 288
Laperrière, Michel, 81
Laporte, Pierre, 113
Larue-Langlois, Jacques, 287
Laurendeau, André, 17–22, 28, 76, 103
Layton, Irving, 129–31
Leclerc, Félix, 249
Leclerc, Gilles, 58–60, 163, 183
Léger, Pierre, 87
Lesage, Jean, 240, 266
Léveillée, Claude, 85, 132, 223
Lévesque, Raymond, 132, 251
Lévesque, René, 21–24, 79, 109, 232, 240, 291, 306
Limoges, Camille, 28, 262
Lockwell, Brother Clément, 67

Maheu, Pierre, 27, 28–33, 35, 36, 40, 58, 80, 89, 90, 94, 109, 113, 132–33, 171, 192, 222, 233, 248, 256, 260–61, 272, 279, 288, 290, 291–301
Maheu, Robert, 62, 261, 295
Major, André, 27, 63, 65, 66, 67, 68, 74, 81, 88, 103, 113, 127, 128, 131, 146–81, 185, 200, 213, 215, 228, 231, 235, 243, 244, 245, 253, 256, 261, 263
Malraux, André, 162, 164–67
Marchand, Jean, 305
Marcotte, Gilles, 52
Marie-Victorin, Brother, 104–6
Marcuse, Herbert, 111
Maspero, François, 21, 211–12
Memmi, Albert, 37, 49, 200, 237, 287
Mill, Michel, 288–89
Miron, Gaston, 43, 64, 134, 163, 168, 183–93, 215, 226, 230, 245, 253, 282, 288, 303
Moscovitch, Henry, 131–32

Nadeau, Jean-Marie, 109, 293
Nelligan, Emile, 178–79, 207

Pelletier, Gérard, 23, 39, 163, 193, 221, 230, 259, 285
Péloquin, Claude, 111–12
Piotte, Jean-Marc, 27, 40, 43–44, 113, 138, 143, 144, 149, 176, 256, 260, 261, 264, 288, 290

Racine, Jean, 44, 265, 267–70, 288–92
Rémillard, Jean-Robert, 223–25
Renaud, Jacques, 52, 58, 61, 62–81, 86–93, 95–96, 103, 127, 136, 138, 150, 153, 155, 159, 161, 169, 170, 172, 215, 228, 243, 251, 253, 272, 297
Richard, Jean-Jules, 61, 193–97, 221
Richard, Maurice, 107
Richler, Mordecai, 129–31
Ringuet (Philippe Panneton), 108
Rioux, Marcel, 303
Roy, Gabrielle, 93–94, 203
Roy, Raoul, 65, 164, 197–202, 258, 302

Sartre, Jean-Paul, 26, 36, 90, 99, 113, 128, 164, 167, 240, 295, 300
Saulnier, Michèle, 268

Sauvage, Catherine, 245
Schirm, François, 271
Schneider, Pierre, 164–65
Schoeters, Georges, 21, 177
Scott, Frank, 103, 218–19, 221
Séguin, Robert-Lionel, 109
Smith, Bernard, 263
Souster, Raymond, 188
Straram, Patrick, 303

Tranquille, Henri, 161
Trudeau, Pierre-Elliott, 23–24, 59, 164, 240, 259, 285, 305
Trudel, Jacques, 289

Vadeboncoeur, Pierre, 143, 149–50, 247–48
Vallières, Pierre, 198–99, 222, 235, 254, 267–68, 270, 271, 276–88, 303, 305–6
van Schendel, Michel, 110, 226–27, 261
Venne, Stephane, 249
Vian, Boris, 143
Vigneault, Gilles, 132, 158, 243, 244–49, 251, 252
Villeneuve, Raymond, 263

Wagner, Claude, 126, 217–18, 220
Wilson, Edmund, 33, 34, 206